ABOUT THIS PUBLICATION

FOR SERVICE ASSISTANCE

Customer Service Department
1.704.898.0770

North Carolina General Statues is published by The Muliti-Media Group of Greater Charlotte in Charlotte, North Carolina. Copyright 2015 by the Multi-Media Group of Greater Charlotte. This book or parts thereof may not be reproduced in any form, stored in a retrieval system, or transmitted in any form by any means—electronic, mechanical, photocopy, recording or otherwise—without prior written permission of the publisher, except as provided by United States of America copyright law.

The records required by U.S. Code 2257(a) through (c) and the pertinent regulations 28 C.F.R. Cli. 1, Part 75 with respect to this publication and all materials associated with such records are maintained by The Multi-Media Group of Greater Charlotte, Publisher and available for review by Attorney General.

www.visionbooks.org

Copyright © 2015 by MMGGC
All rights reserved!

TID: 5061369
ISBN (10) digit: 1502912678
ISBN (13) digit: 9781502912671

123-4-56789-01239-Paperback
123-4-56789-01239-Hardback

First Edition

090520140547

Printed in the United States of America

2015 EDITION

North Carolina Criminal Law And Procedure-Pamphlet # 28

Printed In conjunction with the Administration of the Courts

North Carolina Criminal Law and Procedure
Pamphlet Reference Guide

Chapters	Pamphlet
Chapter 1 Civil Procedure	1
Chapter 1 Civil Procedure (Continue)	2
Chapter 1A Rules of Civil Procedure	2
Chapter 1B Contribution.	2
Chapter 1C Enforcement of Judgments.	2
Chapter 1D Punitive Damages.	2
Chapter 1E Eastern Band of Cherokee Indians.	2
Chapter 1F North Carolina Uniform Interstate Depositions and Discovery Act.	2
Chapter 2 - Clerk of Superior Court [Repealed and Transferred.]	3
Chapter 3 - Commissioners of Affidavits and Deeds [Repealed.]	3
Chapter 4 - Common Law	3
Chapter 5 - Contempt [Repealed.]	3
Chapter 5A - Contempt	3
Chapter 6 - Liability for Court Costs	3
Chapter 7 - Courts [Repealed and Transferred.]	3
Chapter 7A – Judicial Department	3
Chapter 7A – Continuation (Judicial Department)	4
Chapter 7A – Continuation (Judicial Department)	5
Chapter 7B - Juvenile Code	5
Chapter 8 - Evidence	6
Chapter 8A - Interpreters for Deaf Persons [Recodified.]	6
Chapter 8B - Interpreters for Deaf Persons	6
Chapter 8C - Evidence Code	6
Chapter 9 - Jurors	6
Chapter 10 - Notaries [Repealed.]	6
Chapter 10A - Notaries [Recodified.]	6
Chapter 10B - Notaries	6
Chapter 11 - Oaths	6
Chapter 12 - Statutory Construction	6
Chapter 13 - Citizenship Restored	6
Chapter 14 - Criminal Law	7
Chapter 14 –Criminal Law (Continuation)	8
Chapter 15 - Criminal Procedure	9
Chapter 15A - Criminal Procedure Act (Continuation)	10
Chapter 15A - Criminal Procedure Act (Continuation)	11
Chapter 15B - Victims Compensation	11
Chapter 15C - Address Confidentiality Program	11
Chapter 16 - Gaming Contracts and Futures	11
Chapter 17 - Habeas Corpus	11

Chapter 17A - Law-Enforcement Officers [Recodified.]	11
Chapter 17B - North Carolina Criminal Justice Education and Training System [Recodified.] Chapter 17C - North Carolina Criminal Justice Education and Training Standards Commission	11
	11
Chapter 17D - North Carolina Justice Academy	11
Chapter 17E - North Carolina Sheriffs' Education and Training Standards Commission	11
Chapter 18 - Regulation of Intoxicating Liquors [Repealed.]	12
Chapter 18A - Regulation of Intoxicating Liquors [Repealed.]	12
Chapter 18B - Regulation of Alcoholic Beverages	12
Chapter 18C - North Carolina State Lottery	12
Chapter 19 - Offenses against Public Morals	12
Chapter 19A - Protection of Animals	12
Chapter 20 - Motor Vehicles	13
Chapter 20 - Motor Vehicles (Continuation)	14
Chapter 20 - Motor Vehicles (Continuation)	15
Chapter 20 - Motor Vehicles (Continuation)	16
Chapter 21 - Bills of Lading	17
Chapter 22 - Contracts Requiring Writing	17
Chapter 22A - Signatures	17
Chapter 22B - Contracts Against Public Policy	17
Chapter 22C - Payments to Subcontractors	17
Chapter 23 - Debtor and Creditor	17
Chapter 24 – Interest	17
Chapter 25 – Uniform Commercial Code	18
Chapter 25 – Uniform Commercial Code (Continuation)	19
Chapter 25A – Retail Installment Sales Act	20
Chapter 25B - Credit	20
Chapter 25C - Sales of Artwork	20
Chapter 26 - Suretyship	20
Chapter 27 - Warehouse Receipts [Repealed.]	20
Chapter 28 - Administration [Repealed.]	20
Chapter 28A - Administration of Decedents' Estates	20
Chapter 28B - Estates of Absentees in Military Service	20
Chapter 28C - Estates of Missing Persons	20
Chapter 29 - Intestate Succession	21
Chapter 30 - Surviving Spouses	21
Chapter 31 - Wills	21
Chapter 31A - Acts Barring Property Rights	21
Chapter 31B - Renunciation of Property and Renunciation of Fiduciary Powers Act	21
Chapter 31C - Uniform Disposition of Community Property Rights at Death Act	21
Chapter 32 - Fiduciaries	21
Chapter 32A - Powers of Attorney	21
Chapter 33 - Guardian and Ward [Repealed and Recodified.]	21

Chapter 33A - North Carolina Uniform Transfers to Minors Act	21
Chapter 33B - North Carolina Uniform Custodial Trust Act	21
Chapter 34 - Veterans' Guardianship Act	22
Chapter 35 - Sterilization Procedures	22
Chapter 35A - Incompetency and Guardianship	22
Chapter 36 - Trusts and Trustees [Repealed.]	22
Chapter 36A - Trusts and Trustees	22
Chapter 36B - Uniform Management of Institutional Funds Act [Repealed.]	22
Chapter 36C - North Carolina Uniform Trust Code	22
Chapter 36D - North Carolina Community Third Party Trusts, Pooled Trusts	23
Chapter 36E - Uniform Prudent Management of Institutional Funds Act	23
Chapter 37 - Allocation of Principal and Income [Repealed.]	23
Chapter 37A - Uniform Principal and Income Act	23
Chapter 38 - Boundaries	23
Chapter 38A - Landowner Liability	23
Chapter 38B - Trespasser Responsibility	23
Chapter 39 - Conveyances	23
Chapter 39A - Transfer Fee Covenants Prohibited	23
Chapter 40 - Eminent Domain [Repealed.]	23
Chapter 40A - Eminent Domain	23
Chapter 41 - Estates	23
Chapter 41A - State Fair Housing Act	23
Chapter 42 - Landlord and Tenant	23
Chapter 42A - Vacation Rental Act	23
Chapter 43 - Land Registration	23
Chapter 44 - Liens	24
Chapter 44A - Statutory Liens and Charges	24
Chapter 45 - Mortgages and Deeds of Trust	24
Chapter 45A - Good Funds Settlement Act	24
Chapter 46 - Partition	24
Chapter 47 - Probate and Registration	25
Chapter 47A - Unit Ownership	25
Chapter 47B - Real Property Marketable Title Act	25
Chapter 47C - North Carolina Condominium Act	25
Chapter 47D - Notice of Settlement Act [Expired.]	25
Chapter 47E - Residential Property Disclosure Act	25
Chapter 47F - North Carolina Planned Community Act	25
Chapter 47G - Option to Purchase Contracts	25
Chapter 47H - Contracts for Deed	25
Chapter 48 - Adoptions +	26
Chapter 48A - Minors	26
Chapter 49 - Bastardy	26
Chapter 49A - Rights of Children	26
Chapter 50 - Divorce and Alimony	26

Chapter 50A - Uniform Child-Custody Jurisdiction and Enforcement Act	26
Chapter 50B - Domestic Violence	26
Chapter 50C - Civil No-Contact Orders	26
Chapter 51 - Marriage	26
Chapter 52 - Powers and Liabilities of Married Persons	27
Chapter 52A - Uniform Reciprocal Enforcement of Support Act [Repealed.]	27
Chapter 52B - Uniform Premarital Agreement Act	27
Chapter 52C - Uniform Interstate Family Support Act	27
Chapter 53 - Banks	27
Chapter 53A - Business Development Corporations and North Carolina Capital Resource Corporations	28
Chapter 53B - Financial Privacy Act	28
Chapter 54 - Cooperative Organizations	28
Chapter 54A - Capital Stock Savings and Loan Associations [Repealed.]	28
Chapter 54B - Savings and Loan Associations	29
Chapter 54C - Savings Banks	29
Chapter 55 - North Carolina Business Corporation Act	30
Chapter 55A - North Carolina Nonprofit Corporation Act	31
Chapter 55B - Professional Corporation Act	31
Chapter 55C - Foreign Trade Zones	31
Chapter 55D - Filings, Names, and Registered Agents for Corporations, Nonprofit Corporations, and Partnerships	31
Chapter 56 - Electric, Telegraph and Power Companies [Repealed.]	31
Chapter 57 - Hospital, Medical and Dental Service Corporations [Recodified.]	31
Chapter 57A - Health Maintenance Organization Act [Recodified.]	31
Chapter 57B - Health Maintenance Organization Act [Recodified.]	31
Chapter 57C - North Carolina Limited Liability Company Act.	31
Chapter 58 - Insurance.	32
Chapter 58 - Insurance (Continuation)	33
Chapter 58 - Insurance (Continuation)	34
Chapter 58 - Insurance (Continuation)	35
Chapter 58 - Insurance (Continuation)	36
Chapter 58 - Insurance (Continuation)	37
Chapter 58 - Insurance (Continuation)	38
Chapter 58A - North Carolina Health Insurance Trust Commission [Recodified.]	38
Chapter 59 - Partnership.	39
Chapter 59B - Uniform Unincorporated Nonprofit Association Act.	39
Chapter 60 - Railroads and Other Carriers [Repealed and Transferred.]	39
Chapter 61 - Religious Societies	39
Chapter 62 - Public Utilities	39

Chapter 62 - Public Utilities (Continuation)	40
Chapter 62A - Public Safety Telephone Service And Wireless Telephone Service	40
Chapter 63 - Aeronautics	40
Chapter 63A - North Carolina Global TransPark Authority	40
Chapter 64 - Aliens	40
Chapter 65 – Cemeteries	40
Chapter 66 - Commerce and Business	41
Chapter 67 - Dogs	41
Chapter 68 - Fences and Stock Law	41
Chapter 69 - Fire Protection	41
Chapter 70 - Indian Antiquities, Archaeological Resources and Unmarked Human Skeletal Remains Protection	42
Chapter 71 - Indians [Repealed.]	42
Chapter 71A - Indians	42
Chapter 72 - Inns, Hotels and Restaurants	42
Chapter 73 - Mills	42
Chapter 74 - Mines and Quarries	42
Chapter 74A - Company Police [Repealed.]	42
Chapter 74B - Private Protective Services Act [Repealed.]	42
Chapter 74C - Private Protective Services	42
Chapter 74D - Alarm Systems	42
Chapter 74E - Company Police Act	42
Chapter 74F - Locksmith Licensing Act	42
Chapter 74G - Campus Police Act	42
Chapter 75 - Monopolies, Trusts and Consumer Protection	42
Chapter 75A - Boating and Water Safety	43
Chapter 75B - Discrimination in Business	43
Chapter 75C - Motion Picture Fair Competition Act	43
Chapter 75D - Racketeer Influenced and Corrupt Organizations	43
Chapter 75E - Unlawful Activities in Connection With Certain Corporate Transactions	43
Chapter 76 - Navigation	43
Chapter 76A - Navigation and Pilotage Commissions	43
Chapter 77 - Rivers, Creeks, and Coastal Waters	43
Chapter 78 - Securities Law [Repealed.]	43
Chapter 78A - North Carolina Securities Act	43
Chapter 78B - Tender Offer Disclosure Act [Repealed.]	43
Chapter 78C - Investment Advisers	43
Chapter 78D - Commodities Act	43
Chapter 79 - Strays [Repealed.]	43
Chapter 80 - Trademarks, Brands, etc.	44
Chapter 81 - Weights and Measures [Recodified.]	44
Chapter 81A - Weights and Measures Act of 1975.	44
Chapter 82 - Wrecks [Repealed.]	44
Chapter 83 - Architects [Recodified.]	44

Chapter 83A - Architects	44
Chapter 84 - Attorneys-at-Law	44
Chapter 84A - Foreign Legal Consultants	44
Chapter 85 - Auctions and Auctioneers [Repealed.]	44
Chapter 85A - Bail Bondsmen and Runners [Recodified.]	44
Chapter 85B - Auctions and Auctioneers	44
Chapter 85C - Bail Bondsmen and Runners [Recodified.]	44
Chapter 86 - Barbers [Recodified.]	44
Chapter 86A - Barbers	44
Chapter 87 - Contractors	44
Chapter 88 - Cosmetic Art [Repealed.]	44
Chapter 88A - Electrolysis Practice Act	44
Chapter 88B - Cosmetic Art	45
Chapter 89 - Engineering and Land Surveying [Recodified.]	45
Chapter 89A - Landscape Architects	45
Chapter 89B - Foresters	45
Chapter 89C - Engineering and Land Surveying	45
Chapter 89D - Landscape Contractors	45
Chapter 89E - Geologists Licensing Act	45
Chapter 89F - North Carolina Soil Scientist Licensing Act	45
Chapter 89G - Irrigation Contractors	45
Chapter 90 - Medicine and Allied Occupations	45
Chapter 90 - Medicine and Allied Occupations (Continuation)	46
Chapter 90 - Medicine and Allied Occupations (Continuation)	47
Chapter 90 - Medicine and Allied Occupations (Continuation)	48
Chapter 90A - Sanitarians and Water and Wastewater Treatment Facility Operators	48
Chapter 90B - Social Worker Certification and Licensure Act	48
Chapter 90C - North Carolina Recreational Therapy Licensure Act	48
Chapter 90D - Interpreters and Transliterators	48
Chapter 91 - Pawnbrokers [Repealed.]	48
Chapter 91A - Pawnbrokers Modernization Act of 1989	48
Chapter 92 - Photographers [Deleted.]	48
Chapter 93 - Certified Public Accountants	48
Chapter 93A - Real Estate License Law	49
Chapter 93B - Occupational Licensing Boards	49
Chapter 93C - Watchmakers [Repealed.]	49
Chapter 93D - North Carolina State Hearing Aid Dealers and Fitters Board.	49
Chapter 93E - North Carolina Appraisers Act	49
Chapter 94 - Apprenticeship	49
Chapter 95 - Department of Labor and Labor Regulations	49
Chapter 95 - Department of Labor and Labor Regulations (Continuation)	50
Chapter 96 - Employment Security	50
Chapter 97 - Workers' Compensation Act	50
Chapter 97 - Workers' Compensation Act (Continuation)	51

Chapter 98 - Burnt and Lost Records	51
Chapter 99 - Libel and Slander	51
Chapter 99A - Civil Remedies for Criminal Actions	51
Chapter 99B - Products Liability	51
Chapter 99C - Actions Relating to Winter Sports Safety and Accidents	51
Chapter 99D - Civil Rights	51
Chapter 99E - Special Liability Provisions	51
Chapter 100 - Monuments, Memorials and Parks	51
Chapter 101 - Names of Persons	51
Chapter 102 - Official Survey Base	51
Chapter 103 - Sundays, Holidays and Special Days	51
Chapter 104 - United States Lands	51
Chapter 104A - Degrees of Kinship	51
Chapter 104B - Hurricanes or Other Acts of Nature	51
Chapter 104C - Atomic Energy, Radioactivity and Ionizing Radiation [Repealed and Recodified.]	51
Chapter 104D - Southern States Energy Compact	51
Chapter 104E - North Carolina Radiation Protection Act	51
Chapter 104F - Southeast Interstate Low-Level Radioactive Waste Management Compact [Repealed]	51
Chapter 104G - North Carolina Low-Level Radioactive Waste Management Authority Act of 1987 [Repealed]	51
Chapter 105 - Taxation	51
Chapter 105 - Taxation (Continuation)	52
Chapter 105 - Taxation (Continuation)	53
Chapter 105 - Taxation (Continuation)	54
Chapter 105A - Setoff Debt Collection Act	55
Chapter 105B - Defaulted Student Loan Recovery Act	55
Chapter 106 - Agriculture	55
Chapter 106 - Agriculture (Continue)	56
Chapter 106 - Agriculture (Continue)	57
Chapter 107 - Agricultural Development Districts [Repealed.]	57
Chapter 108 - Social Services [Repealed and Recodified.]	57
Chapter 108A - Social Services	57
Chapter 108B - Community Action Programs	58
Chapter 108C Medicaid and Health Choice Provider Requirements.	58
Chapter 108D Medicaid Managed Care for Behavioral Health Services.	58
Chapter 109 - Bonds [Recodified.]	58
Chapter 110 - Child Welfare	58
Chapter 111 - Aid to the Blind	58
Chapter 112 - Confederate Homes and Pensions [Repealed.]	58
Chapter 113 - Conservation and Development	58
Chapter 113 - Conservation and Development (Continuation)	59

Chapter 113A - Pollution Control and Environment	59
Chapter 113A - Pollution Control and Environment (Continuation)	60
Chapter 113B - North Carolina Energy Policy Act of 1975	60
Chapter 114 - Department of Justice	60
Chapter 115 - Elementary and Secondary Education [Repealed.]	60
Chapter 115A - Community Colleges, Technical Institutes, and Industrial Education Centers [Repealed.]	60
Chapter 115B - Tuition and Fee Waivers	60
Chapter 115C - Elementary and Secondary Education	60
Chapter 115C - Elementary and Secondary Education (Continuation)	61
Chapter 115C - Elementary and Secondary Education (Continuation)	62
Chapter 115C - Elementary and Secondary Education (Continuation)	63
Chapter 115D - Community Colleges	63
Chapter 115E - Private Educational Facilities Finance Act [Recodified]	63
Chapter 116 - Higher Education	63
Chapter 116 - Higher Education (Continuation)	63
Chapter 116A - Escheats and Abandoned Property [Repealed.]	64
Chapter 116B - Escheats and Abandoned Property	64
Chapter 116C - Continuum of Education Programs	64
Chapter 116D - Higher Education Bonds	64
Chapter 117 - Electrification	64
Chapter 118 - Firemen's and Rescue Squad Workers' Relief and Pension Funds [Recodified.]	64
Chapter 118A - Firemen's Death Benefit Act [Repealed.]	64
Chapter 118B - Members of a Rescue Squad Death Benefit Act [Repealed.]	64
Chapter 119 - Gasoline and Oil Inspection and Regulation	64
Chapter 120 - General Assembly	65
Chapter 120 - General Assembly (Continuation)	66
Chapter 120 - General Assembly (Continuation)	67
Chapter 120C - Lobbying	67
Chapter 121 - Archives and History	67
Chapter 122 - Hospitals for the Mentally Disordered [Repealed.]	67
Chapter 122A - North Carolina Housing Finance Agency	67
Chapter 122B - North Carolina Agricultural Facilities Finance Act [Repealed.]	67
Chapter 122C - Mental Health, Developmental Disabilities, and Substance Abuse Act of 1985	67
Chapter 122C - Mental Health, Developmental Disabilities, and Substance Abuse Act of 1985 (Continuation)	68
Chapter 122D - North Carolina Agricultural Finance Act	68

Chapter 122E - North Carolina Housing Trust and Oil Overcharge Act	68
Chapter 123 - Impeachment	69
Chapter 123A - Industrial Development [Repealed.]	69
Chapter 124 - Internal Improvements	69
Chapter 125 - Libraries	69
Chapter 126 - State Personnel System	69
Chapter 127 - Militia [Repealed.]	69
Chapter 127A - Militia	69
Chapter 127B - Military Affairs	69
Chapter 127C - Advisory Commission on Military Affairs	69
Chapter 128 - Offices and Public Officers	69
Chapter 128 - Offices and Public Officers (Continuation)	70
Chapter 129 - Public Buildings and Grounds	70
Chapter 130 - Public Health [Repealed.]	70
Chapter 130A - Public Health	70
Chapter 130A - Public Health (Continuation)	71
Chapter 130A - Public Health (Continuation)	72
Chapter 130B - Hazardous Waste Management Commission [Repealed.]	72
Chapter 131 - Public Hospitals [Repealed.]	72
Chapter 131A - Health Care Facilities Finance Act	72
Chapter 131B - Licensing of Ambulatory Surgical Facilities [Repealed.]	72
Chapter 131C - Charitable Solicitation Licensure Act [Repealed.]	72
Chapter 131D - Inspection and Licensing of Facilities	72
Chapter 131E - Health Care Facilities and Services	72
Chapter 131E - Health Care Facilities and Services (Continuation)	73
Chapter 131F - Solicitation of Contributions	73
Chapter 132 - Public Records	73
Chapter 133 - Public Works	74
Chapter 134 - Youth Development [Recodified.]	74
Chapter 134A - Youth Services [Repealed.]	74
Chapter 135 - Retirement System for Teachers and State Employees; Social Security; Health Insurance Program for Children	74
Chapter 135 - Retirement System for Teachers and State Employees; Social Security; Health Insurance Program for Children	75
Chapter 136 - Transportation	75
Chapter 136 - Transportation (Continuation)	76
Chapter 137 - Rural Rehabilitation [Repealed.]	76
Chapter 138 - Salaries, Fees and Allowances	76
Chapter 138A - State Government Ethics Act	76
Chapter 139 - Soil and Water Conservation Districts	76

Chapter 140 - State Art Museum; Symphony and Art Societies	76
Chapter 140A - State Awards System	76
Chapter 141 - State Boundaries	76
Chapter 142 - State Debt	76
Chapter 143 - State Departments, Institutions, and Commissions	77
Chapter 143 - State Departments, Institutions, and Commissions (Continuation)	78
Chapter 143 - State Departments, Institutions, and Commissions (Continuation)	79
Chapter 143 - State Departments, Institutions, and Commissions (Continuation)	80
Chapter 143A - State Government Reorganization	80
Chapter 143B - Executive Organization Act of 1973	80
Chapter 143B - Executive Organization Act of 1973 (Continuation)	81
Chapter 143B - Executive Organization Act of 1973 (Continuation)	82
Chapter 143C - State Budget Act	83
Chapter 143D - The State Governmental Accountability and Internal Control Act	83
Chapter 144 - State Flag, Official Governmental Flags, Motto, and Colors	83
Chapter 145 - State Symbols and Other Official Adoptions.	83
Chapter 146 - State Lands	83
Chapter 147 - State Officers	83
Chapter 148 - State Prison System	84
Chapter 149 - State Song and Toast	84
Chapter 150 - Uniform Revocation of Licenses [Repealed.]	84
Chapter 150A - Administrative Procedure Act [Recodified.]	84
Chapter 150B - Administrative Procedure Act	84
Chapter 151 - Constables [Repealed.]	84
Chapter 152 - Coroners	84
Chapter 152A - County Medical Examiner [Repealed.]	84
Chapter 152A - County Medical Examiner [Repealed.] (Continuation)	85
Chapter 153 - Counties and County Commissioners [Repealed.]	85
Chapter 153A - Counties	85
Chapter 153B - Mountain Resources Planning Act	85
Chapter 153C - Uwharrie Regional Resources Act	85
Chapter 154 - County Surveyor [Repealed.]	85
Chapter 155 - County Treasurer [Repealed.]	85
Chapter 156 - Drainage	85
Chapter 156 – Drainage (Continuation)	86

Chapter 157 - Housing Authorities and Projects	86
Chapter 157A - Historic Properties Commissions [Transferred.]	86
Chapter 158 - Local Development	86
Chapter 159 - Local Government Finance	86
Chapter 159 - Local Government Finance (Continuation)	87
Chapter 159A - Pollution Abatement and Industrial Facilities Financing Act [Unconstitutional.]	87
Chapter 159B - Joint Municipal Electric Power and Energy Act	87
Chapter 159C - Industrial and Pollution Control Facilities Financing Act	87
Chapter 159D - The North Carolina Capital Facilities Financing Act	87
Chapter 159E - Registered Public Obligations Act	87
Chapter 159F - North Carolina Energy Development Authority [Repealed.]	87
Chapter 159G - Water Infrastructure	87
Chapter 159H - [Reserved.]	87
Chapter 159I - Solid Waste Management Loan Program and Local Government Special Obligation Bonds	87
Chapter 160 - Municipal Corporations [Repealed And Transferred.]	87
Chapter 160A - Cities and Towns	88
Chapter 160A - Cities and Towns (Continuation)	89
Chapter 160B - Consolidated City-County Act	89
Chapter 160C - Baseball Park Districts [Repealed.]	90
Chapter 161 - Register of Deeds	90
Chapter 162 - Sheriff	90
Chapter 162A - Water and Sewer Systems	90
Chapter 162B Continuity of Local Government in Emergency.	90
Chapter 163 Elections and Election Laws.	90
Chapter 163 Elections and Election Laws. (Continuation)	91
Chapter 164 Concerning the General Statutes of North Carolina.	92
Chapter 165 Veterans.	92
Chapter 166 Civil Preparedness Agencies [Repealed.]	92
Chapter 166A North Carolina Emergency Management Act.	92
Chapter 167 State Civil Air Patrol [Repealed.]	92
Chapter 168 Persons with Disabilities.	92
Chapter 168A Persons With Disabilities Protection Act.	92

Chapter 53A

Business Development Corporations and North Carolina Capital Resource Corporations.

Article 1.

Business Development Corporations.

§§ 53A-1 through 53A-19: Repealed by Session Laws 1995, c. 46, s. 1.

§ 53A-20: Expired.

§ 53A-21: Expired.

§ 53A-22: Expired.

§ 53A-23: Expired.

§ 53A-24: Expired.

§ 53A-25: Expired.

§ 53A-26: Expired.

§ 53A-27: Expired.

§ 53A-28: Expired.

§ 53A-29: Expired.

§ 53A-30: Expired.

§ 53A-31: Expired.

§ 53A-32: Expired.

§ 53A-33: Expired.

§ 53A-34: Expired.

Article 3.

North Carolina Enterprise Corporations.

§ 53A-35. Short Title.

This Article shall be known and may be cited as the North Carolina Enterprise Corporation Act. (1987 (Reg. Sess., 1988), c. 882, s. 1.)

§ 53A-36. Legislative findings and purpose.

(a) The General Assembly finds and declares that there exists in the State of North Carolina a serious shortage of mezzanine finance capital and credit available for investment in rural areas in the State. This shortage of mezzanine finance capital and credit is severe throughout the rural areas of the State, has persisted for a number of years, and constitutes a grave threat to the welfare and prosperity of all residents of the State.

(b) The General Assembly finds and declares further that private enterprise and existing federal and State governmental programs have not adequately alleviated the severe shortage of mezzanine finance capital and credit available for investments in rural areas in the State.

(c) The General Assembly finds and declares that it is a matter of grave public necessity that North Carolina Enterprise Corporations be authorized to be created and to be empowered to alleviate these severe shortages of mezzanine finance capital and credit for investment in rural areas of the State. North Carolina Enterprise Corporations shall help eliminate barriers to rural economic development by providing mezzanine finance capital and credit, and other types of financing as appropriate, to businesses in rural areas that have been unable to obtain sufficient financing through traditional financial institutions. (1987 (Reg. Sess., 1988), c. 882, s. 1.)

§ 53A-37. Definitions.

The following definitions apply in this Article:

(1) Business. A corporation, partnership, association, or sole proprietorship operated for profit.

(2) Equity security. Common stock, preferred stock, an interest in a partnership, subordinated debt, or a warrant that is convertible into, or entitles

the holder to receive upon its exercise, common stock, preferred stock, or an interest in a partnership.

(3)   Mezzanine finance. An investment in the equity securities or subordinated debt of a Qualified North Carolina Business.

(4)   Qualified North Carolina Business. A business whose headquarters and principal business operations are located in North Carolina and which, together with its affiliates on a consolidated basis, had gross income during the immediately preceding fiscal year, determined in accordance with generally accepted accounting principles without taking into account extraordinary items, of less than forty million dollars ($40,000,000).

(5)   Rural areas. Any county in North Carolina which does not include within its boundaries a city, as defined by G.S. 160A-1(2), with a population greater than one percent (1%) of the population of North Carolina.

(6)   Security. A security as defined in G.S. 78A-2(11).

(7)   Subordinated debt. Indebtedness that is or will be subordinated to other indebtedness of the issuer. Subordinated debt may be convertible into common stock, preferred stock, or an interest in a partnership.

(8)   Traditional Financial Institutions. Corporations or associations chartered under Chapters 53 or 54B of the General Statutes. (1987 (Reg. Sess., 1988), c. 882, s. 1.)

§ 53A-38. Incorporation authorized.

(a)   One or more persons, a majority of whom are residents of this State, may, by filing a certificate of incorporation as provided in subsection (b), incorporate a North Carolina Enterprise Corporation under the provisions of this Article.

(b)   Persons who wish to associate themselves for the purpose of establishing a North Carolina Enterprise Corporation shall file a certificate of incorporation with the Secretary of State. The certificate shall be in accordance with G.S. 55-7. (1987 (Reg. Sess., 1988), c. 882, s. 1.)

§ 53A-39. Purpose.

The purpose of a North Carolina Enterprise Corporation shall be to promote, stimulate, develop, and advance economic prosperity and stimulate job creation in North Carolina's rural areas primarily through mezzanine finance investments in Qualified North Carolina Businesses. To stimulate development broadly across the State, a North Carolina Enterprise Corporation, to the maximum extent feasible consistent with sound business practices, will make mezzanine financing and other types of financing available to small businesses and to businesses located throughout all the rural areas of North Carolina. (1987 (Reg. Sess., 1988), c. 882, s. 1.)

§ 53A-40. Corporate name.

The name of the corporation shall include the words "North Carolina Enterprise Corporation". (1987 (Reg. Sess., 1988), c. 882, s. 1.)

§ 53A-41. Governing law.

Except as otherwise provided in this Article, a North Carolina Enterprise Corporation shall be governed by Chapter 55 of the General Statutes. (1987 (Reg. Sess., 1988), c. 882, s. 1.)

§ 53A-42. Powers.

A North Carolina Enterprise Corporation created under this Article shall have all the powers conferred on business corporations by Chapter 55 of the General Statutes. (1987 (Reg. Sess., 1988), c. 882, s. 1.)

§ 53A-43. Primary investments.

The primary investments of a North Carolina Enterprise Corporation shall be in Qualified North Carolina Businesses that have significant potential to create jobs and diversify and stabilize the economy of rural areas of this State. (1987 (Reg. Sess., 1988), c. 882, s. 1.)

§ 53A-44. Prohibited investments.

Investments by a North Carolina Enterprise Corporation shall not be made in any business unless the business can demonstrate to the satisfaction of the North Carolina Enterprise Corporation that the business cannot obtain sufficient financing through traditional financial institutions. (1987 (Reg. Sess., 1988), c. 882, s. 1.)

§ 53A-45. Board of directors.

The business and affairs of a North Carolina Enterprise Corporation shall be managed and conducted by a board of directors and by such officers and agents as the corporation by its bylaws shall authorize. The initial board of directors shall be those listed in the Articles of Incorporation. At the initial shareholders meeting, and thereafter annually, the voting common stock shareholders shall elect a board of directors comprised of not less than thirteen (13) members in accordance with the following conditions:

(1) Not less than five (5) members who are employed by the North Carolina banks that invest in the common stock of the North Carolina Enterprise Corporation;

(2) Not less than five (5) members who are representatives of North Carolina savings and loans, insurance companies, utility companies, endowment funds, public investors, private businesses, private individuals, or others that invest in the common stock of the North Carolina Enterprise Corporation;

(3) Not less than two (2) members who are the representatives of appropriate public interests, which persons shall not be employed by any bank, entity, or person that owns common stock of the North Carolina Enterprise Corporation;

(4) One member who is the President or the Chief Executive Officer of the North Carolina Enterprise Corporation. (1987, Reg. Sess., 1988), c. 882, s. 1.)

§ 53A-46: Repealed by Session Laws 1996, Second Extra Session, c. 14, s. 8.

§ 53A-47. Charter void unless business begun; Article void unless corporation organized.

If a corporation organized pursuant to this Article fails to begin business within three years after the effective date of its charter then its charter is void. If, at the expiration of three years after July 1, 1988, no corporation has been organized pursuant to this Article, then on that date this Article shall expire. (1987 (Reg. Sess., 1988), c. 882, s. 1.)

Chapter 53B.

Financial Privacy Act.

§ 53B-1. Short title.

This act may be cited as the North Carolina Financial Privacy Act. (1985 (Reg. Sess., 1986), c. 1002, s. 1.)

§ 53B-2. Definitions.

As used in this Chapter, unless the context otherwise requires, the term:

(1) "Customer" means a person who has transacted business with a financial institution or has used the services offered by a financial institution.

(2) "Financial institution" means a banking corporation, trust company, savings and loan association, credit union, or other entity principally engaged in the business of lending money or receiving or soliciting money on deposit.

(3) "Financial record" means an original of, a copy of, or information derived from, a record held by a financial institution pertaining to a customer's relationship with the financial institution and identified with or identifiable with the customer. Financial record shall not include forged or counterfeit financial instruments or records relating to an account established under a fictitious name or another person's name without proper authorization.

(4) "Government authority" means an agency or department of the State or of any of its political subdivisions, including any officer, employee, or agent thereof.

(5) "Government inquiry" means a lawful investigation by a government agency or official proceeding inquiring into a violation of, or failure to comply with, any criminal or civil statute, law, or rule.

(6) "Supervisory agency" means a State agency or department having the statutory authority to examine the financial condition or business operation of a financial institution. (1985 (Reg. Sess., 1986), c. 1002, s. 1; 2006-259, s. 14(a).)

§ 53B-3. Public policy.

It is the policy of this State that financial records should be treated as confidential and that no financial institution may provide to any government authority and no government authority may have access to any financial records except in accordance with the provisions of this Chapter. (1985 (Reg. Sess., 1986), c. 1002, s. 1.)

§ 53B-4. Access to financial records.

Notwithstanding any other provision of law, no government authority may have access to a customer's financial record held by a financial institution unless the financial record is described with reasonable specificity and access is sought pursuant to any of the following:

(1) Customer authorization that meets the requirements of the Right to Financial Privacy Act § 1104, 12 U.S.C. § 3404, provided, however, a customer authorization received by a State agency or a county department of social

services for the purpose of determining eligibility for the programs of public assistance under Chapter 108A of the General Statutes, or for purposes of a government inquiry concerning these same programs of public assistance, cannot be revoked and shall remain valid for 12 months unless a shorter period is specified in the authorization, or a customer authorization that is given by a licensed attorney with respect to an account in which the attorney holds funds as a fiduciary.

(2) Authorization under G.S. 105-242 or G.S. 105-258.

(3) Search warrant as provided in Article 11 of Chapter 15A of the General Statutes.

(4) Statutory authority of a supervisory agency to examine or have access to financial records in the exercise of its supervisory, regulatory, or monetary functions with respect to a financial institution.

(5) The authority granted under G.S. 116B-72 and G.S. 116B-75.

(6) Examination and review by the State Auditor or his authorized representative under G.S. 147-64.6(c)(9) or G.S. 147-64.7(a).

(7) Request by a government authority authorized to buy and sell student loan notes under Article 23 of Chapter 116 of the General Statutes for financial records relating to insured student loans.

(8) Pending litigation to which the government authority and the customer are parties.

(9) Subpoena or court order in connection with a grand jury proceeding.

(10) A writ of execution under Article 28 of Chapter 1 of the General Statutes.

(11) Other court order or administrative or judicial subpoena authorized by law if the requirements of G.S. 53B-5 are met.

(12) The authority granted to the Attorney General under Chapter 75 of the General Statutes.

(13) A subpoena delivered to the financial institution pursuant to G.S. 108A-116 by (i) a county department of social services director investigating a credible

report of financial exploitation of a disabled adult or (ii) a law enforcement agency investigating a credible report of financial exploitation of a disabled adult or older adult.

As used in this section, the term "reasonable specificity" means that degree of specificity reasonable under all the circumstances, and, with respect to requests under G.S. 116B-72 and G.S. 116B-75, may include designation by general type or class. (1985 (Reg. Sess., 1986), c. 1002, s. 1; 1999-460, s. 11; 2006-259, s. 14(b); 2007-527, s. 1; 2010-31, s. 31.8(j); 2013-337, s. 2(a).)

§ 53B-5. Service on customer certification.

A government authority may have access to a customer's financial record pursuant to G.S. 53B-4(11) only if:

(1) The court order or subpoena describes with reasonable specificity the financial record to which access is sought;

(2) A copy of the court order or subpoena has been served on the customer pursuant to G.S. 1A-1, Rule 4 (j) of the N.C. Rules of Civil Procedure or by certified mail to the customer's last known address and the court order or subpoena states the name of the government authority seeking access to the financial record and the purpose for which access is sought;

(3) The following notice has been served on the customer pursuant to G.S. 1A-1, Rule 4 (j) of the N.C. Rules of Civil Procedure or by certified mail to the customer's last known address together with the court order or subpoena:

"Records or information held by the financial institution named in the attached process are being sought by government authority in accordance with the North Carolina Financial Privacy Act. You may have rights under the act to challenge access to the records or information. You must, however, act within 10 days from the date this notice was served on you to make a challenge in court or the records or information will be made available. You may wish to employ an attorney to represent you and protect your rights.";

(4) The customer has not challenged the court order or subpoena within 10 days after service by certified mail which is presumed to be received three days from mailing;

(5) The government authority has certified in writing to the financial institution that it has complied with the applicable provisions of this Chapter. (1985 (Reg. Sess., 1986), c. 1002, s. 1; 1995, c. 222, s. 1.)

§ 53B-6. Delayed notice.

Upon application of a government authority, a superior court judge may order that the customer notice required by G.S. 53B-5 be delayed if the court finds there is reason to believe that:

(1) The financial record to which access is sought is relevant to a legitimate government inquiry; and

(2) Notice to the customer will:

a. Endanger life or physical safety of any person;

b. Result in flight from prosecution;

c. Lead to intimidation of a witness;

d. Result in destruction of or tampering with evidence; or

e. Otherwise seriously jeopardize the government inquiry or an official proceeding or investigation.

A court order granting delay of notice to a customer under this section shall set out the specific facts supporting its findings, specify the period of delay, and direct that the government authority shall serve on the customer at the end of that period a copy of the court order or subpoena and a notice that the records have been furnished. (1985 (Reg. Sess., 1986), c. 1002, s. 1.)

§ 53B-7. Customer challenge.

(a) Within 10 days after service of a court order or subpoena under this Chapter a customer may apply to the superior court of the county in which he resides for an order quashing or modifying the court order or subpoena. The customer shall deliver or mail a copy of the application to the government authority and the financial institution named in the court order or subpoena. The superior court shall grant or deny the application within 10 days after it is filed.

(b) Nothing in this Chapter affects the right of a financial institution to challenge a request for financial records by a government authority under existing law. (1985 (Reg. Sess., 1986), c. 1002, s. 1.)

§ 53B-8. Disclosure of financial records.

No financial institution or its officer, employee, or agent may disclose a customer's financial record to a government authority except as provided in this Chapter. This section does not prohibit a financial institution from giving notice of or disclosing a financial record to a government authority, as defined in G.S. 53B-2(4), to the same extent as is authorized with respect to federal government authorities in the Right to Financial Privacy Act § 1103(d), 12 U.S.C. § 3403(d). Nothing in this section shall prohibit a financial institution or its officer, employee or agent from disclosing, or require the disclosure of, the name, address, and existence of an account of any customer to a government authority that makes a written request stating the reason for the request. Nothing in this Chapter shall prohibit a financial institution or its officer, employee, or agent from notifying a government authority that the financial institution or its officer, employee, or agent has information that may be relevant to a possible violation of law or regulation. The information shall be limited to a description of the suspected illegal activity and the name or other identifying information concerning any individual, corporation, or account involved in the activity. Any financial institution or its officer, employee, or agent making a disclosure of information pursuant to this section shall not be liable to the customer under the laws and rules of the State of North Carolina or any political subdivision of the State for disclosure or for failure to notify the customer of the disclosure. (1985 (Reg. Sess., 1986), c. 1002, s. 1; 1995, c. 222, s. 2; 1998-119, s. 3.)

§ 53B-9. Duty of financial institutions; fee; limitation of liability.

(a) Upon service of a subpoena or court order pursuant to G.S. 53B-4(1), (3), (9), or (11) and receipt of certification pursuant to G.S. 53B-5(5), or upon receipt of a subpoena pursuant to G.S. 53B-4(13), a financial institution shall locate the financial records requested and prepare to make them available to the government authority seeking access to them. Upon receipt of notice that a customer has challenged the court order or subpoena, the financial institution may suspend its efforts to make the records available until after final disposition of the challenge.

(b) Upon receipt of access to financial records pursuant to G.S. 53B-4(1), (3), (9), (11), or (13), a government authority shall pay the financial institution that provided the financial records a fee for costs directly incurred in assembling and delivering the financial records. The fee shall be at the rate established pursuant to the Right to Financial Privacy Act § 1115(a), 12 U.S.C. § 3415, and 12 C.F.R. 219, unless waived, in whole or in part, by the financial institution.

(c) A financial institution that discloses a financial record pursuant to this Chapter in good faith reliance upon certification by a government authority pursuant to G.S. 53B-5(5) is not liable for damages resulting from the disclosure. (1985 (Reg. Sess., 1986), c. 1002, s. 1; 2013-337, s. 2(b).)

§ 53B-10. Penalty.

(a) Any financial institution disclosing financial records or information contained therein in violation of this Chapter shall be liable to the customer to whom the records relate in an amount equal to the sum of:

(1) One thousand dollars ($1,000);

(2) Any actual damages sustained by the customer as a result of the disclosure; and

(3) Such punitive damages as the court may allow, where the violation is found to have been willful or intentional.

(b) Any government authority that participates in or induces or solicits a violation of this Chapter shall be liable to the customer to whom the violation relates in the amount set out in subsection (a) above. It shall be a defense to an action under this subsection that the government authority acted in good faith in obtaining and relying upon process issued pursuant to G.S. 53B-4. (1985 (Reg. Sess., 1986), c. 1002, s. 1.)

Chapter 53C.

Regulation of Banks.

Article 1.

General Provisions.

§ 53C-1-1. Title.

This Chapter shall be known and may be cited as Regulation of Banks and Other Financial Services. (2012-56, s. 4.)

§ 53C-1-2. Scope and applicability of Chapter.

(a)   Unless the context specifies otherwise, this Chapter shall apply to the following:

(1)   All existing banks organized or created under the laws of this State.

(2)   All banks created under the provisions of Article 3 of this Chapter.

(3)   All persons who subject themselves to the provisions of this Chapter.

(4)   All persons who become subject to the penalties provided for in this Chapter as a consequence of violating any of the provisions of this Chapter.

(b)   Transactions validly entered into before October 1, 2012, and the rights, duties, and interests flowing from them remain valid and may be terminated, completed, or enforced as required or permitted by any statute amended or repealed by the law by which this act was enacted as though the amendment or repeal had not occurred.

(c)   Except as restricted by federal law, a federally chartered depository institution that has a branch in this State shall have all the rights, powers, and privileges and shall be entitled to the same exemptions and immunities as banks organized or created under the laws of this State.

(d) Except as restricted by federal law or the laws of another state in which it was organized or created, an out-of-state bank that has a branch in this State shall have, with respect to activities conducted through such branch, all the rights, powers, and privileges and shall be entitled to the same exemptions and immunities as banks organized and created under the laws of this State.

(e) Any reference in this Chapter to a state or federal law, regulation, or agency shall be deemed to refer to any replacement law or regulation or any successor agency, whether or not this Chapter explicitly provides for that reference. (2012-56, s. 4.)

§ 53C-1-3. Existing banks; prohibitions, injunctions.

(a) No depository institution organized or created under the laws of this State may operate as a bank except in accordance with this Chapter. Banks established prior to October 1, 2012, may continue operation under their existing organizational documents but shall be subject to all other requirements of this Chapter.

(b) No person shall operate in this State as a "bank," "savings bank," "savings and loan association," "trust company," or otherwise as a depository institution or trust institution unless established as a depository institution or trust institution under the laws of this State or another state or established under federal law. Unless so authorized, no person doing business in this State shall do either of the following:

(1) Use in its name the term "bank," "savings and loan," "savings bank," "banking company," "trust company," or words of similar meaning that lead the public reasonably to believe that it conducts the business of a depository institution or trust institution.

(2) Use any sign, letterhead, circular, or Web site content or advertise or communicate in any manner that would lead the public reasonably to believe that it conducts the business of a depository institution or trust institution.

(c) Upon application by the Commissioner, a court of competent jurisdiction may issue an injunction to restrain any person from violating or from continuing to violate this section. (2012-56, s. 4.)

§ 53C-1-4. Definitions and application of terms.

Unless the context requires otherwise, the following definitions apply in this Chapter:

(1) Acquire. - To obtain the right or power to vote or to direct the voting of voting securities of a bank or holding company as follows:

a. Through a purchase of or share exchange for shares.

b. By reason of an issuance of shares or the exercise of a right under a warrant, option, or convertible security or instrument to acquire shares.

c. Pursuant to an agreement or trust or through any similar transaction, event, or contractual right.

(2) Acting in concert. - Knowing participation in a joint activity or interdependent conscious parallel action toward the common goal of obtaining control of a bank or holding company, whether or not pursuant to an express agreement, including participation in a combination or pooling of voting securities of a bank holding company for such common purpose pursuant to any contract, understanding, relationship, agreement, or other arrangement, whether written or otherwise.

(3) Affiliate. - A person that, directly or indirectly, controls, is controlled by, or is under common control with another person. Each member of a group of persons acting in concert shall be deemed an affiliate of the group.

(4) Bank. - Any corporation, other than a credit union, savings institution, or trust company, that is organized under the laws of this State and is engaged in the business of receiving deposits (other than trust funds), paying monies, and making loans.

(5) Bank operating subsidiary. - A subsidiary that is under the control of a bank and engages only in activities in which a bank may engage pursuant to G.S. 53C-5-1.

(6) Bank premises. - Any improved or unimproved real estate, whether or not open to the public, that is utilized or intended to be utilized by a bank, including additional space to rent as a source of income.

(7) Bank supervisory agency. - Any of the following agencies:

a. The CFPB, FDIC, Federal Reserve Board, OCC, and any successor to these agencies.

b. Any agency of another state with primary responsibility for chartering and supervising depository institutions organized under the laws of that state.

c. Any agency of a sovereign nation with primary responsibility for chartering and supervising depository institutions organized under the laws of that nation.

(8) Bankers' bank. - As defined in Regulation D of the Federal Reserve Board, 12 C.F.R. § 204.121.

(9) Banking laws. - All laws which the Commissioner or the OCOB is authorized to enforce under any applicable statute.

(10) Board of directors. - A governing board of a company that is responsible for policy, oversight, and compliance.

(11) Branch. - An office of any bank or a depository institution organized under the banking laws of the United States, another state, or another sovereign nation, other than that depository institution's principal office, in which deposits are received. A branch may also engage in any of the functions or services authorized to be engaged in by the bank of which it is a branch. The term "branch" does not include a non-branch bank business office, automated teller machine, remote deposit facility, remote service unit, customer-bank communications terminal, point-of-sale terminal, automated banking facility or other direct or remote information processing device or machine, whether manned or unmanned, by means of which information relating to any financial service or transaction rendered to the public is stored and transmitted, instantaneously or otherwise, to or from a bank or other nonbank terminal.

(12) Capital. - An amount equal to the bank's "total capital" as that term is used by the FDIC in 12 C.F.R. Part 325; provided, that if the term "total capital" is replaced by a term including substantially the same elements as "total capital," the term "capital" as used in this Chapter shall mean an amount equal to the amount calculated by application of the definition of such replacement term.

(13) Capital impairment. - The reduction of a bank's capital at any time below its required capital.

(14) Central reserve bank. - A depository institution of which at least fifty percent (50%) of its shares are owned by other depository institutions.

(15) CFPB. - The Consumer Financial Protection Bureau or its successor.

(16) Charter. - A document issued by the Commissioner in accordance with Article 3 of this Chapter permitting a bank to conduct banking business.

(17) Combination. - A merger, share exchange, or transfer or acquisition of all or substantially all assets and liabilities of a person undertaken in compliance with such federal laws and laws of this State or other states as may be applicable.

(18) Commission. - The State Banking Commission provided for in G.S. 53C-2-1.

(19) Commissioner. - The Commissioner of Banks provided for in G.S. 53C-2-2.

(20) Company. - A corporation, limited liability company, partnership, joint venture, business trust, trust, syndicate, association, unincorporated organization, or other form of business entity.

(20a) Consumer finance licensee. - An individual associated with a "licensee," as that term is defined in G.S. 53-165(h).

(21) Control. - The possession, directly or indirectly, of the power or right to direct or to cause the direction of the management or policies of a person by reason of an agreement, understanding, proxy, or power of attorney or through

the ownership of or voting power over ten percent (10%) or more of any class of the voting securities of the person.

(22) Control transaction. - The acquisition of control over a bank or a holding company other than pursuant to a combination.

(23) Credit union. - A credit union as defined in G.S. 54-109.1.

(24) De novo branch. - A branch of a bank or of an out-of-state bank within this State that is established as a branch, and not (i) by virtue of an acquisition of the existing branch of another bank or out-of-state bank, (ii) by a combination involving the bank or out-of-state bank, or (iii) by the conversion of a non-branch bank business office to a branch.

(25) Deposit. - A "deposit" as defined in Section 3(1) of the Federal Deposit Insurance Act, 12 U.S.C. § 1813(1).

(26) Deposit insurance. - Insurance of a bank's deposit accounts where the beneficiaries are the holders of the insured accounts.

(27) Depository institution. - A bank, out-of-state bank, savings institution, or federally chartered institution, the deposits of which are insured by the FDIC.

(28) Deputy commissioner. - An individual appointed by the Commissioner to such office as provided by G.S. 53C-2-3.

(29) Distribution. - With respect to a bank, "distribution" has the same meaning as set forth in Chapter 55.

(30) DPC subsidiary. - A debt previously contracted subsidiary of a bank that acquires in good faith an equity ownership interest through foreclosure or other realization on collateral, by way of a compromise of a disputed or contested claim, or to avoid a loss in connection with a debt previously contracted or to which the bank transfers an equity ownership interest so acquired by the bank.

(31) Equity ownership interest. - Any beneficial equity or similar interest, whether direct or indirect, including shares, limited or general partnership interests, and membership interests in a limited liability company.

(32) Examination. - A supervisory inspection of a bank, a proposed bank, a holding company, or a branch of an out-of-state bank operating in this State that

may include inspection of all relevant information, including information of or about the subsidiaries and affiliates of the bank, proposed bank holding company, or branch. "Examination" also includes an investigation of any person with respect to any violation or suspected violation of any provision of this Chapter by such person, or a review of facts and circumstances relevant to the Commissioner's consideration of the issuance of an order pursuant to this Chapter.

(33)   Farm credit system institution. - A lending institution regulated by the Farm Credit Administration.

(34)   FDIC. - The Federal Deposit Insurance Corporation or its successor.

(35)   Federal Reserve Board. - The Board of Governors of the Federal Reserve System or its successor.

(36)   Federal savings association. - A federal savings association or federal savings bank chartered under Section 5 of the Home Owners' Loan Act, 12 U.S.C. § 1464.

(37)   Federally chartered institution. - A national bank or federal savings association.

(38)   Financial subsidiary. - A "financial subsidiary" as defined in 12 U.S.C. § 24a(g).

(39)   Holding company. - A company that controls a depository institution or that controls a company that directly or indirectly controls a depository institution.

(40)   Immediate family. - An individual's spouse, father, mother, children, brothers, sisters, and grandchildren; the father, mother, brothers and sisters of the individual's spouse; and the spouse of the individual's child, brother, or sister.

(41)   Inadequate capital. - An amount of capital equal to at least seventy-five percent (75%) but less than one hundred percent (100%) of required capital.

(42)   Individual. - A human being.

(43) Insufficient capital. - An amount of capital less than seventy-five percent (75%) of required capital.

(44) Lower-tier subsidiary. - Any company which is controlled by a subsidiary.

(45) National bank. - A banking association organized under 12 U.S.C. § 21.

(46) Non-branch bank business office. - Any staffed physical location open to the public in this State in which an office of a bank, out-of-state bank, depository institution established under the laws of another state, or federally chartered institution that is not a branch, an office of a separately organized subsidiary of such depository institution, or an office of the holding company of such depository institution, at which one or more banking or banking-related products or services are offered, other than the taking of deposits. The provision of remote deposit capture facilities or services by a non-branch bank business office shall not be deemed to be a taking of deposits. Non-branch bank business offices include loan production offices, mortgage loan offices, and insurance agency offices, or a combination thereof.

(47) North Carolina financial institution. - A bank, savings institution, or trust company organized under the laws of this State. For purposes of the Securities Act of 1933 and the Securities Exchange Act of 1934, any North Carolina financial institution is a banking institution.

(48) OCC. - The Office of the Comptroller of the Currency or its successor.

(49) OCOB. - The Office of the Commissioner of Banks as provided in G.S. 53C-2-3.

(50) Organizational documents. - The charter, certificate of organization, articles of incorporation, articles of association, certificate of limited partnership, bylaws, operating agreement, partnership agreement, and any other similar documents required to be prepared or adopted by a company in connection with its organization, and as thereafter amended from time to time.

(51) Organizational law. - The laws of the jurisdiction of organization of a company applicable to the organization of the company and its governance, including approval of transactions by its board of directors, shareholders, partners, members, or beneficiaries, as applicable.

(52) Organizers. - One or more individuals who are the organizers of a proposed bank responsible for the business of the proposed bank from the filing of the application to the Commission's final decision on the application.

(53) Out-of-state bank. - A bank that is organized, chartered, or created under the laws of a state other than this State and the deposits of which are insured by the FDIC.

(54) Person. - An individual, a company, or a group of persons who are acting in concert.

(55) Plan of conversion. - A detailed outline of the procedure of the conversion of a depository institution from one to another charter.

(56) Practical banker. - An individual who at the time of appointment to the Commission is, or has been during the five years preceding the appointment, a president, chief executive officer, director, or holder of five percent (5%) or more of any class of voting securities of a North Carolina financial institution.

(57) Principal office. - The office that houses the headquarters of a bank.

(58) Public member. - A member of the Commission who is not a practical banker or a consumer finance licensee and who is not at the time of appointment to the Commission, nor was within the five years preceding the appointment, an employee of a North Carolina financial institution.

(59) Public notice. - Notice to the public of the applicable information specified in this Chapter by (i) a single publication in a newspaper of general circulation in the county in which the bank that is the subject of the publication has its principal office or in such other county as may be directed by the Commissioner to best meet the purposes for which the notice is required and (ii) a posting in the notices section of the Commissioner's Web site for at least 15 days.

(60) Record. - Information, reports, memoranda, charts, letters, messages, extracts, summaries, analyses, compilations, transaction documentation, account statements, financial statements, and other documents, including customer financial and other information, whether created, transmitted, distributed, retained, or stored in tangible or digital form.

(61) Registered agent. - The person named in the organizational documents of a company upon whom service of legal process is deemed binding upon the company.

(62) Required capital. - Required capital means either of the following:

a. In the case of a proposed bank, the amount of capital required by the Commissioner as a prerequisite to the commencement of the business of banking.

b. In all other cases, an amount of capital equal to at least the amount of capital required for a bank to be deemed "adequately capitalized" under applicable federal regulatory capital standards.

(63) Savings institution. - A savings and loan association or a savings bank organized under the laws of this State or of another state, or a federal savings association or savings bank.

(64) Shareholder. - Any person in whose name shares are registered in the records of a corporation, or the beneficial owner of shares to the extent of the rights granted by a nominee certificate on file with a corporation.

(65) Shares. - The units into which the equity ownership interests of a corporation are divided.

(66) State. - Any state of the United States, the District of Columbia, or any territory of the United States other than this State.

(67) State trust company. - A company organized under the provisions of Article 24 of Chapter 53 of the General Statutes and a trust company previously organized under other provisions of this Chapter to operate only as a trust company and not as a commercial bank.

(68) Subsidiary. - A company over which a bank has control, including a lower-tier subsidiary.

(69) This State. - The State of North Carolina.

(70) Trust business. - Acting as a fiduciary or in other capacities permissible for a trust institution under G.S. 53-331.

(71)   Trust company. - A trust institution that is neither a depository institution nor a foreign bank, as defined in 12 U.S.C. § 1813(s)(1), but not including a bank organized under the laws of a territory of the United States.

(72)   Trust funds. - Trust funds as defined in Section 3(p) of the Federal Deposit Insurance Act, 12 U.S.C. § 1813(p).

(73)   Trust institution. - Any company lawfully acting as a fiduciary in a state or in a foreign country.

(74)   Voting securities. - A security that (i) confers upon the holder the right to vote for the election of members of the board of directors or similar governing body of the company or (ii) is convertible into, or entitles the holder to receive upon its exercise, a security that confers such a right to vote.

(75)   Well-capitalized. - The term "well-capitalized" has the same meaning as defined in Regulation Y of the Federal Reserve Board, 12 C.F.R. § 225.2(r).

(76)   Well-managed. - Except as otherwise provided in this Chapter, a company or depository institution is well-managed if the following apply:

a.   At its most recent examination, the company or institution received at least a satisfactory composite rating and at least a satisfactory rating for management, if such rating is given.

b.   In the case of a company or depository institution that has not received an inspection or examination rating, a company or depository institution is well-managed if the Commissioner has determined, after a review of the managerial and other resources of the company or depository institution and after consulting with any other appropriate bank supervisory agency for the company or institution, that the company or institution is well-managed.

A depository institution that results from the merger of two or more depository institutions that are well-managed shall be considered to be well-managed unless the Commissioner determines otherwise after consulting with any other appropriate bank supervisory agency for each depository institution involved in the merger. A depository institution that results from the merger of a depository institution that is well-managed with one or more depository institutions that are not well-managed or have not been examined shall be considered to be well-managed if the Commissioner determines, after a review of the managerial and other resources of the resulting depository institution and after consulting with any other appropriate bank supervisory agency for the institutions involved in the merger, as applicable, that the resulting institution is well-managed. (2012-56, s. 4; 2013-29, s. 1.)

§ 53C-1-5. Severability.

If any provision of this Chapter is found by any court of competent jurisdiction to be invalid as to any person or circumstance, or to be preempted by federal law, the remaining provisions of this Chapter shall not be affected and shall continue to apply to any other person or circumstance. (2012-56, s. 4.)

Article 2.

Commission and Commissioner.

§ 53C-2-1. The Commission.

(a) The Commission consists of 15 members, including the State Treasurer, who shall serve as an ex officio member; 12 members appointed by the Governor; and two members appointed by the General Assembly under G.S. 120-121, one of whom shall be appointed upon the recommendation of the President Pro Tempore of the Senate and one of whom shall be appointed upon the recommendation of the Speaker of the House of Representatives. The Governor shall appoint three practical bankers, one consumer finance licensee, and eight public members to the Commission. The member appointed upon the recommendation of the President Pro Tempore of the Senate shall be a practical banker, and the member appointed upon the recommendation of the Speaker of the House shall be a practical banker. Members shall serve terms of four years. No individual shall serve more than two complete consecutive terms on the Commission. Any vacancy occurring in the membership of the Commission shall be filled by the appropriate appointing officer for the unexpired term, except that vacancies among members appointed by the General Assembly shall be filled in accordance with G.S. 120-122. The appointed members of the Commission shall receive subsistence and travel expenses at the rates set forth in G.S. 120-3.1. This compensation shall be paid from the revenues of the OCOB.

(b)   The Commission shall meet at such times, but not less than once every three months, as the Commission may by resolution prescribe, and the Commission shall be convened in special session at the call of the Governor or the Commissioner. The State Treasurer shall be chair of the Commission. The Commission shall meet in person, provided that it may, so long as consistent with applicable law regarding public meetings, meet by telephone or video conference, including attendance of one or more members by telephone or video conferencing.

(c)   Except as required by State or federal law, no member of the Commission shall divulge or make use of any information designated by this Chapter or by the Commissioner as confidential, and no member shall give out any such information unless the information shall be required of the member at a hearing at which the member is duly subpoenaed or by a court of competent jurisdiction.

(d)   A quorum of the Commission shall consist of a majority of its total membership. Subject to the standards of Chapter 138A of the General Statutes, a majority vote of the members qualified with respect to a matter who are present at the meeting where such matter is considered shall constitute valid action of the Commission. In accordance with G.S. 138A-38(a)(6), the State Treasurer and all disqualified members who are present at a meeting shall be counted for purposes of determining whether a quorum is present.

(e)   The Commission is authorized to supervise, direct, and review the exercise by the Commissioner of all powers, duties, and functions vested in or exercised by the Commissioner under the banking laws of this State. (2012-56, s. 4; 2013-29, s. 2.)

§ 53C-2-2. The Commissioner.

(a)   Effective April 1, 2011, and quadrennially thereafter, the Governor shall appoint a Commissioner, which appointment shall be subject to confirmation by the General Assembly by joint resolution. The name of the individual appointed to be Commissioner shall be submitted to the General Assembly on or before February 1 of the year in which the individual's term of office begins. The term of office for the Commissioner shall be four years. In case of a vacancy in the office of Commissioner, the Governor shall appoint an individual to serve as Commissioner on an interim basis pending confirmation of a nominee by the General Assembly.

(b)   The Commissioner has the powers enumerated in this Chapter and otherwise provided by North Carolina law and such other powers as may be necessary for the proper discharge of the Commissioner's duties, including the power to enter into contracts. The Commissioner shall act as the executive officer of the Commission.

(c)   The Commissioner is authorized to subpoena witnesses and compel their attendance, require the production of evidence, administer oaths, and examine any person under oath in connection with any subject related to any power vested or duty imposed on the Commissioner under this Chapter.

(d)   The Commissioner may sue and prosecute or defend in any action or proceeding in any courts of this State or any other state and in any court of the United States for the enforcement or protection of any right or pursuit of any remedy necessary or proper in connection with the subjects committed to the Commissioner for administration or in connection with any bank or the rights, liabilities, property, or assets thereof under the Commissioner's supervision. Nothing herein shall be construed to render the Commissioner liable to be sued except as other departments and agencies of the State may be liable under the general law. The Commissioner may exercise any jurisdiction, supervise, regulate, examine, or enforce any banking law and any State consumer protection laws or federal laws with respect to which the Commissioner has enforcement jurisdiction.

(e)   The Commissioner shall have a seal of office bearing the legend "State of North Carolina - Commissioner of Banks." The Commissioner may adopt other symbols or marks of office. (2012-56, s. 4; 2013-29, s. 3.)

§ 53C-2-3. The Office of the Commissioner of Banks.

(a)   The Commissioner shall be assisted in the performance of the duties of office by (i) one or more deputy commissioners and (ii) examiners, investigators, counsel, and other employees under the supervision of the Commissioner, all of whom, together with the Commissioner, shall comprise the "Office of the

Commissioner of Banks." In addition, the work of the OCOB may be conducted by employees of other agencies of government and by agents and independent contractors of the OCOB. The Commissioner may appoint or remove at his or her discretion any deputy commissioner.

(b)   The Commissioner shall appoint, with the approval of the Governor, and may remove at the Commissioner's discretion, a chief deputy commissioner. The chief deputy commissioner may perform such duties and exercise such powers of the Commissioner as the Commissioner may direct. In the event of the absence, death, resignation, disability, or disqualification of the Commissioner, or in case the office of Commissioner otherwise becomes vacant, the chief deputy commissioner shall perform the duties and exercise all the powers vested in the Commissioner until the Governor appoints an acting Commissioner.

(c)   Except as otherwise provided in this Chapter, the OCOB and its employees are exempt from the classification and compensation rules established by the State Human Resources Commission pursuant to G.S. 126-4(1) through (4); G.S. 126-4(5) only as it applies to hours and days of work, vacation, and sick leave; G.S. 126-4(6) only as it applies to promotion and transfer; G.S. 126-4(10) only as it applies to the prohibition of the establishment of incentive pay programs; and Article 2 of Chapter 126 of the General Statutes, except for G.S. 126-7.1. The salary of the Commissioner shall be fixed by the General Assembly.

(d)   The Attorney General shall assign an attorney from the Department of Justice to work full time with the Commission. The attorney shall be subject to all provisions of Chapter 126 of the General Statutes relating to the State Personnel System. The Commission shall fully reimburse the Department of Justice for the compensation, secretarial support, equipment, supplies, records, and other property to support the attorney. (2012-56, s. 4; 2013-382, s. 9.1(c).)

§ 53C-2-4. Administration of the Office of the Commissioner of Banks.

(a)   As authorized in Chapters 54B, 54C, and this Chapter, the OCOB shall be funded by annual or periodic assessments, licensing fees and charges, and reimbursements for examination costs. This list is not exclusive. The OCOB may not levy assessments, fees, or other charges except as expressly provided in this Chapter or by rule adopted in accordance with the provisions of Chapter

150B of the General Statutes and the provisions of this section. The Commissioner is authorized, in the exercise of reasonable discretion, to establish the time, place, and method for the payment of assessments, fees, charges, and costs.

(b) Not less than 30 days prior to the commencement of each fiscal year, the OCOB shall prepare and submit to the Commission a budget for the upcoming fiscal year, including the estimated revenues and expenses for the year. The Commission shall review the budget in a meeting prior to the commencement of the fiscal year with respect to which the budget has been presented and shall approve or modify the budget at the meeting. (2012-56, s. 4.)

§ 53C-2-5. Rule making.

(a) The Commissioner, subject to review and approval by the Commission, may make all necessary rules with respect to the establishment, operation, conduct, and termination of any and all activities and businesses that are subject to licensing, regulation, supervision, or examination by the Commissioner under this Chapter.

(b) The rule-making authority conferred on the Commissioner by this section shall be in addition to and not in derogation of any specific rule-making authority by any other provision of this Chapter or otherwise provided by North Carolina law. (2012-56, s. 4.)

§ 53C-2-6. Hearings and appeals.

(a) Any administrative hearing required or permitted to be held by the Commissioner shall be conducted in accordance with Article 3A of Chapter 150B of the General Statutes.

(b) Upon an appeal to the Commission by any party from an order entered by the Commissioner following an administrative hearing pursuant to Article 3A of Chapter 150B of the General Statutes, the chair of the Commission may appoint an appellate review panel of not fewer than three members to review the record on appeal, hear oral arguments, and make a recommended decision to the Commission. Unless another time period for appeals is provided by this Chapter, any party to an order by the Commissioner may, within 20 days after the order and upon written notice to the Commissioner, appeal the Commissioner's order to the Commission for review. The notice of appeal shall state the grounds for the appeal and set forth in numbered order the assignments of error for review by the Commission. Failure to state the grounds for the appeal and assignments of error shall constitute grounds to dismiss the appeal. Failure to comply with the briefing schedule provided by the Commission shall also constitute grounds to dismiss the appeal. Upon receipt of a notice of appeal, the Commissioner shall, within 30 days of the notice, certify to the Commission the record on appeal. Any party to a proceeding before the Commission may, within 20 days after final order of the Commission, petition the Superior Court of Wake County for judicial review of a final determination of any question of law that may be involved. The petition for judicial review shall be entitled "(insert name) Petitioner v. State of North Carolina on Relation of the Commission." A copy of the petition for judicial review shall be served upon the Commissioner pursuant to G.S. 150B-46. The petition shall be placed on the civil issue docket of the court and shall have precedence over other civil actions. Within 15 days of service of the petition for judicial review, the Commissioner shall certify the record to the Clerk of Superior Court of Wake County. The standard of review of a petition for judicial review of a final order of the Commission shall be as provided in G.S. 150B-51(b).

(c) The hearing officer at administrative hearings conducted under the authority of the Commissioner may be the Commissioner, a deputy commissioner, or other suitable person designated by the Commissioner to serve as a hearing officer.

(d) The Commission may conduct public hearings on matters within its purview. (2012-56, s. 4.)

§ 53C-2-7. Official record.

(a) The Commissioner shall keep a record in the OCOB of the Commissioner's official acts, rulings, and transactions that, except as otherwise provided, shall be open to inspection and copying by any person. The Commissioner may condition the provision of copies of records upon the payment by the person requesting the documents of an amount sufficient to cover the cost of retrieving, copying, and if requested, mailing the documents.

(b) Notwithstanding any laws to the contrary, the following records of the Commissioner shall be confidential and shall not be disclosed or be subject to discovery or public inspection:

(1) Records compiled during or in connection with an examination, audit, or investigation of any person, including records relating to any application for licensure or otherwise to the conduct of business.

(2) Records containing information compiled in preparation for or anticipation of or in the course of litigation, examination, audit, or investigation.

(3) Records containing nonpublic personal information about a customer, whether in paper, electronic, or other form, that is maintained by or on behalf of the financial institution; provided, however, that every report made by a North Carolina financial institution, with respect to a transaction between it and an officer, director, or affiliate thereof, which report is required to be filed with the Commissioner pursuant to this Chapter, shall be filed with the Commissioner in a form prescribed by the Commissioner and shall be open to inspection and copying by any person.

(4) Records containing information furnished in connection with an application bearing on the character, competency, or experience, or information about the personal finances of an existing or proposed organizer, officer, or director of a depository institution, federally chartered institution, trust institution, holding company, or any other person subject to the Commissioner's jurisdiction.

(5) Records containing information about the character, competency, experience, or finances of the directors, officers, or other persons having control over a person giving notice or filing an application to engage in a control transaction pursuant to this Chapter.

(6) Records containing information about the character, competency, or experience of the directors, executive officers, or other persons having control over any of the parties to a combination subject to the Commissioner's jurisdiction.

(7) Records of North Carolina financial institutions in dissolution that have liquidated, that are under the Commissioner's supervisory control, or that are in

receivership and that contain the names or other personal information of any customers of the institutions.

(8) Records prepared by a compliance review committee or other committee of the board of directors of a North Carolina financial institution or established at the direction of such a board of directors that have been obtained by the Commissioner.

(9) Records prepared during or as a result of an examination or investigation of any person by an agency of the United States, or jointly by the agency and the Commissioner, if the records would be confidential under federal law or regulation.

(10) Records prepared during or as a result of an examination or investigation of any person by a regulatory agency with jurisdiction of a state other than this State or of a foreign country if the records would be confidential under that jurisdiction's law or regulations.

(11) Records of information and reports submitted to federal regulatory agencies by any depository institution or trust institution, or its affiliates, holding company or its subsidiaries, or any other person subject to the Commissioner's jurisdiction, if the records would be confidential under federal law or regulation.

(12) Records of complaints from the public received by the OCOB.

(13) Any record that would disclose any information set forth in any of the confidential records referred to in this subsection.

(c) For purposes of this section, "any person subject to the Commissioner's jurisdiction" includes any person who is licensed or registered or should be licensed or registered under this Chapter.

(d) Notwithstanding the provisions of subsection (b) of this section, the Commissioner may, by written agreement with any state or federal law enforcement or regulatory agency, share with that agency any confidential record set out in subsection (b) of this section or any information contained therein, on the condition that such record or information shared shall be treated as confidential under the applicable laws and regulations governing the recipient agency.

(e) Notwithstanding the provisions of subsection (b) of this section which limit discovery of confidential records held by the Commissioner, such records may be produced for discovery in a criminal or enforcement proceeding if both of the following occur:

(1) After reviewing the discovery request, the court orders the Commissioner to submit the confidential records to the court for in camera review and the court finds that the interests of justice require that the documents be discoverable or admissible in evidence.

(2) After making the finding provided by subdivision (1) of this subsection, the court enters a protective order restricting access and public distribution or any republication of the confidential materials requested.

(f) Nothing in this section shall prohibit a bank, upon approval of the Commissioner, from disclosing to an insurance carrier, for the purpose of obtaining insurance coverage required by this Chapter, the bank's regulatory rating prepared by the OCOB; provided, however, that the insurance carrier must agree in writing to maintain the confidentiality of the information and not to disclose it in any manner whatsoever. (2012-56, s. 4.)

Article 3.

Organization of a Bank.

§ 53C-3-1. Application to organize a bank.

(a) An applicant for permission to organize a bank and for a charter must file an application with the Commissioner. The application shall be in the form required by the Commissioner and shall contain such information as the Commissioner requires, set forth in sufficient detail to enable the Commissioner to evaluate the applicant's satisfaction of the criteria set forth in G.S. 53C-3-4. The applicant shall pay a nonrefundable application fee as provided by rule at the time of filing the application.

(b) Upon receipt of an application, the Commissioner shall conduct an examination of the applicant and any other matters deemed relevant by the

Commissioner. The Commissioner may require additional information and may require the amendment of the application in the course of the examination. An applicant's failure to furnish all required information or to pay the required fee within 30 days after filing the application may be considered an abandonment of the application. (2012-56, s. 4.)

§ 53C-3-2. Permission to organize a bank.

(a) With the approval of the Commissioner, the organizers may file articles of incorporation for the proposed bank with the Secretary of State. The Commissioner shall authorize the organization of the proposed bank if the Commissioner is satisfied that each of the following conditions is met:

(1) The application is complete.

(2) The Commissioner's examination as provided for in G.S. 53C-3-1 indicates that the requirements for the issuance of a charter to the applicant are reasonably probable of satisfaction.

(3) The proposed name of the proposed bank is not likely to mislead the public as to its character or purpose and is not the same as a name already adopted by an existing depository institution or trust institution operating in this State.

(b) If the Commissioner approves the organization of the proposed bank, the Commissioner shall issue a certificate to the Secretary of State. The Secretary of State shall transmit to the Commissioner a certified copy of the filed articles of incorporation of the proposed bank.

(c) Unless and until the Commissioner issues a charter to the proposed bank:

(1) The proposed bank shall not transact any business except such as is incidental and necessary to its organization or the application for a charter or preparation for commencing the business of banking.

(2) All funds paid for shares of the proposed bank shall be placed in escrow under a written escrow with a third-party escrow agent satisfactory to the Commissioner.

(3) All funds for shares placed into escrow, and all dividends or interest on such funds, may be removed from escrow only with the Commissioner's approval except to the extent that such funds are refunded to subscribers or as otherwise required by law.

(d) A proposed bank is subject to the jurisdiction of the Commissioner. (2012-56, s. 4.)

§ 53C-3-3. Articles of incorporation of a proposed bank.

(a) The articles of incorporation of a proposed bank shall be signed and acknowledged by or on behalf of an organizer and shall contain the following:

(1) The information required to be set forth in articles of incorporation under Chapter 55 of the General Statutes.

(2) Any provision consistent with Chapter 55 of the General Statutes and other applicable law that the organizers elect to set forth for the regulation of the internal affairs of the proposed bank and that the Commissioner authorizes or requires.

(3) Any provision the Commissioner requires or authorizes as a substitute for a provision that otherwise would be required by Chapter 55 of the General Statutes.

(b) Before the chartering of a proposed bank, the articles of incorporation filed under the provisions of G.S. 53C-3-2 shall be sufficient certification to the FDIC that the proposed bank is a legal entity. (2012-56, s. 4.)

§ 53C-3-4. Commissioner's approval of charter issuance.

(a) The Commissioner may approve a charter for a proposed bank only when the Commissioner has determined that all the following requirements have been satisfied or are reasonably probable to be satisfied within a reasonable period of time specified by the Commissioner in the order of approval:

(1) The proposed bank has solicited or will solicit subscriptions for purchases of shares sufficient to provide an amount of required capital satisfactory to the Commissioner for the commencement of the business of banking.

(2) All prior public solicitations for purchases of shares and all future solicitations will be solicited with appropriate disclosure, taking into account all the circumstances of the public solicitation, including a prominent statement in any solicitation document to the effect that the solicitation has not been approved by the Commissioner or the Commission and that a representation to the contrary is a criminal offense.

(3) All payments for purchases of shares in a bank in organization are made in United States currency.

(4) The proposed bank has an operational expense fund from which to pay organizational expenses, in an amount determined by the Commissioner to be sufficient for the safe and sound operation of the proposed bank while the charter application is pending.

(5) The proposed bank has been formed for legitimate and lawful business purposes.

(6) The character, competence, and experience of the organizers, proposed directors, proposed officers, and initial holders of more than ten percent (10%) of the voting securities of the proposed bank will command the confidence of the public.

(7) The proposed officers and directors, as a group, have degrees of character, competence, and experience sufficient to justify a belief that the proposed bank will be free from improper or unlawful influence and otherwise will operate safely, soundly, and in compliance with law.

(8) The anticipated volume and nature of business of the proposed bank projected in the application are reasonable and indicate a reasonable probability of safe, sound, and profitable operation of the proposed bank.

(9) If the proposed bank intends to conduct "trust business," as defined by G.S. 53C-1-4(70), it appears that trust powers should be granted based on consideration of the various factors set forth in Article 24 of Chapter 53 of the

General Statutes for considering applications and setting capital for a State trust company.

(b)   The Commissioner's determination that the requirements described in subsection (a) are reasonably probable of satisfaction may be based on partial satisfaction of the requirements at a level set by the Commissioner as a prerequisite for approval of the charter, and also may be based on presentation of a plan for the full satisfaction of the requirements.

(c)   If it appears to the Commissioner that the proposed bank has satisfied or is reasonably probable to satisfy the requirements for issuance of a charter, the Commissioner shall issue an order approving the application for a charter and such order shall be submitted to the Commission for its review at a public hearing. The Commissioner may, in the order approving the proposed bank's charter, impose other reasonable conditions or restrictions upon the proposed bank or the new bank, consistent with this Chapter.

(d)   If it appears to the Commissioner that the proposed bank has not satisfied and is not reasonably probable of satisfying the requirements for issuance of a charter, the Commissioner shall issue an order denying approval of the application. The applicant may, within 10 days of issuance of the order, give notice of appeal of this decision to the Commission pursuant to G.S. 53C-2-6. (2012-56, s. 4.)

§ 53C-3-5. Notice; public hearing.

(a)   Not less than 30 days before the public hearing of the Commission to review the Commissioner's approval of an application, the applicant shall cause to be published a public notice containing the following:

(1)   A statement that the application has been filed with the Commissioner.

(2)   The name of the community where the proposed bank intends to locate its principal office.

(3)   A statement that a public hearing will be held to review the Commissioner's approval of the application.

(4) A statement that any interested person may file a written statement either favoring or protesting the chartering of the proposed bank. The statement shall note that, in order to be considered at the public hearing, all written statements from interested persons must be filed with the Commission within 30 days of the date of publication of the public notice.

(b) At the public hearing, the Commission shall consider the findings and order of the Commissioner and shall hear such testimony as the Commissioner may wish to give or be called upon to give. To the extent that the Commission deems the information and testimony relevant to its review of the Commissioner's order, the Commission shall receive information and hear testimony from the organizers and shall hear from any other interested persons. (2012-56, s. 4.)

§ 53C-3-6. Commission decision.

(a) The Commission shall consider the findings and order of the Commissioner, oral testimony, and any other information and evidence, either written or oral, that comes before it at the public hearing to review the Commissioner's approval of an application for a charter. The Commission may adjourn and reconvene the public hearing in unusual circumstances. The Commission shall affirm or reverse the Commissioner's order. The Commission may adopt the Commissioner's recommendation with respect to conditions for issuance of a charter, or it may modify the conditions recommended by the Commissioner. The Commission shall render its decision at the public hearing, unless unusual circumstances require postponement of the decision. The Commission's review shall be limited to a determination of whether the criteria set forth in G.S. 53C-3-4 have been met and whether the provisions of this Article have been followed.

(b) If the Commission denies an application for a charter or if the Commission approves an application with conditions not set forth in the Commissioner's approval, the applicant may appeal the denial or approval containing such conditions, as provided in G.S. 53C-2-6. (2012-56, s. 4.)

§ 53C-3-7. Issuance of charter.

(a)   A proposed bank shall not engage in business except as allowed under G.S. 53C-3-2(c)(1), until it receives a charter issued by the Commissioner. The Commissioner shall not issue the charter until the Commissioner is satisfied that the proposed bank has done each of the following:

(1)   Received payment in United States currency for the purchase of shares and will have satisfactory required capital upon commencing business, in each case in at least the amount required by the Commission's order approving the application.

(2)   Elected the proposed officers and directors named in the application or other officers and directors approved by the Commissioner.

(3)   Secured deposit insurance from the FDIC.

(4)   Complied with all requirements of the Commission's order approving the application for a charter.

(5)   Appears to be ready to commence the business of banking in the reasonable discretion of the Commissioner upon a pre-opening examination.

(b)   The charter issued by the Commissioner shall set forth any trust powers of the bank that may be full or partial trust powers.

(c)   If a bank does not open and engage in the business of banking within six months after the date its charter is issued or within such longer period as may be permitted by the Commissioner, the Commissioner shall revoke the charter.

(d)   If the Commissioner determines that a charter should not be issued following Commission approval, the applicant may appeal that decision to the Commission as provided in G.S. 53C-2-6.

(e)   Following the exhaustion of all appeals, the Commissioner may dissolve and liquidate the proposed bank as provided in G.S. 53C-9-301, or order the organizers to dissolve and liquidate the proposed bank pursuant to G.S. 53C-9-201, if any one of the following occurs:

(1)   The Commissioner does not recommend the issuance of a charter.

(2)   The Commission denies approval of a charter.

(3) The charter is revoked by the Commissioner pursuant to subsection (c) of this section or other applicable law. (2012-56, s. 4.)

Article 4.

Governance of Banks.

§ 53C-4-1. Banks - Form of organization.

(a) A bank shall be formed as, and shall maintain the form of, a corporation formed under the laws of this State.

(b) The provisions contained in Chapter 55 of the General Statutes shall apply to banks, except where provisions of this Chapter provide differently or where the Commissioner determines that any provision of Chapter 55 is inconsistent with the business of banking or the safety and soundness of banks. (2012-56, s. 4.)

§ 53C-4-2. Banks controlled by boards of directors.

(a) The corporate powers of a bank shall be exercised by or under the authority of, and the business and affairs of the bank shall be managed by or under the direction of, its board of directors.

(b) A bank's board of directors shall consist of not fewer than five individuals. For good cause shown, the Commissioner may approve boards of directors consisting of fewer than five individuals to the extent consistent with other applicable law.

(c) The board of directors shall meet at least quarterly, provided that the executive committee shall meet in any month in which there is no meeting of the board of directors, and the loan committee shall meet monthly.

(d)   Except to the extent the provisions of this Chapter or other applicable federal or state laws and regulations impose a different standard, bank directors shall have the duties, authority, and liabilities of directors of corporations organized under Chapter 55 of the General Statutes.

(e)   The board of directors of a bank may appoint directors with respect to such of the bank's branches as it deems useful to the business of the bank. No such advisory director shall be liable for acts or omissions undertaken as an advisory director under the laws applicable to the performance of the duties of a director of a bank, unless and only to the extent he or she undertakes or is delegated authority as a director of the bank. (2012-56, s. 4.)

§ 53C-4-3. Committees of boards of directors.

(a)   The board of directors shall appoint, at a minimum, an audit committee, an executive committee, and a loan committee (which may be the executive committee or the board of directors as a whole) and may appoint such other committees as it deems appropriate to provide for the safe and sound operation of the bank in a manner consistent with applicable laws and regulations.

(b)   The Commissioner may require the board of directors of a bank to establish one or more additional committees if, in the judgment of the Commissioner, such committees are reasonably necessary or appropriate for good corporate governance, for the safe and sound operation of the bank, or to ensure the bank's compliance with applicable laws and regulations. In the exercise of his or her judgment under this subsection, the Commissioner may consider, among other factors, the asset size of the bank, the range and complexity of the activities in which the bank is engaged, the various risks undertaken by the bank, the experience and abilities of the bank's directors and officers, and the adequacy of the bank's existing policies, procedures, and internal controls. (2012-56, s. 4.)

§ 53C-4-4. Minutes of meetings of directors and committees.

Minutes shall be recorded and retained for all meetings of the board of directors and board committees and kept on file at the bank. The minutes shall show a record of actions taken. (2012-56, s. 4.)

§ 53C-4-5. Qualifications of bank directors.

(a) At least three-fourths of the directors of a bank shall be citizens of the United States of America.

(b) A director must satisfy eligibility requirements for bank directors imposed by federal law, including Section 19 of the Federal Deposit Insurance Act, 12 U.S.C. § 1829(a).

(c) Following a director's election or appointment as a director, the director shall, solely for purposes of any action or proceeding that may thereafter be brought by the Commissioner, and on a form satisfactory to the Commissioner, do all of the following:

(1) Consent to the jurisdiction of the Commissioner and the General Court of Justice for the State of North Carolina in any such action or proceeding.

(2) Consent to venue in Wake County, North Carolina, in any such action or proceeding.

(3) Unless the director appoints an agent pursuant to subsection (f) of this section, appoint the Commissioner as the director's agent for service of process in any such action or proceeding and authorize and instruct the Commissioner or the Commissioner's duly appointed deputy or agent to accept service of process for the director in any such action or proceeding.

(d) When service of legal process in an action or proceeding brought by the Commissioner is made on a director by service and acceptance of service of process in the manner provided in subdivision (3) of subsection (c) of this section, the Commissioner shall, within three business days thereafter, give notice to the director of such service and acceptance of service of process by depositing a copy of the process served and accepted, together with any pleading, order, or other item accompanying the process, with a "designated delivery service" as defined in 26 U.S.C. § 7502(f)(2) and directed to the director's last known address in the Commissioner's records. The Commissioner shall keep a record which shall show the day and hour of such acceptance of service of process, any pleading, order, or other item accompanying the process, and the date upon which the above notice was given. When service of process is made pursuant to subdivision (3) of subsection (c) of this section, the time within which the director may file a responsive pleading or similar response, as provided by Chapter 1A or Chapter 150B of the General Statutes, shall be extended by 12 days.

(e)   The consent and appointment described in subsections (c) and (f) of this section shall be deemed irrevocable and shall not be affected by the termination of the director's service as a director.

(f)   In lieu of meeting the requirements of subdivision (3) of subsection (c) of this section, a director may appoint an agent for service of such process in Wake County, North Carolina. (2012-56, s. 4; 2013-29, s. 4.)

§ 53C-4-6. Liability of directors.

(a)   The standard of conduct for directors shall be as set forth in G.S. 55-8-30.

(b)   Any director of any bank who shall knowingly violate, or who shall knowingly permit to be violated by any officers, agents, or employees of the bank, any of the provisions of this Chapter shall be held personally and individually liable for all damages which the bank, its shareholders, or any other person shall have sustained in consequence of such violation. Any aggrieved shareholder of any bank in liquidation may prosecute an action for the enforcement of the provisions of this section. Only one such action may be brought. (2012-56, s. 4.)

§ 53C-4-7. Directors may declare distributions.

Provided a bank does not make distributions that reduce its capital below its applicable required capital, the board of directors of a bank may declare such distributions as it deems proper. (2012-56, s. 4.)

§ 53C-4-8. Officers and employees shall give bond.

(a)   A bank shall require security in the form of a bond for the fidelity and faithful performance of duties by its officers and employees. The bond shall be issued by a bonding company authorized to do business in this State and upon such form as may be approved by the Commissioner. Otherwise, the amount, form, and terms of the bond shall be such as the board of directors may require. The premium for the bond is to be paid by the bank.

(b)   To provide for the safety and soundness of a bank, the Commissioner may require an increase in the amount of the bond or additional or different security. (2012-56, s. 4.)

§ 53C-4-9. Affiliate transactions.

A bank may extend credit to, and engage in transactions with, its affiliates, directors, executive officers, principal shareholders, and their respective immediate family members only to the extent permitted by, and subject to such restrictions and conditions as are imposed by, applicable State and federal laws and regulations. (2012-56, s. 4.)

§ 53C-4-10. Examination of board composition, structure, and conduct.

(a)   As part of its examinations of a bank, the OCOB may assess the competence, composition, structure, and conduct of such bank's board of directors, including the following:

(1)   The number of directors.

(2)   The independence of directors.

(3)   The committee structure of the board.

(4)   The education and training of board members.

(5)   Compliance with the bank's code of ethics.

(b)   In making the assessment authorized by subsection (a) of this section, the OCOB shall take into consideration publicly issued regulations and guidance of the Commissioner and the bank's primary federal supervisor and may consider, among other factors, the asset size of the bank, the range and complexity of the activities in which the bank is engaged, the various risks undertaken by the bank, the experience and abilities of the bank's directors and officers, and the adequacy of the bank's existing policies, procedures, and internal controls. (2012-56, s. 4.)

§ 53C-4-11. Reserve fund.

(a) Each bank shall maintain a reserve fund as follows:

(1) If the bank is a member of the Federal Reserve System, it shall maintain a reserve fund in accordance with the requirements of the Federal Reserve Board.

(2) All other banks shall maintain a reserve fund as required by the Commissioner.

(b) The Commissioner may require a level of reserve fund for nonmember banks as provided in subsection (a)(2) of this section, taking into consideration the level of liquidity the Commissioner deems necessary for the safe and sound operation of the banks.

(c) In establishing the required level of reserve fund, the Commissioner shall include the following types of liquid reserves:

(1) Cash on hand, which shall include both United States currency and exchange of any clearinghouse association or similar intermediary, and balances maintained at any federal reserve bank, either directly or on a pass-through basis, to meet federal reserve system reserve requirements.

(2) Balances payable on demand from designated depository institutions.

(3) Obligations of the United States Treasury, any agency of the United States government that is guaranteed by the United States government, and any general obligation of this State or any political subdivision thereof that has an investment grade rating of A or higher by a nationally recognized rating service.

(d) Notwithstanding any other provision of this Chapter, in the event the reserve fund of a bank falls below the level required under subsection (b) of this section, the Commissioner may require the bank to do the following:

(1) Discontinue making any new extension of credit.

(2) Promptly restore its reserve fund to the applicable required level.

(e) In the event a bank shall fail to promptly restore its reserve fund to the applicable level required within 10 days after the Commissioner directs it to do so, the Commissioner may take such actions under Article 8 of this Chapter as the Commissioner deems necessary. (2012-56, s. 4; 2013-29, s. 5.)

§ 53C-4-12. Compliance review committee.

(a) For purposes of this section, the following definitions apply:

(1) "Compliance review committee" means an audit, loan review, or compliance committee appointed by the board of directors of a bank, or any other person to the extent the person acts at the direction of or reports to such a committee, whose functions are to audit, evaluate, report, or determine compliance with any of the following:

a. Loan underwriting standards.

b. Asset quality.

c. Financial reporting to federal or State regulatory agencies.

d. Adherence to the bank's investment, lending, accounting, ethical, or risk assessment, and financial standards.

e. Compliance with federal or State statutory requirements.

(2) "Compliance review documents" means documents prepared for or created by a compliance review committee.

(3) "Government agency" means a state or federal regulatory body that is not a bank supervisory agency that has jurisdiction over a bank's compliance

with state or federal laws or regulations, including those dealing with taxes, securities, or financial reporting.

(4)   "Loan review committee" means a person or group of persons who, on behalf of a bank, reviews assets, including loans held by the bank, for the purpose of assessing the credit quality of the loans or the loan application process, compliance with the bank's investment and loan policies, and compliance with applicable law and regulations.

(b)   Banks shall maintain complete records of compliance review documents, and the documents shall be available for examination by the Commissioner or any bank supervisory agency or government agency having jurisdiction. Notwithstanding Chapter 132 of the General Statutes, compliance review documents in the custody of a bank, the Commissioner, a government agency, or a bank supervisory agency are confidential, are not open for public inspection, and are not discoverable or admissible in evidence in a civil action against a bank, its directors, officers, or employees, unless the court finds that the interests of justice require that the documents be discoverable or admissible in evidence. (2012-56, s. 4.)

§ 53C-4-13. Immediate report of changes in directors and certain officers.

Each bank shall report to the Commissioner any changes in its (i) directors, (ii) president, (iii) chief executive officer, (iv) chief financial officer, (v) chief loan officer, or (vi) chief credit officer by the close of the second day on which the bank is open for business following such change. (2013-29, s. 6.)

Article 5.

Powers of Banks.

§ 53C-5-1. Powers.

(a)   Except as otherwise specifically provided by this Chapter, a bank shall have the powers conferred upon business corporations organized under the laws of this State. In addition, and not by way of limitation, a bank shall have the power to do the following:

(1) Carry on the business of banking, which includes such activities as discounting and negotiating promissory notes, drafts, bills of exchange, and other evidences of indebtedness; receiving deposits; issuing, advising, and confirming letters of credit; receiving money for transmission; and loaning money on personal security or on real or personal property.

(2) Make any loan that could be made by a federally chartered institution doing business in this State.

(3) Purchase or invest in loans, or a participating interest in loans, of a type that the bank could itself make.

(4) Sell any loan, including one or more participating interests in a loan.

(5) Make any investments authorized by G.S. 53C-5-2 or any other section of this Chapter.

(6) Through information technology systems, processes, and capabilities, provide, deliver, or otherwise make available banking services and products, enhance the effectiveness or efficiency of its operations, and provide other benefits to its customers. Additionally, a bank may utilize its information technology systems, processes, capabilities, and capacities in the same manner and to the same extent as is permitted for national banks.

(7) Engage in any other activities approved by rule, order, or interpretation of the Commissioner.

(b) A bank shall also have the power to engage:

(1) As principal in any activity permissible for a national bank under any law, including the National Bank Act, 12 U.S.C. § 24, as well as any activity recognized as permissible for a national bank in any regulation, order, or written interpretation issued by the OCC.

(2) As principal in any activity that is permissible or determined by the FDIC to be permissible for a bank under the Federal Deposit Insurance Act, 12 U.S.C. § 1831a, or in any regulation, order, or written interpretation thereunder.

(3) As principal in any activity that is permissible for a savings institution organized under Chapters 54B or 54C of the General Statutes, or that is permissible for a federal savings association under the Home Owners' Loan Act of 1933, 12 U.S.C. § 1464, or in any regulation, order, or written interpretation thereunder.

(4) In any activity other than as principal permitted under the Federal Deposit Insurance Act, 12 U.S.C. § 1831a.

(c) In addition to the other powers described in this section, a bank shall have the power to exercise all other powers that are reasonably necessary or incident to the exercise of the powers authorized in subsections (a) and (b) of this section.

(d) Except as provided in subsection (e) of this section, a bank that proposes to engage in any new activity shall apply to the Commissioner for approval to engage in the activity before its commencement. If the new activity will be conducted in a new or existing subsidiary in which the bank intends to make an investment, the bank shall apply to the Commissioner for approval to engage in the new activity before entering into the investment. The bank shall not engage in the new activity or make the investment unless and until the Commissioner issues a written approval of the application. An application for approval shall contain a description of the proposed activity and any other information required by the Commissioner. A copy of any notice or application the bank is required to file with any bank supervisory agency with respect to the proposed activity shall also be provided to the Commissioner. For the purpose of this section, a "new activity" is any business activity in which the bank is not currently engaged. The extension or relocation of an existing activity into a new department, division, or subsidiary of the bank shall not be considered a new activity. A bank may appeal a denial of an application by the Commissioner pursuant to G.S. 53C-2-6.

(e) No application for approval to engage in a new activity shall be required, provided all of the following conditions are met as of the date the activity is commenced:

(1) The new activity is one described in subsection (a), (b), or (c) of this section.

(2) The bank is well-capitalized and well-managed as demonstrated by the supervisory rating it received during its most recent safety and soundness examination.

(3) No notice or application to engage in the new activity is required to be filed by the bank with any federal banking regulator.

(f) A bank permitted to commence a new activity without prior application and approval pursuant to subsection (e) of this section shall notify the Commissioner in writing of the commencement of the new activity no later than the 30th day after the earlier of (i) commencing the new activity or (ii) if applicable, making an investment in a subsidiary through which the new activity will be conducted. (2012-56, s. 4; 2013-29, s. 7.)

§ 53C-5-2. Investment authority.

(a) In addition to any powers or investments authorized by any other section of this Chapter, a bank may invest in the following:

(1) The shares or other securities of the following:

a. Any other depository institution.

b. Any industrial bank, bankers' bank, or other deposit-taking entity chartered or existing under any federal or State law, including the shares or other securities of clearing corporations defined in G.S. 25-8-102, the shares or other securities of central reserve banks, and the shares of an Edge Act bank. The investment of any bank in the shares of a central reserve bank or bank organized under the Edge Act, 12 U.S.C. § 611, et seq., shall at no time exceed ten percent (10%) of the required capital of the bank making the investment.

c. Any company in which a federally chartered institution is authorized to invest under any statute or any regulation, official circular, bulletin, order, or written interpretation issued by the OCC.

(2) Bonds or notes issued by or fully and unconditionally guaranteed as to principal and interest by the United States Treasury. No bank shall be required to maintain a reserve against deposits secured by United States Treasury bonds or notes equal in market value to the amount of such deposits, and such bonds

or notes shall be valid security for all loans and deposits to the same extent as are any obligations of the United States.

(3)   Federal farm loan bonds, notes, or similar obligations issued by a farm credit system institution.

(4)   Securities issued by federal home loan banks pursuant to the Federal Home Loan Bank Act of 1932, as amended.

(5)   Bonds or notes secured by a mortgage or deed of trust insured or guaranteed by the Federal Housing Administration, Secretary of Housing and Urban Development, or the Veterans Administration, or in mortgages or deeds of trust on real estate that have been accepted for insurance or guarantee by the Federal Housing Administration, Secretary of Housing and Urban Development, or Veterans Administration, or in obligations of a national mortgage association, which obligations are insured or guaranteed by the United States government. No law of this State prescribing the nature, amount, or form of security or requiring security upon which loans or investments may be made, or prescribing the rates or time of payment of the interest any obligation may bear, or prescribing the period for which loans or investments may be made, shall apply to investments made pursuant to this subsection.

(6)   Mutual funds, but subject to rules or orders adopted by the Commissioner.

(b)   A bank may make an investment in a subsidiary that will be operated as any of the following:

(1)   Bank operating subsidiary.

(2)   Financial subsidiary.

(3)   DPC subsidiary, as defined by G.S. 53C-1-4(30).

(c)   No investment shall be made by a bank or a subsidiary pursuant to subsection (b) or (d) of this section unless the following apply:

(1)   The investment is approved by the board of directors of the bank or a board-authorized committee.

(2) The bank has carefully investigated the business or activity in which the subsidiary established by the investment will engage.

(3) The bank has established the risk management and financial controls necessary to engage in the business or activity in a safe and sound manner.

(4) The bank has, and following the making of the investment and the application of the provisions of this subsection, will continue to satisfy the capital requirements of this Chapter.

(d) A subsidiary may invest in a lower-tier subsidiary, subject to the same requirements and limitations applicable to a bank's investment in a subsidiary.

(e) Except as provided in subsection (f) of this section, a bank or subsidiary proposing to make an investment described in subsection (b) or (d) of this section shall give prior written notice to the Commissioner, providing such detail as the Commissioner may require. Unless the Commissioner, within 30 days following receipt of the notice, notifies the bank or subsidiary that the Commissioner objects to the proposed investment, the bank or subsidiary may complete the investment. However, the Commissioner may extend the period within which to object to the proposed investment if the Commissioner determines that it raises issues that require additional information or additional time for analysis. While the objection period is so extended, the bank or subsidiary may not proceed with respect to the proposed investment. A bank may appeal an objection by the Commissioner pursuant to G.S. 53C-2-6.

(f) The prior notice requirement provided by subsection (e) of this section shall not apply if all of the following apply:

(1) The bank is well-capitalized and well-managed as demonstrated by the supervisory rating it received during its most recent examination.

(2) Each activity of the subsidiary in which the investment is to be made is either of the following:

a. One in which the bank is then engaged or has previously been engaged, directly or through a different subsidiary, and for which all necessary approvals of bank supervisory agencies and of the Commissioner have previously been obtained and remain in effect.

b. One for which no prior notice or application for approval to any federal bank supervisory authority is required.

(3) A bank that makes an investment pursuant to the exception created by this subsection shall nevertheless notify the Commissioner in writing of the investment within 30 days thereafter.

(g) Any bank, out-of-state bank, national bank, or any subsidiary thereof that engages in an activity subject to licensure and/or regulation under the laws of this State, other than this Chapter, shall be subject to licensure and/or regulation on a basis that does not arbitrarily discriminate by the appropriate regulatory agency which licenses and/or regulates nonbanks that engage in the same activity.

(h) The Commissioner shall monitor the impact of investment activities of banks and their subsidiaries under this section on the safety and soundness of such banks. Any securities owned or hereafter acquired in excess of the limitations herein imposed shall be disposed of at public or private sale within six months after the date of acquiring the securities and, if not so disposed of, they shall be charged to profit and loss account and no longer carried on the books as an asset. The limit of time in which securities shall be disposed of or charged off the books of the bank may be extended by the Commissioner if in the Commissioner's judgment it is for the best interest of the bank that the extension be granted, provided that the limitations imposed in this section on the ownership of shares or other equity ownership interest in companies are suspended only to the extent that any bank operating under the supervision of the Commissioner may subscribe for and purchase shares and other equity ownership interests in, or debentures, bonds, or other types of securities of, any company organized under the laws of the United States for the purposes of insuring the depositors a part or all of their funds on deposit in banks to the extent as security ownership is required in order to obtain the benefits of deposit insurance for such depositors.

(i) A bank may purchase, hold, and convey real estate other than bank premises for the following purposes:

(1) As security for extensions of credit made or moneys due to it when that real estate has been mortgaged to it in good faith.

(2) When the real estate has been purchased at sales upon foreclosures of mortgages and deeds of trust held or owned by it, or on judgments or decrees

obtained and rendered for debts due to it, or through deeds in lieu of foreclosure or other settlements affecting security of those debts. All real property acquired under this subdivision shall be sold by the bank within five years after it is acquired unless, upon application by the bank, the Commissioner extends the time within which the sale shall be made.

(j)   A bank's investment in any bonds or other debt obligations of any one person, other than obligations of the United States government or an agency thereof, or other obligations guaranteed by the United States, this State, another state, or other political subdivision of this State or another state, shall at no time exceed ten percent (10%) of the sum of (i) the bank's "capital," as that term is defined in G.S. 53C-1-4, plus (ii) those portions of the bank's allowance for loan and lease losses, deferred tax assets, and intangible assets that are excluded from the bank's capital under 12 C.F.R. Part 325. (2012-56, s. 4; 2013-29, s. 8.)

§ 53C-5-3. Banks, fiduciaries authorized to invest in securities approved by the Secretary of Housing and Urban Development, Federal Housing Administration, Veterans Administration.

(a)   Insured Mortgages and Obligation of National Mortgage Associations and Federal Home Loan Banks. - It shall be lawful for all commercial and industrial banks, trust companies, building and loan associations, savings and loan associations, insurance companies, mortgagees and loan correspondents approved by the Secretary of Housing and Urban Development or Federal Housing Administration, and other financial institutions engaged in business in this State, and for guardians, executors, administrators, trustees, or others acting in a fiduciary capacity in this State to invest, to the same extent that such funds may be invested in interest-bearing obligations of the United States, their funds or moneys in their custody or possession that are eligible for investment, in bonds or notes secured by a mortgage or deed of trust insured or guaranteed by the Federal Housing Administration, Secretary of Housing and Urban Development, or the Veterans Administration, or in mortgages or deeds of trust on real estate which have been accepted for insurance or guarantee by the Federal Housing Administration, Secretary of Housing and Urban Development, or Veterans Administration, and in obligations of a national mortgage association, which obligations are insured or guaranteed by the United States Government, or bonds, debentures, consolidated bonds, or other obligations of any federal home loan bank or banks.

(b) Insured or Guaranteed Loans; Loans Purchased by National Mortgage Associations and Federal Home Loan Banks. - All such banks, trust companies, building and loan associations, savings and loan associations, insurance companies, mortgagees and loan correspondents approved by the Secretary of Housing and Urban Development or Federal Housing Administration, and other financial institutions, and also all such guardians, executors, administrators, trustees, or others acting in a fiduciary capacity in this State, may make such loans, secured by real estate, as the Secretary of Housing and Urban Development, the Federal Housing Administration, a national mortgage association, or the Veterans Administration has insured or guaranteed, or has made a commitment to insure or guarantee, and may obtain such insurance or guarantee; provided, further, that the above designated financial institutions may make loans, secured by real estate, that are eligible and committed for sale to a national mortgage association, federal home loan bank, federal home loan mortgage corporation, or other agency or instrumentality of the United States.

(c) Eligibility for Credit Insurance. - All banks, trust companies, building and loan associations, savings and loan associations, insurance companies, mortgagees and loan correspondents approved by the Secretary of Housing and Urban Development or Federal Housing Administration, and other financial institutions, on being approved as eligible for credit insurance by the Secretary of Housing and Urban Development, the Federal Housing Administration, or the Veterans Administration, may make such loans as are insured by the Secretary of Housing and Urban Development or Federal Housing Administration or insured or guaranteed by the Veterans Administration.

(d) Certain Securities Made Eligible for Collaterals. - Whenever by statute of this State collateral is required as security for the deposit of public or other funds; or deposits are required to be made with any public official or department; or an investment of capital or surplus, or a reserve or other fund is required to be maintained, consisting of designated securities, bonds, and notes secured by a mortgage or deed of trust insured or guaranteed by the Secretary of Housing and Urban Development, Federal Housing Administration, or Veterans Administration, debentures issued by the Secretary of Housing and Urban Development or the Federal Housing Administration and obligations of a national mortgage association shall be eligible for such purposes.

(e) General Laws Not Applicable. - No law of this State prescribing the nature, amount, or form of security or requiring security upon which loans or investments may be made, or prescribing or limiting the rates or time of payment of the interest any obligation may bear, or prescribing or limiting the period for which loans or investments may be made, shall be deemed to apply to loans or investments made pursuant to the foregoing paragraphs. (2012-56, s. 4.)

Article 6.

Bank Operations.

§ 53C-6-1. Loans and extensions of credit.

(a) A bank may make a loan or extension of credit secured by the pledge of its own shares or the shares of its holding company, provided:

(1) When a bank exercises its security interest in shares of the bank or its holding company, it shall dispose of all of the shares within a period of six months. If the shares have not been disposed of within six months, the shares shall be charged to profit and loss and no longer carried as an asset of the bank. The Commissioner may extend the six-month period not to exceed an additional six months.

(2) A bank may not extend credit to finance the purchase of or to carry shares of the bank or the shares of its holding company. For purposes of this subsection, the phrase "to carry" has the meaning set forth in 12 C.F.R. Part 221, as promulgated by the Federal Reserve Board.

(b) Loans and Extensions of Credit - Limitations:

(1) The total loans and extensions of credit, both direct and indirect, by a bank to a person, other than a municipal corporation for money borrowed, including in the liabilities of a company the liabilities of the several members of the company, outstanding at one time and not fully secured, as determined in a manner consistent with subdivision (2) of this subsection, by collateral having a market value at least equal to the amount of the loan or extension of credit, shall not exceed the greater of (i) fifteen percent (15%) of the sum of the bank's capital plus those portions of the bank's allowance for loan and lease losses, deferred tax assets, and intangible assets that are excluded from the bank's

capital under 12 C.F.R. Part 325 or (ii) the amount permitted for national banks in this State by statute or regulation of the Comptroller of the Currency.

(2)   The total loans and extensions of credit, both direct and indirect, by a bank to a person outstanding at one time and fully secured by readily marketable collateral having a market value, as determined by reliable and continuously available price quotations, at least equal to the amount of the loan or extension of credit outstanding, shall not exceed the greater of (i) ten percent (10%) of the sum of the bank's capital plus those portions of the bank's allowance for loan and lease losses, deferred tax assets, and intangible assets that are excluded from the bank's capital under 12 C.F.R. Part 325 or (ii) the amount permitted for national banks by statute or regulation of the Comptroller of the Currency. This limitation shall be separate from and in addition to the limitation contained in subdivision (1) of this subsection.

(3)   The following shall not be considered as extensions of credit within the meaning of this section; provided that the limitations of this subsection shall not apply to loans or obligations to the extent that they are secured or covered by guarantees or by commitments or agreements to take over or purchase the same made by any federal reserve bank or by the United States or any department, board, bureau, commission, or establishment of the United States, including any corporation wholly owned, directly or indirectly, by the United States:

a.   The discount of bills of exchange drawn in good faith against actual existing values.

b.   The discount of solvent trade acceptances or other solvent commercial or business paper actually owned by the person negotiating the same.

c.   Loans or extensions of credit secured by a segregated deposit account in the lending bank.

d.   The purchase of bankers' acceptances of the kind described in section 13 of the Federal Reserve Act and issued by other depository institutions.

e.   The purchase of any notes and the making of any loans secured by not less than a like face amount of bonds of the United States or any agency of the United States; or other obligations guaranteed by the United States government or the State of North Carolina; or certificates of indebtedness of the United

States, or agency thereof; or other obligations guaranteed by the United States government.

(4)   For purposes of this subsection, the following definitions and conditions apply:

a.   "Person" includes an individual or a corporation, partnership, trust, association, joint venture, pool, syndicate, sole proprietorship, unincorporated organization, or any other form of entity not specifically listed; provided, the term "person" shall not include (i) a clearing organization registered with the Commodity Futures Trading Commission (or its successor) or the Securities and Exchange Commission (or its successor) or any federal banking agency or (ii) a bank's affiliates.

b.   Loans or extensions of credit to one person include loans made to other persons when the proceeds of the loans or extensions of credit are to be used for the direct benefit of the first person or the persons are engaged in a common enterprise.

c.   For purposes of this section, extensions of credit by a bank to a person shall include the bank's credit exposures to the person in derivative transactions with the bank.

d.   "Derivative transaction" includes any transaction that is a contract, agreement, swap, warrant, note, or option that is based, in whole or in part, on the value of, any interest in, or any quantitative measure or the occurrence of any event relating to one or more commodities, securities, debt instruments, currencies, interest or other rates, indices, or assets.

e.   Credit exposure to a person in connection with a derivative transaction shall be determined based on an amount that the bank reasonably determines, in accordance with customary industry practices under the terms of the derivative transaction or otherwise, would be its loss if the person were to default on the date of determination, taking into account any netting and collateral arrangements and any guarantees or other credit enhancements, provided that the bank may elect to determine credit exposure on the basis of such other method of determining credit exposure as may be permitted by the bank's primary federal regulator.

(c) The Commissioner shall monitor the lending activities of banks under this section for undue credit concentrations and inadequate risk diversification that could adversely affect the safety and soundness of the banks.

(d) Rules adopted by the Commissioner to ensure that extensions of credit made by banks are in keeping with sound lending practices and to promote the purposes of this Chapter shall not prohibit a bank from making any extension of credit that is a permitted extension of credit for a federally chartered institution.

(e) Any bank may, by resolution duly passed at a meeting of its board of directors or a board-authorized committee, request the Commissioner to suspend the limitations on loans set forth in this section as the limitations may apply to any particular loan (i) on the bank's books that then exceeds such limitations, or (ii) which the bank desires to make or modify in a manner that would not otherwise be permitted in the absence of a suspension of such limitations. Upon receipt of a duly certified copy of such resolution, the Commissioner may, in the Commissioner's discretion and subject to such requirements, limitations, and conditions as the Commissioner deems appropriate, suspend the limitations on loans set forth in this section insofar as they apply to the loan in question. (2012-56, s. 4; 2013-29, ss. 9, 10.)

§ 53C-6-2. Deposits.

(a) A bank may, consistent with applicable law and safe and sound banking practices, offer all types of deposit accounts upon such terms and conditions as the bank considers appropriate.

(b) A bank shall secure insurance for its deposits from the FDIC. (2012-56, s. 4.)

§ 53C-6-3. Securing deposits.

(a) A bank may not create a lien on its assets or otherwise secure the repayment of a deposit, except as authorized or required by this section, other laws of this State, or federal law.

(b) A bank may pledge its assets to secure a deposit of the government of this State or any other state, any agency or political subdivision of this State or any other state, the United States government, any agency or instrumentality of the United States, or any Indian tribe recognized by the United States government as eligible for the services provided to Indian tribes by the Secretary of the Interior because of its status as an Indian tribe.

(c) This section does not prohibit the pledge of assets by a bank to secure the repayment of money borrowed.

(d) An act, deed, conveyance, pledge, or contract in violation of this section is void. (2012-56, s. 4.)

§ 53C-6-4. Minors.

(a) A bank may issue and operate a deposit account in the name of a minor or in the name of two or more individuals, one or more of whom are minors, and receive payments, pay withdrawals, accept a pledge of the account, issue automated teller machine (ATM) and debit cards, contract for overdraft protection, and act in any other manner with respect to the account on the order of the minor with like effect as if the minor were of full age and legal capacity. Any payment to or at the direction of a minor is a discharge of the bank to the extent thereof. The account shall be held for the exclusive right and benefit of the minor and any joint owners, free from the control of all other persons except creditors. A minor who obtains a deposit account from a bank under this subsection, whether individually or together with others, is bound by the terms of the deposit account agreement to the same extent as if the minor were of full age and legal capacity.

(b) Any bank may lease a safe deposit box to a minor or to two or more individuals, one or more of whom are minors. With respect to any such lease, a bank may deal with the minor in all regards as if the minor were of full age and legal capacity. A minor entering a lease agreement with a bank under this subsection, whether individually or together with others, is bound by the terms of the safe deposit box agreement to the same extent as if the minor were of full age and legal capacity.

(c) If a minor with a deposit account, other than a joint account with right of survivorship or a Payable on Death account, dies, a parent or legal guardian of the minor may access and withdraw the funds on deposit, and the bank is discharged to the extent of any withdrawal. If a minor with a safe deposit box dies, the provisions of G.S. 28A-15-13 shall control the opening, inventory, and release of contents of the safe deposit box.

(d)   This section shall not affect the law governing transactions with minors in cases outside the scope of this section, including transactions that constitute an extension of credit to the minor. (2012-56, s. 4.)

§ 53C-6-5: Reserved for future codification purposes.

§ 53C-6-6. Joint accounts.

(a)   Any two or more individuals may establish a joint deposit account by written contract. The deposit account shall be held for them as joint tenants. The account also may be held pursuant to G.S. 41-2.1 of the General Statutes and have the incidents set forth in that section. If the account is held pursuant to G.S. 41-2.1, the contract shall set forth that fact.

(b)   Unless the individuals establishing a joint account have agreed with the bank that withdrawals require more than one signature, payment by the bank to, or at the direction of, any joint tenant designated in the contract authorized by this section shall be a total discharge of the bank's obligation as to the amount so paid.

(c)   Funds in a joint account established with right of survivorship shall belong to the surviving joint tenant or tenants upon the death of a joint tenant, and the funds shall be subject only to the personal representative's right of collection as set forth in G.S. 28A-15-10(a)(3), or as provided in G.S. 41-2.1 if the account is established pursuant to the provisions of that section. Payment by the bank of funds in the joint account to a surviving joint tenant or tenants shall terminate the personal representative's authority under G.S. 28A-15-10(a)(3) to collect against the bank for the funds so paid, but the personal representative's authority to collect such funds from the surviving joint tenant or tenants is not terminated.

(d) A pledge of a joint account by any one or more of the joint tenants, unless otherwise specifically agreed between the bank and all joint tenants in writing, shall be a valid pledge and transfer of the account or of the amount so pledged, shall be binding upon all joint tenants, shall not operate to sever or terminate the joint ownership of all or any part of the account, and shall survive the death of any joint tenant.

(e) A bank is not liable to joint tenants for complying in good faith with a writ of execution, garnishment, attachment, levy, or other legal process that appears to have been issued by a court or other authority of competent jurisdiction and seeks funds held in the name of any one or more of the joint tenants.

(f) Persons establishing a joint account with right of survivorship under this section shall sign a statement showing their election of the right of survivorship in the account and containing language set forth in a conspicuous manner and substantially similar to the following:

"BANK (or name of institution)

JOINT ACCOUNT WITH RIGHT OF SURVIVORSHIP

G.S. 53C-6-6

We understand that by establishing a joint account under the provisions of North Carolina General Statute 53C-6-6 that:

(1) The bank (or name of institution) may pay the money in the account to, or on the order of, any person named as a joint holder of the account unless we have agreed with the bank that withdrawals require more than one signature; and

(2) Upon the death of one joint owner, the money remaining in the account will belong to the surviving joint owners and will not pass by inheritance to the heirs of the deceased joint owner or be controlled by the deceased joint owner's will.

_____

_____ "

(g) This section does not repeal or modify any provision of law relating to estate taxes.

(h) Any joint tenant may terminate a joint account.

(i) Where a joint account is held by two or more individuals and a joint tenant does not wish for the account to be terminated but requests to be removed from the account, the bank shall remove the joint tenant from the account. The joint account shall continue in the names of the remaining tenant or tenants. Any joint tenant who requested to be removed from an account remains liable for any debts incurred in connection with the joint account during the period in which the individual was a named joint tenant.

(j) Any joint account created under the provisions of G.S. 53-146.1 as it existed prior to October 1, 2012, shall for all purposes be governed by the provisions of this section on and after October 1, 2012, and any reference to G.S. 53-146.1 in any document concerning the account shall be deemed a reference to this section.

(k) This section shall not be deemed exclusive. Deposit accounts not conforming to this section shall be governed by other applicable provisions of the General Statutes or the common law, as appropriate. (2012-56, s. 4; 2013-29, s. 11.)

§ 53C-6-7. Payable on Death accounts.

(a) If any natural person establishing a deposit account shall execute a written agreement with the bank containing a statement that it is executed pursuant to the provisions of this section and providing for the account to be held in the name of the natural person as owner for one or more beneficiaries, the account and any balance thereof shall be held as a Payable on Death account. The account shall have the following incidents:

(1) Any owner during the owner's lifetime may change any designated beneficiary by a written direction to the bank.

(2) If there are two or more owners of a Payable on Death account, the owners shall own the account as joint tenants with right of survivorship and,

except as otherwise provided in this section, the account shall have the incidents set forth in G.S. 53C-6-6.

(3)   Any owner may withdraw funds by writing checks or otherwise, as set forth in the account contract, and receive payment in cash or check payable to the owner's personal order.

(4)   If the beneficiary is a natural person, there may be one or more beneficiaries, and the following shall apply:

a.   If only one beneficiary is living and of legal age at the death of the last surviving owner, the beneficiary shall be the owner of the account and payment by the bank to the owner shall be a total discharge of the bank's obligation as to the amount paid. If two or more beneficiaries are living at the death of the last surviving owner, they shall be owners of the account as joint tenants with right of survivorship as provided in G.S. 53C-6-6, and payment by the bank to the owners or any of the owners shall be a total discharge of the bank's obligation as to the amount paid.

b.   If only one beneficiary is living and that beneficiary is not of legal age at the death of the last surviving owner, the bank shall transfer the funds in the account to the general guardian or guardian of the estate, if any, of the minor beneficiary. If no guardian of the minor beneficiary has been appointed, the bank shall hold the funds in a similar interest-bearing account in the name of the minor until the minor reaches the age of majority or until a duly appointed guardian withdraws the funds.

(5)   If the beneficiary is an entity other than a natural person, there shall be only one beneficiary.

(6)   If one or more owners survive the last surviving beneficiary who was a natural person, or if a beneficiary who is an entity other than a natural person should cease to exist before the death of the owner, the account shall become an individual account of the owner, or a joint account with right of survivorship of the owners, and shall have the legal incidents of an individual account in a case of a single owner or a joint account with right of survivorship, as provided in G.S. 53C-6-6, in the case of multiple owners.

(7)   Prior to the death of the last surviving owner, no beneficiary shall have any ownership interest in a Payable on Death account. Funds in a Payable on Death account established pursuant to this subsection shall belong to the

beneficiary or beneficiaries upon the death of the last surviving owner, and the funds shall be subject only to the personal representative's right of collection as set forth in G.S. 28A-15-10(a)(1). Payment by the bank of funds in the Payable on Death account to the beneficiary or beneficiaries shall terminate the personal representative's authority under G.S. 28A-15-10(a)(1) to collect against the bank for the funds so paid, but the personal representative's authority to collect such funds from the beneficiary or beneficiaries is not terminated.

The natural person establishing an account under this subsection shall sign a statement containing language set forth in a conspicuous manner and substantially similar to the language set out below. The language may be on a signature card or in an explanation of the account that is set out in a separate document whose receipt is acknowledged by the person establishing the account:

"BANK (or name of institution)

PAYABLE ON DEATH ACCOUNT

G.S. 53C-6-7

I (or we) understand that by establishing a Payable on Death account under the provisions of North Carolina General Statute 53C-6-7 that:

1. During my (or our) lifetime I (or we), individually or jointly, may withdraw the money in the account.

2. By written direction to the bank (or name of institution) I (or we), individually or jointly, may change the beneficiary or beneficiaries.

3. Upon my (or our) death, the money remaining in the account will belong to the beneficiary or beneficiaries, and the money will not be inherited by my (or our) heirs or be controlled by will.

_____ "

(b) This section shall not be deemed exclusive. Deposit accounts not conforming to this section shall be governed by other applicable provisions of the General Statutes or the common law, as appropriate.

(c) No addition to the accounts, nor any withdrawal, payment, or change of beneficiary, shall affect the nature of the account as Payable on Death accounts or affect the right of any owner to terminate the account.

(d) This section does not repeal or modify any provisions of law relating to estate taxes.

(e) Any Payable on Death account created under the provisions of G.S. 53-146.2, as it existed prior to October 1, 2012, shall for all purposes be governed by the provisions of this section on and after October 1, 2012, and any reference to G.S. 53-146.2 in any document concerning the account shall be deemed a reference to this section. (2012-56, s. 4; 2013-29, s. 12.)

§ 53C-6-8. Personal agency accounts.

(a) Any person may establish a personal agency account by written contract containing a statement that it is executed pursuant to the provisions of this section. A personal agency account may be any type of deposit account. The written contract shall name an agent who shall have authority to act on behalf of the depositor in the manner set out in this subsection. The agent shall have the authority to do the following:

(1) Make, sign, or execute checks drawn on the account or otherwise make withdrawals from the account.

(2) Endorse checks made payable to the principal for deposit only into the account.

(3) Deposit cash or negotiable instruments, including instruments endorsed by the principal, into the account.

(b) A person establishing an account under this section shall sign a statement containing language substantially similar to the following in a conspicuous manner:

"BANK (or name of institution)

PERSONAL AGENCY ACCOUNT

G.S. 53C-6-8

The undersigned understands that by establishing a personal agency account under the provisions of North Carolina General Statute 53C-6-8, the agent named in the account may:

1. Sign checks drawn on the account.

2. Make deposits into the account.

The undersigned also understand that if the undersigned is a natural person, upon his or her death, the money remaining in the account will be controlled by his or her will or inherited by his or her heirs.

_____ "

(c) An account created under the provisions of this section grants no ownership right or interest in the agent. Upon the death of the principal, there is no right of survivorship to the account, and the authority set out in subsection (a) of this section terminates.

(d) The written contract referred to in subsection (a) of this section shall provide that the principal may elect to extend the authority of the agent set out in subsection (a) of this section to act on behalf of the principal in regard to the account, notwithstanding the subsequent incapacity or mental incompetence of the principal. If the principal is a natural person and elects to extend the authority of the agent, then upon the subsequent incapacity or mental incompetence of the principal, the agent may continue to exercise the authority, without the requirement of bond or of accounting to any court, until such time as the agent shall receive actual knowledge that the authority has been terminated. The duly qualified guardian of the estate of the incapacitated or incompetent principal, or the duly appointed attorney-in-fact for the incapacitated or incompetent principal acting pursuant to a durable power of attorney, as defined in G.S. 32A-8, which grants to the attorney-in-fact the authority in regard to the account that is granted to the agent by the written contract executed pursuant to the provisions of this section, shall have the power, upon notifying the agent and providing written notice to the bank where the personal agency account is established, to terminate the agent's authority to act on behalf of the principal with respect to the account. Upon termination of the agent's authority, the agent shall account to the guardian or attorney-in-fact for all actions of the agent in regard to the account during the incapacity or incompetence of the principal. If the principal is a natural person and does not elect to extend the authority of the agent, then upon the subsequent incapacity or mental incompetence of the principal, the authority of the agent set out in subsection (a) of this section terminates.

(e)   When an account under this section has been established, all or part of the account or any interest or dividend may be paid on a check made, signed, or executed by the agent. In the absence of actual knowledge that the principal has died or that the agency created by the account has been terminated, the payment shall be valid and sufficient discharge to the bank for payment so made.

(f)   A personal agency account shall have only one owner and one agent. The owner shall retain the authority to change the named agent on the personal agency account.

(g)   Any personal agency account created under the provisions of G.S. 53-146.3, as it existed prior to October 1, 2012, shall for all purposes be governed by the provisions of this section on and after October 1, 2012, and any reference to G.S. 53-146.3 in any document concerning the account shall be deemed a reference to this section. (2012-56, s. 4; 2013-29, s. 13.)

§ 53C-6-9. Accounts opened by adults for minors.

(a)   One or more adults may open and maintain a custodial deposit account for or in the name of a minor and using the minor's taxpayer identification number. Unless otherwise provided in the agreement governing the account the following terms apply:

(1)   Beneficial ownership of the account vests exclusively in the minor. All interest credited to the account shall belong to the minor and shall be reported to the appropriate taxing authorities in the name of the minor using the minor's taxpayer identification number.

(2)   Except as otherwise provided, control of the account vests exclusively in the custodian whose name appears on the bank's records for the account. If there is more than one custodian named on the bank's account records, each may act independently. Any one or more of the custodians named on the bank's

records may turn over control of the account to the minor at any time, either before or after the minor reaches the age of majority.

(3) If the custodian has not already transferred control, then after the minor beneficiary reaches the age of majority, the beneficiary may instruct the bank to transfer control to the beneficiary and remove the named custodian.

(4) If the custodian or, if more than one custodian is on the account, the last of the custodians to survive dies before the minor reaches the age of majority, the minor's parent or the minor's legal guardian may act as custodian or name another custodian on the account.

(b) This section shall not be deemed exclusive. Accounts not conforming to this section shall be governed by other applicable provisions of the General Statutes, including Chapter 33A, the North Carolina Uniform Transfers to Minors Act, or the common law, as appropriate. (2012-56, s. 4.)

§ 53C-6-10. Payment of balance of deceased person or person under disability to personal representative or guardian.

(a) A bank may pay any balance on deposit to the credit of any deceased individual to the duly qualified personal representative, collector, or public administrator of the decedent who is qualified as such under the laws of any state.

(b) A bank may pay any balance on deposit to the credit of any individual judicially declared incompetent or otherwise under a legal disability to the duly qualified personal representative, guardian, curator, conservator, or committee of the person declared incompetent or under disability who is qualified as such under the laws of any state.

(c) The presentation of a letter of qualification as personal representative, collector, public administrator, guardian, curator, conservator, or committee of the person issued or certified by the appointing court shall be conclusive proof of the jurisdiction of the court issuing the same and sufficient authority for the payment.

(d) Payment by a bank in good faith under the authority of this section discharges the liability of the bank to the extent of the payment. (2012-56, s. 4.)

§ 53C-6-11. Powers of attorney; notice of revocation; payment after notice.

(a)   Any bank may continue to recognize any act of an attorney-in-fact or other agent until the bank receives actual notice of the principal's death or a written notice of revocation signed by the principal who granted the authority or, in the case of a company, evidence satisfactory to the bank of the revocation. Payment by the bank to or at the direction of an attorney-in-fact or other agent before receipt of the notice is a total discharge of the bank's obligation as to the amount so paid.

(b)   Notwithstanding that a bank has received written notice of revocation of the authority of an attorney-in-fact or other designated agent, a bank may, until 10 days after receipt of notice, pay any item made, drawn, accepted, or endorsed by the attorney-in-fact or agent prior to the revocation, provided that the item is otherwise properly payable. (2012-56, s. 4.)

§ 53C-6-12. Account statements to be rendered annually or on request.

(a)   Every bank shall render an account statement for each deposit account at least annually to the depositor; provided, however, the statements are not required for time deposits. Every bank shall render a statement of account for each deposit account, including time deposits upon receipt of an appropriate request reasonably made by a depositor.

(b)   For purposes of this section, an account statement is deemed to have been "rendered" to a depositor as of the earlier of the date the statement is mailed to the depositor's address as shown on bank records and the date the account is posted to the bank's Web site in a manner and a form ensuring the statement to be readily available to the depositor; provided however, the bank and the depositor may agree that an account statement may be rendered by other means.

(c)   Nothing in this section shall be construed to relieve the depositor from the duty of exercising due diligence in the review of an account statement rendered by the bank and of timely notification to the bank upon discovery of any error. (2012-56, s. 4.)

§ 53C-6-13. Safe deposit boxes; unpaid rentals; procedure; escheats.

(a)   If the rental due on a safe deposit box is 90 days or more past due, the lessor bank may send a notice by registered mail or certified mail, return receipt requested, to the last known address of the lessee or by another means agreed to in writing by the lessor bank and the lessee, stating that the safe deposit box will be opened and its contents stored at the expense of the lessee unless payment of the rental is made within 30 days of the date of the mailing of the notice or the date such notice is given by the means otherwise previously agreed to in writing by the lessor bank and the lessee. If the rental is not paid within the stated period, the box may be opened in the presence of an officer of the bank and of a notary public who is not a director, officer, employee, or shareholder of the bank. The contents shall be sealed in a package by the notary public, who shall write on the outside the name of the lessee and the date of the opening. The notary public shall execute a certificate reciting the name of the lessee, the date of the opening of the box, and a list of its contents. The certificate shall be included in the package, and a copy of the certificate shall be sent by registered mail or certified mail, return receipt requested, to the last known address of the lessee or by the means otherwise previously agreed to in writing by the lessor bank and the lessee. The package then shall be placed in the general vaults of the bank at a rental not exceeding the rental previously charged for the box.

(b)   If the contents of the safe deposit box have not been claimed within two years of the mailing or other permissible delivery of the copy of the certificate to the lessee, the bank may send a further notice to the last known address of the lessee by registered mail or certified mail, return receipt requested, to the last known address of the lessee or by a means otherwise previously agreed to in writing by the lessor bank and the lessee, stating that unless the accumulated charges are paid within 30 days of the date of the mailing of the notice, the contents of the box will be delivered to the State Treasurer as abandoned property under the provisions of Chapter 116B of the General Statutes.

(c)   The bank shall submit to the State Treasurer a verified inventory of all of the contents of the safe deposit box upon delivery of the contents of the box or such part thereof as shall be required by the State Treasurer under G.S. 116B-55, but the bank may deduct from any cash of the lessee in the safe deposit box an amount equal to accumulated charges for rental and shall submit to the State

Treasurer a verified statement of the charges and deduction. If there is no cash or insufficient cash to pay accumulated charges in the safe deposit box, the bank may submit to the State Treasurer a verified statement of accumulated charges or balance of the accumulated charges due, and the State Treasurer shall remit to the bank the charges or balance due, up to the value of the property in the safe deposit box delivered to the State Treasurer, less any costs or expenses of sale; but if the charges or balance due exceeds the value of the property, the State Treasurer shall remit only the value of the property, less costs or expenses of sale. Any accumulated charges for safe deposit box rental paid by the State Treasurer to the bank shall be deducted from the value of the property of the lessee delivered to the State Treasurer.

(d) Any property, including documents or writings of a private nature, that has little or no apparent financial value need not be sold but may be destroyed by the bank if the State Treasurer declines to receive the property under G.S. 116B-69(a).

(e) An explanation of the contractual provisions pertaining to default, together with reference to this section, shall be printed on every contract for rental of a safe deposit box. (2012-56, s. 4.)

§ 53C-6-14. Reproduction and retention of records; admissibility of copies in evidence; disposition of originals; record production generally.

(a) Any bank may cause any or all records kept by it to be recorded, copied, or reproduced by any photographic, reproduction, electronic, or digital process or method, or by any other records retention technology approved by rule or order of the Commissioner, of a kind that is capable of accurately converting the records into tangible form within a reasonable time. Each such converted tangible form of record also shall be deemed a record.

(b) Any tangible form of a record shall be deemed for all purposes to be an original record and shall be admissible in evidence in all courts and administrative agencies in this State, if otherwise admissible, and the bank may destroy or otherwise dispose of the original form of the record; provided, however, that a bank shall retain either the originals or convertible form of its records for such period as may be required by law or by rule or order of the Commissioner. Any bank may dispose of any original or convertible form of a record that has been retained for the period prescribed by law or by rule or order of the Commissioner for its class.

(c) Originals and converted tangible forms of records shall not be held inadmissible in any court action or proceeding on the grounds that they lack certification, identification, or authentication and shall be received as evidence if otherwise admissible in any court or quasi-judicial proceeding if they have been identified and authenticated by the live testimony of a competent witness or if the records are accompanied by a certificate substantially in the following form:

"CERTIFICATE REGARDING BANK RECORDS

1. The accompanying documents are true and correct copies of the records of [name of bank]. The records were made in the regular course of business of the bank at or near the time of the acts, events, or conditions they reflect.

2. The undersigned is authorized to execute this certificate.

3. This certificate is issued pursuant to G.S. 53C-6-14.

I certify, under penalty of perjury under the laws of the State of North Carolina, that the foregoing statements are true and correct.

Date: _____

_____

Signature

_____

Print or type name

_____

Title

[Notarize as required by law for an affidavit]"

(d) This section supplements and does not supersede G.S. 8-45.1. (2012-56, s. 4.)

§ 53C-6-15. Establishment of branches.

(a)   A bank may establish one or more branches in this State, whether de novo or by acquisition of existing branches of another depository institution, with the prior written approval of the Commissioner. The Commissioner's approval may be given or withheld, in the Commissioner's discretion, in accordance with the provisions of subsection (c) of this section.

(b)   A bank may establish branches in another state, whether de novo or by acquisition of existing branches of another depository institution, in accordance with the provisions of applicable federal law and the laws of the other state, upon prior written approval of the Commissioner. The Commissioner's approval may be given or withheld in the Commissioner's discretion in accordance with the provisions of subsection (c) of this section.

(c)   A bank seeking authority to establish a branch shall make application to the Commissioner in a form acceptable to the Commissioner. Not more than 30 days before nor less than 10 days after the filing of the application with the Commissioner, the applicant shall publish public notice of the filing of the application. The public notice shall contain all of the following:

(1)   A statement that the application has been filed with the Commissioner.

(2)   The physical address or location of the proposed branch, including street and city or town.

(3)   A statement that any interested person may make written comment on the application to the Commissioner and that comments received by the Commissioner within 14 days of the date of publication of the public notice shall be considered. The public notice shall provide the then current mailing address of the Commissioner.

(d)   A bank may conduct any activities at a branch in another state authorized under this section that are permissible for a bank chartered by the other state where the branch is located, except to the extent the activities are expressly prohibited by the laws of this State or by any rule or order of the Commissioner applicable to the bank.

(e) Upon receipt of an application to establish a branch, the Commissioner shall conduct an examination of the pertinent facts and information and may request such additional information as the Commissioner deems necessary to make a decision on the application. In deciding whether to approve a branch application, the Commissioner shall take into account such factors as the financial condition and history of the applicant; the adequacy of its capital; the applicant's future earnings prospects; the character, competency, and experience of its management; the probable impact of the branch on the condition of the applicant bank and existing depository institutions in the community to be served; and the convenience and needs of the community the proposed branch is to serve. (2012-56, s. 4.)

§ 53C-6-16. Change of location of a branch or principal office.

(a) A bank may change the location of its principal office or a branch with the prior written approval of the Commissioner. A request to relocate the principal office or a branch of a bank shall be made in a form acceptable to the Commissioner and shall include information regarding the reason for the proposed relocation, the distance and direction of the move, and such other information as the Commissioner may require in order to reach a decision in the matter.

(b) Not more than 30 days before nor less than 10 days after filing a request to relocate the principal office or a branch of a bank, the applicant shall publish public notice of the request. The public notice shall contain all of the following:

(1) A statement that the request has been filed with the Commissioner.

(2) The physical address of the principal office or branch to be relocated and the physical address of the proposed new location.

(3) A statement that any interested person may make written comment on the request to the Commissioner and that comments received by the Commissioner within 14 days of the date of publication of the public notice will be considered. The statement shall provide the then current mailing address of the Commissioner.

(c) The Commissioner shall approve a request to relocate the principal office or a branch of a bank if the relocation is to a site within the same vicinity as the original location, or does not result in a material change in the primary service area of the principal office or branch, or is considered important to the economic viability of the bank or the branch, or is otherwise found not to be inconsistent with the public need and convenience. (2012-56, s. 4.)

§ 53C-6-17. Branch closings.

A bank may close a branch upon providing written notice to the Commissioner and the customers of the branch at least 90 days prior to the proposed closing. The notice shall include the date the branch will close and posting, in a conspicuous manner on the branch premises for a period of 30 days prior to the proposed closing date, a notice of its intent to close the branch. The consolidation of two or more branches into a single location in the same vicinity shall not be considered a closure subject to the 90-day and 30-day notice requirements of this section. To be considered a consolidation, the bank shall request consolidation treatment from the Commissioner, who shall decide, in his or her discretion, whether the branches to be consolidated are considered to be in the same vicinity, with due consideration to the distance between the branches and the nature of the market in which the branches are situated. (2012-56, s. 4.)

§ 53C-6-18. Non-branch bank business offices.

(a) A bank may establish one or more non-branch bank business offices as defined by G.S. 53C-1-4(46):

(1) If a proposed non-branch bank business office will offer a product, service, or other type of business not previously engaged in by the bank, the bank shall provide the Commissioner with written notification of the intent to open the office. The notification shall include the proposed location of the office and a description of the business to be conducted at the office. If the Commissioner does not request additional information or object to its establishment within 10 days of the date of receipt of the notification, the non-branch bank business office shall be deemed approved. In deciding whether to object to the establishment of a non-branch bank business office, the Commissioner shall consider, without limitation, whether the business proposed to be conducted at the non-branch bank business office is permissible for a

bank, the costs of its establishment and ongoing operation and the impact of the costs on the bank's capital and profitability, and the ability of the bank's management to conduct the proposed business.

(2) If a proposed non-branch bank business office will offer only products, services, or other types of business already engaged in by the bank, the bank shall provide the Commissioner with written notification of the intent to open the office.

(b) An out-of-state bank may establish and operate a non-branch bank business office in this State upon written notice to the Commissioner.

(c) A bank or an out-of-state bank may close a non-branch bank business office at any time with notice to the Commissioner.

(d) No deposits may be taken at a non-branch bank business office. (2012-56, s. 4.)

§ 53C-6-19. Operations; suspension.

(a) A bank, any of its branches, and any of its non-branch bank business offices may operate on such days and during such hours, and may observe such holidays, as the bank's board of directors shall designate.

(b) Whenever the Commissioner determines that an emergency exists or is pending in this State or any part thereof, the Commissioner may authorize banks operating in the affected area or areas to suspend any or all of their operations in such area or areas for such period or periods as the Commissioner establishes. An emergency is any condition or occurrence that may interfere with a bank's operations or poses an existing or imminent threat to the safety or security of persons or property, or both.

(c) In the event that an emergency exists or is pending in this State or any part thereof and a bank operating in the affected area or areas is unable to communicate the existence or pendency of the emergency to the OCOB, an officer of the bank may suspend any or all of the bank's operations in the affected area or areas without the prior approval of the Commissioner. The bank shall give notice of such closing to the Commissioner as soon as practicable. (2012-56, s. 4.)

Article 7.

Control Transactions; Combinations; Conversions.

Part 1. Change in Control.

§ 53C-7-101. Control transactions.

(a)   Except as otherwise expressly permitted by this section, a person shall not engage in a control transaction, as defined by G.S. 53C-1-4(22), involving a bank without the prior approval of the Commissioner. A person may contract to engage in a control transaction with the consummation of such control transaction being subject to receipt of the approval of the Commissioner.

(b)   The Commissioner may require a person who is obligated to file an application under this Part to appoint an agent resident in this State for service of process upon the filing of such notice or as a condition to the acceptance of such application for review. The application for approval shall be in a form required by the Commissioner and shall be accompanied by such fee as may be required by rule.

(c)   The following transactions shall not constitute a control transaction requiring the prior approval of the Commissioner:

(1)   The acquisition of control over voting securities in connection with securing, collecting, or satisfying a debt previously contracted for in good faith and not for the purpose of acquiring control of the bank, if the acquiring person files a notice with the Commissioner, in the form required by the Commissioner, describing such transaction at least 10 days before the acquiring person first votes or directs the voting of the voting securities.

(2)   The acquisition of control over voting securities by a person who has previously engaged in a control transaction with respect to the bank after receiving the approval of the Commissioner under this Article, which approval permits the acquisition of control over additional voting securities, or any person who is an affiliate of the person previously engaging in the approved control

transaction with the permission and who is identified in the application submitted for the approval, if the acquiring person files a notice with the Commissioner, in the form required by the Commissioner, describing the transaction at least 10 days before the acquiring person or affiliate thereof first votes or directs the voting of the voting securities.

(3) An acquisition of control over voting securities by operation of law, will, or intestate succession, if the acquiring person files a notice with the Commissioner, in the form required by the Commissioner, describing the acquisition or transfer at least 10 days before the acquiring person first votes or directs the voting of the voting securities.

(4) Bona fide gifts.

(5) A transaction exempted by rules, orders, or declaratory rulings of the Commissioner issued because approval of such a transaction is not necessary to achieve the objectives of this Chapter.

(5a) An acquisition of control over voting shares exempt from the prior approval requirements set forth in section 3 of the Bank Holding Company Act, as amended (12 U.S.C. § 1842), pursuant to the exceptions described in items (A), (B), or (C) of subsection (a) of that section.

(6) An acquisition of control over voting securities in a transaction subject to approval under section 3 of the Bank Holding Company Act, as amended (12 U.S.C. § 1842).

(d) Upon receipt of a notice described in subsection (c), the Commissioner may, before the 10th day following the receipt, notify the acquiring person of the Commissioner's objection to the exercise of control over the voting securities or may require the acquiring party to submit further information before exercising control over the voting securities. An acquiring person receiving a notice of objection shall be required to submit an application for approval of a control transaction. An acquiring person receiving a notice to submit further information may be required to provide any information that would be included in an application for approval of a control transaction. In the event such an acquiring person is comprised of a group of persons, the Commissioner may require each member of the group to submit relevant information.

(e) All voting securities over which control has been acquired by an acquiring person shall not be voted on any matter submitted to a vote of the holders of the outstanding voting securities of the bank and shall be deemed authorized but unissued for purposes of determining the presence of a quorum of holders of voting securities until such time as follows:

(1)   The Commissioner has approved an application for approval of a control transaction with respect to the voting securities.

(2)   The transaction is one listed in subsection (c) of this section that does not require the filing of a notice with the Commissioner.

(3)   The transaction is one listed in subsection (c) of this section that requires a notice to be filed with the Commissioner and the Commissioner has not issued an objection to the notice and any requirement of the Commissioner for the filing of further information has been determined by the Commissioner to have been satisfied. (2012-56, s. 4; 2013-29, s. 14.)

§ 53C-7-102. Application regarding a control transaction.

(a)   A person seeking approval of a control transaction involving a bank under this Article shall file the following with the Commissioner:

(1)   An application in the form prescribed by the Commissioner.

(2)   All filing fees required by a rule of the Commissioner.

(3)   Such information as is required by a rule of the Commissioner or as is deemed by the Commissioner to achieve the objectives of this Chapter.

(b)   In the event a person submitting an application is a group of persons, the Commissioner may require each member of the group to submit information relevant to the application.

(c)   Notwithstanding any laws to the contrary, information about the character, competence, or experience of an acquiring person or its proposed management personnel or affiliates shall be deemed a record of the Commissioner and subject to G.S. 53C-2-7(b). (2012-56, s. 4; 2013-29, s. 15.)

§ 53C-7-103. Public notice.

A person filing an application for approval of a control application shall publish a public notice of the filing of the application not more than 30 days before nor more than 10 days after the filing of the application with the Commissioner. The public notice shall contain the following:

(1)   A statement that the application has been filed with the Commissioner.

(2)   The name of the applicable bank and the address of its principal office.

(3)   A statement that any interested person may make written comment on the proposed control transaction and that comments received by the Commissioner within 14 days of the date of the publication of the public notice shall be considered. The public notice shall provide the current mailing address of the Commissioner. (2012-56, s. 4.)

§ 53C-7-104. Actions on control transaction applications.

(a)   The Commissioner shall examine the proposed control transaction, including the character, competence, and experience of the acquiring person and its proposed management personnel, to determine whether the interests of the customers and communities served by the bank would be adversely affected by the proposed control transaction. Not later than the 60th day following receipt of a completed application for approval of a control transaction, unless extraordinary circumstances require a longer period of review, the Commissioner shall approve or deny the application.

(b)   The Commissioner may deny an application for approval of a control transaction for any of the following reasons:

(1)   The financial condition of the person seeking approval of a control transaction could jeopardize the financial stability of the bank or the financial interests of its customers.

(2)   An examination of the character, competence, and experience of any acquiring person or of any of the proposed management personnel shows that it would not be in the interest of the depositors of the bank, or in the interest of the public, to permit the person to control the bank.

(3) The plans or proposals of the person seeking approval with respect to exercising control over the bank would not be in the best interests of the bank's customers.

(4) Upon the effective date of such proposed control transaction, the bank would not be solvent, have inadequate capital, or not be in compliance with this Chapter or rules of the Commissioner.

(5) The application for approval is incomplete.

(6) If the acquiring person solicits votes for the approval of or consents to the control transaction from the holders of the voting securities of the bank, adequate and complete disclosures of all material information about the proposed control transaction, together with a prominent statement that neither the control transaction nor any solicitation of the holders' votes or consents have been approved by the Commissioner and that any representation to the contrary is a criminal offense, have not been made to the holders.

(c) If an application filed under this Part is approved by the Commissioner, the control transaction may become effective. All conditions to approval set forth in the order of the Commissioner shall be enforceable against the person, and each member of a group of persons, receiving the approval. (2012-56, s. 4.)

§ 53C-7-105. Appeal.

Any order of the Commissioner denying an application for approval of a control transaction may be appealed to the Commission by the person filing the application denied, as provided in G.S. 53C-2-6. (2012-56, s. 4.)

Part 2. Combinations.

§ 53C-7-201. Combination authority.

With the approval of the Commissioner, a bank may combine with one or more depository institutions or non-depository institutions, provided that the bank is the surviving entity in any combination with a non-depository institution. The application for approval shall be in the form required by the Commissioner and shall be accompanied by a fee as set forth by rule. (2012-56, s. 4.)

§ 53C-7-202. Combination application and investigation.

(a)   A bank seeking approval of a combination shall file with the Commissioner an application for approval, copies of the agreement under which the bank proposes to effect the combination, and such additional information as the Commissioner shall require by rule or as is required by the Commissioner in connection with the application in order to achieve the objectives of this Chapter.

(b)   A bank filing an application for approval of a combination shall publish a public notice of the filing of the application not more than 30 days before nor more than 10 days after the filing of the application with the Commissioner. The public notice shall contain the following:

(1)   A statement that the application has been filed with the Commissioner.

(2)   The names of the parties to the proposed combination and the addresses of their principal offices.

(3)   A statement that any interested person may make written comment on the proposed combination and that comments received by the Commissioner within 14 days of the date of the publication of the public notice shall be considered. The public notice shall contain the current mailing address of the Commissioner.

(c)   The Commissioner shall examine the proposed combination, including the character, competency, and experience of the proposed directors and executive officers of the surviving party of the combination, to determine whether the interests of the customers of and communities served by the parties to the combination would be adversely affected by the proposed combination.

(d)   Notwithstanding any laws to the contrary, information about the character, competence, or experience of the directors and executive officers of the parties to a combination received by the Commissioner shall be subject to G.S. 53C-2-7(b). (2012-56, s. 4.)

§ 53C-7-203. Decision on application.

Based on the application and the Commissioner's examination, the Commissioner shall enter an order approving or denying approval of the proposed combination not later than the 60th day following the date the Commissioner notifies the parties that the application is complete, unless extraordinary circumstances require a longer period of review. (2012-56, s. 4.)

§ 53C-7-204. Interim banks.

The Commissioner may approve an application to organize an interim bank solely for the purpose of effecting a combination under this Article. No interim bank shall transact any business except as is incidental and necessary to its organization and the combination. The Commissioner may set forth in the order approving the organization such additional conditions with respect to the interim bank as the Commissioner deems necessary. (2012-56, s. 4.)

§ 53C-7-205. Fiduciary powers and liabilities in a combination or a transferring of assets and liabilities.

Whenever any depository institution or any trust institution shall combine with or shall sell to and transfer its assets and liabilities to any other depository institution, trust institution, or other company, as provided by the laws of this State or the United States, all the then existing fiduciary rights, powers, duties, and liabilities of the combining or transferring institution, including the rights, powers, duties, and liabilities as executor, administrator, guardian, trustee, and/or any other fiduciary capacity, whether under appointment by order of court, will, deed, or other instrument, shall, upon the effective date of the combination or sale and transfer, vest in, devolve upon, and thereafter be performed by the surviving or transferee company, and such latter institution shall be deemed substituted for and shall have all the rights and powers of the transferring institution. (2012-56, s. 4; 2013-29, s. 16.)

§ 53C-7-206. Combination with federally chartered institution.

A combination by a bank with a federally chartered institution in which the federally chartered institution will be the surviving party shall be subject to approval by the chartering authority of the federally chartered institution in accordance with the laws of the United States. (2012-56, s. 4.)

§ 53C-7-207. Combination with a subsidiary.

(a) Except as provided in subsection (c) of this section, a bank proposing to do any of the following combinations shall give prior written notice to the Commissioner that provides such detail of the proposed combination that the Commissioner may require:

(1) Combine with a subsidiary, if the bank is the resulting entity of the combination.

(2) Combine a subsidiary with another company, if a subsidiary is the resulting entity.

(3) Combine two or more subsidiaries of two or more banks under common control of the same holding company.

Unless the Commissioner, within 30 days of receiving the notice, notifies the bank or subsidiary that the Commissioner objects to the proposed combination, the bank or subsidiary may complete the combination. However, the Commissioner may extend the period to object to the proposed combination if the Commissioner determines that it raises issues that require additional information or additional time for analysis. While the objection period is so extended, the bank or subsidiary may not proceed with respect to the proposed combination.

(b) A bank may, pursuant to G.S. 53C-2-6, appeal an objection by the Commissioner.

(c) The prior written notice requirement of subsection (a) of this section is not required for (i) a combination of a subsidiary and another company when the subsidiary is not the resulting entity, (ii) a combination of two or more subsidiaries of the same bank, each of which shall be effected in accordance with applicable organizational law, or (iii) if all of the following apply:

(1)   The bank is well-capitalized and well-managed as demonstrated by the supervisory rating it received during its most recent examination.

(2)   The subsidiary with which the combination is to be made engages in either of the following activities:

a.   One in which the bank is then engaged or has previously been engaged, directly or through a different subsidiary, and for which all necessary approvals of bank supervisory agencies and of the Commissioner have previously been obtained and remain in effect.

b.   One for which no prior notice or application for approval to any federal bank supervisory authority is required.

(3)   The bank notifies the Commissioner in writing of the combination within 30 days thereafter. (2012-56, s. 4; 2013-29, s. 17.)

§ 53C-7-208: Repealed by Session Laws 2013-29, s. 18, effective April 16, 2013.

§ 53C-7-209. Appeal.

Any order of the Commissioner denying an application for approval of a combination may be appealed to the Commission by a party to the combination as provided in G.S. 53C-2-6. (2012-56, s. 4.)

Part 3. Charter Conversion.

§ 53C-7-301. Conversion to a North Carolina bank charter.

(a)   Any depository institution that is not a bank may apply to the Commissioner for permission to convert into a bank and for certification of related amendments to its organizational documents necessary to effect the conversion. The application for approval shall be in the form required by the Commissioner and shall be accompanied by a fee as set forth by rule.

(b)   A plan of conversion shall be submitted as a part of the application filed with the Commissioner. The Commissioner may require amendment of the plan.

(c)   The Commissioner shall approve the plan of conversion, as amended if applicable, if upon examination the Commissioner finds the following:

(1)   The resulting bank will commence operations in a safe, sound, and prudent manner with adequate capital, liquidity, reserves, asset composition, and earnings prospects.

(2)   The directors and officers of the converting institution are qualified by character, competency, and experience to control and operate the resulting bank in a legal and proper manner.

(3)   The interests of the converting institution's customers, creditors, and shareholders will not be materially and adversely affected by the proposed conversion.

(4)   The plan of conversion is not in violation of the converting institution's applicable organizational law.

(5)   Adequate written disclosure of the material terms of the plan of conversion and other relevant material information has been or will be made to the converting institution's equity ownership interest holders as required by the converting institution's organizational law, including a statement in any such written disclosure that any materials used to solicit the votes of the holders have not been approved by the Commission or the Commissioner and that any representation to the contrary is a criminal offense.

(d)   Following approval of the plan of conversion, the Commissioner shall supervise and monitor the conversion process in order to determine compliance by the converting institution with the plan of conversion and applicable law.

(e)   The Commissioner shall authorize by order the consummation of the conversion, issue a charter, and permit the converting institution to file with the Secretary of State and other public officials such documents as are necessary to effect the conversion when the Commissioner determines the conversion process complied with the organizational law applicable to the converting institution and the plan of conversion was approved, if required by applicable organizational law, by such vote of the converting institution's equity ownership interest holders as is required under the organizational law.

(f) The Commissioner may provide in the order authorizing the consummation of conversion for the resulting bank to do the following:

(1) Wind up any activities legally engaged in by the converting institution at the time of conversion but not permitted to banks.

(2) Return any assets and deposit liabilities legally held by the converting institution at the time of the conversion but not permitted to be held by banks.

The length, terms, and conditions of the transitional periods described in this subsection shall be subject to the discretion of the Commissioner.

(g) Upon the effective date of the conversion, the converting institution shall continue in existence as a bank, and all rights, liabilities, and obligations of whatever kind of the converting institution shall continue and remain in its new form of organization. Except as may be authorized by the Commissioner pursuant to subsection (f) of this section, the bank shall have only those rights, powers, and duties authorized for or imposed upon banks by the laws of this State and the United States. All actions and proceedings to which the converting institution was party prior to conversion shall be unaffected by the conversion and shall proceed as if the conversion had not been effected. (2012-56, s. 4.)

§ 53C-7-302. Appeal.

Any order of the Commissioner denying an application for approval of a conversion to a bank may be appealed to the Commission by the party filing the application as provided in G.S. 53C-2-6. (2012-56, s. 4.)

§ 53C-7-303. Conversion by North Carolina bank.

(a) A bank may convert to another form of depository institution under the laws of this State, of another state, or the United States in accordance with applicable law.

(b) Upon the effective date of the conversion, the depository institution shall notify the Commissioner of the effective date and file with the Commissioner a copy of its authorization to operate as a depository institution certified by the applicable federal regulator or financial institution regulator.

(c) Upon the effective date of the conversion, the resulting depository institution shall cease to be a bank.

(d) Upon the effective date of the conversion, all rights, liabilities, and obligations of whatever kind of the bank shall continue and remain in its new form of organization as a depository institution organized under the laws of this State, another state, or the United States. All actions and proceedings to which the bank was party prior to conversion shall be unaffected by the conversion and shall proceed as if the conversion had not been effected. (2012-56, s. 4.)

Article 8.

Bank Supervision.

§ 53C-8-1. Commissioner has authority to supervise banks.

(a) Every bank shall be under the supervision of the Commissioner. It shall be the Commissioner's duty to enforce the banking laws through the employees and agents of the OCOB. All banks shall conduct their business in a manner consistent with the banking laws.

(b) The Commissioner may enter into written agreements, cease and desist order stipulations, cease and desist orders, consent orders, and similar arrangements with banks and their holding companies, or either of them; may request resolutions be approved by boards of directors of banks and their holding companies, or either of them; and may take other similar corrective actions.

(c) Upon written request, the Commissioner may, notwithstanding any other provision of law to the contrary, issue letters of interpretation, advisory opinions, or written guidance on any laws under the Commissioner's jurisdiction, provided that the interpretations, opinions, and guidance shall not have the force and effect of rules of law. (2012-56, s. 4.)

§ 53C-8-2. Assessments and fees.

Banks shall pay the following assessments and fees into the OCOB within 10 days after receipt of an invoice:

(1) Annual assessments. - Each bank shall pay a cumulative assessment based on its total assets as shown on its report of condition made to the Commissioner as of December 31 each year or the date most nearly approximating the same, not to exceed the amount determined by applying the following schedule:

a. On the first fifty million dollars ($50,000,000) of assets, or fraction thereof, ten thousand dollars ($10,000).

b. On assets greater than fifty million dollars ($50,000,000) but not more than two hundred fifty million dollars ($250,000,000), fourteen dollars ($14.00) per hundred thousand dollars ($100,000), or fraction thereof.

c. On assets greater than two hundred fifty million dollars ($250,000,000), but not more than five hundred million dollars ($500,000,000), eleven dollars ($11.00) per hundred thousand dollars ($100,000), or fraction thereof.

d. On assets greater than five hundred million dollars ($500,000,000), but not more than one billion dollars ($1,000,000,000), seven dollars ($7.00) per hundred thousand dollars ($100,000), or fraction thereof.

e. On assets greater than one billion dollars ($1,000,000,000), but not more than ten billion dollars ($10,000,000,000), four dollars ($4.00) per hundred thousand dollars ($100,000), or fraction thereof.

f. On assets greater than ten billion dollars ($10,000,000,000), two dollars ($2.00) per hundred thousand dollars ($100,000), or fraction thereof.

(2) Assessments on trust assets. - Each bank shall pay an assessment on trust assets held by it in the amount of one dollar ($1.00) per hundred thousand dollars ($100,000) of trust assets, or fraction thereof, except that banks are not required to pay assessments on real estate held as trust assets.

(3) Special assessments. - If the Commissioner determines that the financial condition or manner of operation of a bank warrants further examination or an increased level of supervision, or in the event of a combination or conversion, the Commissioner may charge, and the institutions shall pay, an assessment equal to the reasonable cost of further examination, increased level of supervision, or supervision with regard to the combination or conversion. The Commissioner's determination of the cost of further examination shall be, in the absence of manifest error, dispositive of the issue of reasonableness.

(4) In the first half of each calendar year, the Commission shall review the estimated cost of maintaining each division of the OCOB for the next fiscal year. If the estimated assessments provided for under this Chapter for any division shall exceed the estimated cost of maintaining that division for the next fiscal year, then the Commission may reduce by a uniform percentage any assessments provided for in this Chapter for that division. If the estimated assessments provided for in this Chapter for any division shall be less than the estimated cost of maintaining that division for the next fiscal year, then the Commission may increase by a uniform percentage any assessments provided for in this Chapter for that division to an amount that will increase the amount of assessments to be collected to an amount at least equal to the estimated cost of maintaining that division of the OCOB for the next fiscal year. (2012-56, s. 4.)

§ 53C-8-3. Reports required of banks.

(a) Each bank shall file the following with the Commissioner, at such times, on such forms, and in such formats as the Commissioner may require:

(1) Annual reports of conditions.

(2) Periodic reports for interim periods within a year, not less than monthly in any case.

(b)   In addition to the reports filed pursuant to subsection (a) of this section, each bank shall provide to the Commissioner copies of all applications and reports of condition filed by it under applicable federal law contemporaneously with the filing of such application and reports by the bank with its primary federal regulator.

(c)   Nothing in this section shall be interpreted to limit the authority of the Commissioner to request and obtain other information that the Commissioner may deem necessary to discharge the duties of the Commissioner under this Chapter. (2012-56, s. 4.)

§ 53C-8-4. Examination by Commissioner.

(a)   The Commissioner may examine everything relating to the business of a bank or its holding company, and may appoint examiners to make such examination. The examiners shall file with the Commissioner a full report of the findings resulting from the examination, including any violation of law or any unauthorized or unsafe practices of the bank or the holding company disclosed by the examination.

(b)   Examinations under subsection (a) of this section shall be conducted pursuant to practices and procedures established by the OCOB, provided the Commissioner may take into consideration the guidelines and requirements for such activity of the primary federal supervisor of the bank or holding company.

(c)   The Commissioner shall furnish a copy of the report of examination to the bank or the holding company examined and may, upon request, furnish a copy of the report to the primary federal regulator of the bank or its holding company and to the FDIC if not the bank's primary federal regulator. (2012-56, s. 4.)

§ 53C-8-5. Examination of affiliates.

The Commissioner, at his or her discretion, may examine the affiliates of a bank to the extent it is necessary to safeguard the interest of depositors and creditors of the bank and of the general public, and to enforce the provisions of this Chapter. The Commissioner may conduct the examination in conjunction with any examination of the bank or an affiliate thereof conducted by any other state or federal regulatory authority. (2012-56, s. 4.)

§ 53C-8-6. Access to books and records; right to issue subpoenas, administer oaths, and examine witnesses.

(a) The Commissioner and the Commissioner's examiners and agents:

(1) Shall have free access to all books and records of a bank, its holding company, and their affiliates that relate to the business of the bank or the holding company, and the books and records kept by an officer, agent, or employee of the bank or holding company relating to or upon which any record is kept.

(2) May subpoena witnesses and administer oaths or affirmations in the examination of any director, officer, agent, or employee of the bank, its holding company, or their affiliates or of any other person in relation to affairs, transactions, and conditions of the bank, its holding company, or their affiliates.

(3) May require the production of the records, books, papers, contracts, and other documents of a bank, its holding company, and their affiliates.

(4) May order that improper entries be corrected on the books and records of a bank, its holding company, and the bank's affiliates.

(b) The Commissioner may issue subpoenas duces tecum.

(c) If a person fails to comply with a subpoena so issued or a party or witness refuses to testify on any matters, a court of competent jurisdiction, on the application of the Commissioner, may compel compliance by proceedings for contempt as in the case of disobedience of the requirements of a subpoena issued from the court or a refusal to testify in the court. (2012-56, s. 4.)

§ 53C-8-7. Examiner making false report.

If any bank examiner shall knowingly and willfully make any false or fraudulent report of the condition of any bank that the examiner has examined with the intent to aid or abet the bank or its affiliates in committing violations of any provision of this Chapter, or if any examiner shall keep or accept any bribe or gratuity given for the purpose of inducing the examiner not to file any report of examination of any bank, or if any examiner shall neglect to make an examination of any bank by reason of having received or accepted any bribe or gratuity, the examiner shall be guilty of a Class H felony. (2012-56, s. 4.)

§ 53C-8-8. Examiner disclosing confidential information.

If any examiner or other employee of the OCOB fails to keep secret the facts and information obtained in the course of an examination of a bank except as permitted or required by this Chapter, the examiner shall be guilty of a Class 1 misdemeanor. (2012-56, s. 4.)

§ 53C-8-9. Loans or gratuities forbidden.

(a) No bank, or any officer, director, employee, or affiliate thereof, shall make an extension of credit or grant any gratuity to the Commissioner, any deputy commissioner, or any bank examiner. Any person violating this provision shall be guilty of a Class 1 misdemeanor and may be fined a sum equal to the amount of the extension made or the gratuity given. If the Commissioner, any deputy commissioner, or any bank examiner accepts an extension of credit or gratuity from any bank, or from any officer, director, employee, or affiliate thereof, that individual shall be guilty of a Class 1 misdemeanor and may be fined a sum equal to the extension of credit made or the gratuity given.

(b) Notwithstanding the provisions of subsection (a) of this section, the Commissioner may exempt from the application of subsection (a) any deputy commissioner or any bank examiner with respect to any extension of credit existing upon the hiring of the deputy commissioner or bank examiner by the OCOB and any extension of the term or renewal of such extension of credit made thereafter, so long as the extension of term or renewal has terms and conditions generally available to customers of the applicable bank having generally the same creditworthiness as the deputy commissioner or bank examiner. (2012-56, s. 4.)

§ 53C-8-10. Willfully and maliciously making derogatory reports.

Any person who shall willfully and maliciously make, circulate, transmit, or otherwise communicate any statement, rumor, or suggestion to one or more other persons that is directly or by inference false and derogatory to the financial condition, or affects the solvency or financial standing, of any bank, or who shall counsel, aid, procure, or induce another to make, circulate, transmit, or otherwise communicate any such statement or rumor, shall be guilty of a Class 1 misdemeanor. (2012-56, s. 4.)

§ 53C-8-11. Misapplication, embezzlement of funds.

(a) Any person who, with intent to defraud or injure a bank or any other person or with intent to deceive an officer of the bank or an employee of the OCOB appointed to examine the affairs of the bank, commits any of the following acts shall be guilty of a felony:

(1) Embezzles, converts, or misapplies any of the money, funds, credit, or property of the bank, whether owned by it or held in trust.

(2) Issues or puts forth a certificate of deposit; draws an order or bill of exchange; makes an acceptance; assigns a note, bond, draft, bill of exchange, mortgage, judgment, or decree; or fictitiously borrows or solicits, obtains, or receives money for a bank not in good faith.

(3) Makes or permits to be made a false entry in a record of a bank, or conceals or permits to be concealed, by any means or manner, the true and correct entries in a record of a bank.

(4) Knowingly makes an extension of credit, or permits an extension of credit, by a bank to any insolvent person or to a person who has ceased to exist, or that never had any existence, or upon collateral consisting of stocks or bonds of an insolvent or nonexistent person.

(5) Makes or publishes, or knowingly permits to be made or published, a false report, statement, or certificate as to the true financial condition of a bank.

(b)   If an offense committed under this section involves money, funds, credit, or property with a value of one hundred thousand dollars ($100,000) or more, it is a Class C felony. If an offense committed under this section involves money, funds, credit, or property with a value of less than one hundred thousand dollars ($100,000), it is a Class H felony. (2012-56, s. 4.)

§ 53C-8-12. Enforcement of the banking laws.

(a)   When the Commissioner believes that a violation of the banking laws has occurred or is continuing, the Commissioner may order an examination or investigation of the facts and circumstances relating to the suspected violation.

(b)   Every bank failing to make and transmit any report that the Commissioner is authorized to require by this Chapter, and in and according to the form prescribed by the Commissioner, within 10 business days after the receipt of a request or requisition therefor, or within the extension of time granted by the Commissioner, shall be notified by the Commissioner, and if the failure continues for five business days after the receipt of the notice, the delinquent bank shall be subject to a penalty of up to one thousand dollars ($1,000). The penalty provided by this section shall be recovered in a civil action in any court of competent jurisdiction, and it shall be the duty of the Attorney General to prosecute all such actions.

(c)   In addition to any other powers conferred by this Chapter, the Commissioner shall have the power to do the following:

(1)   Order any bank, trust company, or subsidiary thereof, or any director, officer, or employee, or any other person the Commissioner is authorized to regulate, to cease and desist violating any provision of this Chapter or any lawful rule issued thereunder.

(2)   Order any bank, trust company, or subsidiary thereof, or any director, officer, or employee, or any other person the Commissioner is authorized to regulate, to cease and desist from a course of conduct that is unsafe or unsound and that is likely to cause insolvency or dissipation of assets or is likely to jeopardize or otherwise seriously prejudice the interests of a depositor.

(d)   Consistent with Article 3A of Chapter 150B of the General Statutes, notice and opportunity for hearing shall be provided before any of the actions authorized by this section shall be undertaken by the Commissioner. In cases involving extraordinary circumstances requiring immediate action, the Commissioner may take such action but shall promptly afford a subsequent hearing upon application to rescind the action taken.

(e)   The Commissioner shall have the power to subpoena witnesses, compel their attendance, require the production of evidence, administer oaths, and examine any person under oath in connection with any subject related to a duty imposed or a power vested in the Commissioner.

(f)   The Commissioner may impose a civil money penalty of not more than one thousand dollars ($1,000) for each violation by any bank, trust company, or subsidiary thereof, or any director, officer, or employee, or any other person the Commissioner is authorized to regulate, of an order issued under subdivision (1) of subsection (c) of this section. The Commissioner may impose a civil money penalty of not more than five hundred dollars ($500.00) per day for each day that a bank, trust company, or subsidiary thereof, or any director, officer, or employee, or any other person the Commissioner is authorized to regulate, violates a cease and desist order issued under subdivision (2) of subsection (c) of this section. The proceeds of civil money penalties imposed pursuant to this subsection, net of documented expenses of examination and enforcement, shall be remitted to the Civil Penalty and Forfeiture Fund in accordance with G.S. 115C-457.2.

(g)   Administrative orders issued by the Commissioner and civil money penalties imposed for violation of such orders shall be subject to review by the Commission, which shall have power to amend, modify, or disapprove the same at any regular or special meeting.

(h)   Notwithstanding any penalty imposed by the Commissioner, the Commission may, after notice of and opportunity for hearing, impose, enter judgment for, and enforce, by appropriate process, a penalty of not more than ten thousand dollars ($10,000) against any bank, trust company, or subsidiary thereof, or against any of its directors, officers, or employees, or any other person the Commissioner is authorized to regulate, for violating any lawful order of the Commission or Commissioner. The proceeds of civil money penalties imposed pursuant to this subsection, net of documented expenses of examination and enforcement, shall be remitted to the Civil Penalty and Forfeiture Fund in accordance with G.S. 115C-457.2.

(i)   If the Commissioner believes that a violation of a criminal statute has occurred, the Commissioner may refer the matter to the appropriate prosecutorial agency. (2012-56, s. 4.)

§ 53C-8-13. Immediate action orders.

(a)   In the event that the Commissioner determines that a bank has inadequate capital or insufficient capital or determines that immediate action is necessary to cause a bank to conduct its business in a safe and sound manner or to cause a bank or any of its directors, officers, or employees to cease from an act or course of conduct that threatens, or is reasonably probable of threatening, the financial integrity of the bank, the commissioner may order, as applicable, the bank to take such corrective action as the Commissioner deems necessary or may order the bank, director, officer, or employee to immediately cease such conduct, act, or course of conduct and to refrain therefrom in the future.

(b)   Any order made under this section shall be effective upon issuance, provided, however, that the Commissioner shall promptly afford a subsequent hearing upon the order as provided in G.S. 53C-2-6. (2012-56, s. 4.)

§ 53C-8-14. Supervisory control.

(a)   Whenever the Commissioner determines that a bank has insufficient capital and is conducting its business in an unsafe or unsound manner or in any fashion that threatens the financial integrity of the bank, the Commissioner may serve a notice of charges on the bank, requiring it to show cause why it should not be placed under supervisory control. The notice of charges shall specify the grounds for supervisory control and set the time and place for a hearing. A hearing before the Commissioner shall be held no earlier than seven days and no later than 15 days after issuance of the notice of charges.

(b)   If, after the hearing provided in subsection (a) of this section, the Commissioner determines that supervisory control of the bank is necessary to protect the bank's customers, creditors, or the general public, the Commissioner shall issue an order taking supervisory control of the bank. The board of directors of the bank in office on the date of the issuance of the order may appeal the order of the Commissioner to the Commission pursuant to G.S. 53C-2-6 no later than 10 days after the date of the issuance of the order.

(c) The Commissioner may appoint an agent to supervise and monitor the operations of the bank during the period of supervisory control. During the period of supervisory control, the bank shall act in accordance with any instructions and directions as may be given by the Commissioner, directly or through the agent, and shall not act or fail to act except when to do so would violate an outstanding order of its federal bank supervisory agent or the FDIC if the FDIC is not its primary federal regulator.

(d) Within 180 days of the date of the order taking supervisory control, the Commissioner shall issue an order approving a plan for the termination of supervisory control on the 30th day following the issuance of the order. The plan may provide for the following:

(1) The issuance by the bank of debt instruments or shares.

(2) The appointment or removal of one or more officers and/or one or more directors.

(3) The reorganization or combination of the bank.

(4) A control transaction with respect to the bank.

(5) The dissolution and liquidation of the bank.

(e) The reasonable costs of the Commissioner under this section shall be paid by the bank. The Commissioner's determination of the costs shall be, in the absence of manifest error, dispositive of the issue of reasonableness. (2012-56, s. 4.)

§ 53C-8-15. Removal of directors, officers, and employees.

(a) If the Commissioner determines that a director, officer, or employee of a bank has participated in or consented to any violation of this Chapter or an order of the Commissioner, or has engaged in any unsafe or unsound business practice in the operation of the bank, or has been dishonest, incompetent, or reckless in the management of the affairs of the bank, or has persistently violated the laws of this State, or repeatedly violated or failed to comply with any of the bank's organizational documents, and that as a result, a situation exists requiring prompt corrective action in order to protect the bank, its customers, or the public, the Commissioner may issue an order temporarily removing the director, officer, or employee pending a hearing that shall occur not less 10 days after removal. The order shall state that it is a "Temporary Order of Removal" and shall further state the grounds upon which it was issued together with the date, time, and location of a hearing on the matter. For good cause shown, the Commissioner may grant the director, officer, or employee subject to the order a 10-day extension of the hearing date, but the temporary removal order shall remain in full force and effect. Upon a hearing before the Commissioner within the prescribed time, the temporary removal order may be dissolved or made permanent in whole or in part.

(b)   Any removal under this section is effective in all respects as if the removal had been made by the shareholders of the bank in question.

(c)   Without the prior written approval of the Commissioner, no director, officer, or employee subject to an order under this section shall be eligible to be elected, reelected, or appointed any position as a director, officer, or employee of that bank or any other North Carolina financial institution during the period of the order's effect.

(d)   An individual who is the subject of an order of the Commissioner under this section may appeal the order to the Commission pursuant to G.S. 53C-2-6 no later than 10 days after the date of issuance of the order. (2012-56, s. 4.)

§ 53C-8-16. Emergency powers.

In the event of a natural disaster or other national, regional, state, or local emergency, the Commissioner may temporarily waive or suspend requirements for compliance by one or more banks with any provisions of this Chapter. (2012-56, s. 4.)

§ 53C-8-17. Interstate regulatory agreements.

The Commissioner may enter into cooperative, coordinating, and information sharing agreements with (i) any bank supervisory agency having jurisdiction over an out-of-state bank that operates one or more branches in this State and (ii) any bank supervisory agency of another state in which a bank operates one or more branches with respect to the periodic examination or other supervision of the branches of the out-of-state bank operating in this State or the branches of the bank operating in such other state. (2012-56, s. 4.)

Article 9.

Supervisory Liquidation; Voluntary Dissolution and Liquidation.

Part 1. General Provisions.

§ 53C-9-101. Supervisory combinations.

Notwithstanding any other provision of this Chapter, in order to protect the public, including depositors and creditors of a bank, the Commissioner, upon making a finding that a bank is unable to operate in a safe and sound manner and is not reasonably likely to be able to resume safe and sound operations, may authorize or require a combination of the bank, a control transaction, or any other transaction, whether or not the Commissioner has taken supervisory control pursuant to G.S. 53C-8-14. In ordering any such combination, control transaction, or other transaction, the Commissioner may order that a vote of the bank's shareholders shall not be required to effect the combination, control transaction, or other transactions. (2012-56, s. 4.)

§ 53C-9-102. Distributions; assignments restricted.

A bank that is in the process of involuntary or voluntary dissolution pursuant to this Article may not make or pay distributions to its shareholders unless the bank has the prior written approval of the Commissioner. No bank shall make any general assignment for the benefit of its creditors except by surrendering possession of its assets to the Commissioner for dissolution and liquidation pursuant to G.S. 53-9-301, and any other purported assignment by the bank for the benefit of its creditors shall be void. (2012-56, s. 4.)

§ 53C-9-103. Cancellation of charter.

Whenever a combination, dissolution, or other transaction occurs by which a bank ceases to exist or ceases to be eligible for a charter, the Commissioner shall by order cancel the bank's charter and shall publish the order in accordance with G.S. 53-1-4(59). A copy of the order shall be filed by the Commissioner with the Secretary of State. The bank shall continue to exist under Chapter 55 of the General Statutes for the purpose of dissolving and liquidating its business and affairs. (2012-56, s. 4.)

Part 2. Voluntary Dissolution and Liquidation.

§ 53C-9-201. Voluntary dissolution prior to receipt of charter.

A bank in formation may, prior to issuance of its charter, give notice to the Commissioner and, with the Commissioner's consent, abandon its application to the Commissioner and dissolve and liquidate by a majority vote of its board of directors and as provided under Chapter 55 of the General Statutes. (2012-56, s. 4.)

§ 53C-9-202. Voluntary dissolution.

(a)   With the approval of the Commissioner, a bank may engage in a voluntary dissolution and liquidation.

(b)   If, by a majority vote, the board of directors of a bank should determine that in their judgment the bank should be dissolved and liquidated, then the board of directors shall submit immediately to the Commissioner the following documents, certified by an appropriate officer of the bank:

(1)   The board of directors' resolution.

(2) The bank's proposed articles of dissolution.

(3) The board of directors' plan for liquidation.

(4) Any notices or proxy solicitation materials proposed to be sent to shareholders.

(c) The Commissioner shall examine the documents submitted under subsection (b) of this section and such other matters as the Commissioner deems relevant and may issue an order authorizing the bank and its board of directors to proceed with dissolution and liquidation as provided in G.S. 53C-9-203. Examination by the Commissioner of the materials referred to in subsection (b)(4) of this section shall not be deemed to be approval of the documents for any purpose.

(d) At any annual or special meeting of shareholders called for the purpose of voting upon a proposal for voluntary dissolution of a bank, the shareholders of the bank may, by an affirmative vote, in person or by proxy, of the holders of shares representing at least two-thirds of the votes entitled to be cast on such matters, resolve to dissolve and liquidate the bank in accordance with the order of the Commissioner issued under subsection (c) of this section.

(e) If a majority of the board of directors of a bank should determine that in its best judgment the bank should be dissolved and liquidated but deems it impractical or otherwise inadvisable to proceed with a vote upon voluntary dissolution by the shareholders, then the board of directors shall immediately forward a certified copy of its resolution to the Commissioner and the Commissioner shall place the bank in receivership pursuant to G.S. 53C-9-301. (2012-56, s. 4.)

§ 53C-9-203. Voluntary dissolution and liquidation procedure.

(a) At the appropriate time, the Commissioner shall do the following:

(1) Inform the FDIC and the bank's federal supervisory agency if other than the FDIC.

(2) Select and appoint a receiver or receiver in liquidation, just as if the liquidation were involuntary under G.S. 53C-9-301.

(3) Attach a certificate of approval to the articles of dissolution, and the bank shall then file the certified articles with the Secretary of State.

(b) Upon the filing of the articles of dissolution with the Secretary of State, it shall be unlawful for the bank to accept any additional deposit accounts or additions to deposit accounts or make any additional extensions of credit, but all its income and receipts in excess of actual expenses of liquidation of the bank shall be applied to the discharge of its liabilities.

(c) The persons charged with liquidation of the bank in the approved plan of dissolution shall cause to be published a public notice stating the bank has closed and will dissolve and liquidate and notifying its depositors and creditors to present their claims for payment, specifying the method for doing so.

(d) The bank may pay reasonable compensation, subject to the approval of the Commissioner, to the persons charged with its liquidation.

(e) Any bank in the process of voluntary dissolution and liquidation shall be subject to examination by the Commissioner and shall furnish any reports required by the Commissioner.

(f) If the Commissioner determines at any time that the voluntary liquidation plan is not working, the Commissioner may place the bank in receivership pursuant to G.S. 53C-9-301. (2012-56, s. 4.)

Part 3. Receivership; Involuntary Dissolution.

§ 53C-9-301. Receivership.

(a) The Commissioner may take custody of the books, records, and assets of every kind and character of any bank in the instances established in Part 2 of this Article or if it reasonably appears from one or more examinations made by the Commissioner that any of the following conditions exist:

(1) The directors or officers of the bank, or the liquidators of the bank subject to a voluntary plan of liquidation, have neglected, failed, or refused to take action that the Commissioner deems necessary for the protection of the bank.

(2) The directors, officers, or liquidators of the bank have impeded or obstructed an examination.

(3) The business of the bank is being conducted in a fraudulent, illegal, or unsafe manner.

(4) The bank is in an unsafe or unsound condition to transact business and it is not reasonably probable that it will be able to return to a safe and sound condition.

(5) The capital of the bank is impaired such that the likely realizable value of its assets is insufficient to pay and satisfy the claims of all depositors and all creditors.

(6) The directors or officers of the bank, or the liquidators of a bank subject to a voluntary plan of liquidation, have assumed duties or performed acts in excess of those authorized by applicable statutes or regulations, by the bank's organizational documents or plan of liquidation, or without supplying the required bond.

(7) The bank is insolvent or is in imminent danger of insolvency or has suspended its ordinary business transactions due to insufficient funds.

(8) The bank is unable to continue operations.

(b) Unless the Commissioner reasonably finds that an emergency exists that requires that the Commissioner take custody immediately, the Commissioner shall first give written notice to the board of directors of the bank specifying which of those circumstances listed in subdivisions (1) through (8) of subsection (a) have been determined to exist and shall allow a reasonable time in which corrections may be made before a receiver of the bank will be appointed as outlined in subsections (c) and (d) of this section. For these purposes, "written notice" shall be deemed to include any report of examination or other confidential or nonconfidential written communication that is either directly from the Commissioner or is joined in by the Commissioner.

(c) The Commissioner shall appoint as receiver or coreceivers one or more qualified persons for the purpose of receivership and liquidation of the bank of which the Commissioner has taken custody under subsection (a) of this section, which receiver shall furnish a bond in such form and amount, and with such surety, as the Commissioner may require.

(d) The Commissioner may appoint the FDIC or its nominee as the receiver, and the receiver shall be permitted to serve without posting bond. In the event of such an appointment, the Commissioner shall thereafter be forever relieved of any and all responsibility and liability in respect to the receivership and the liquidation of the bank.

(e) In the event the Commissioner takes custody of a bank and then appoints a receiver for the bank, the Commissioner shall serve personally at the bank's principal office through the officer who is present and appears to be in charge, the Commissioner's order taking possession and, if applicable, the Commissioner's order appointing a receiver for the bank in liquidation. The Commissioner shall also mail a certified copy of the order taking possession and the appointing order by certified mail or by express delivery to any previous receiver or other legal custodian of the bank and to the Clerk of Superior Court of Wake County. The Commissioner shall give notice to the public of the Commissioner's actions by posting a notice summarizing the Commissioner's actions near the entrance to each branch of the bank, and the Commissioner shall issue a similar public notice as defined in G.S. 53C-1-4(59).

(f) Whenever a receiver for a bank is duly appointed and qualified under subsection (c) or (d) of this section:

(1) The receiver, by operation of law and without any conveyance or other instrument, act, or deed, shall succeed to all the rights, titles, powers, and privileges of the bank, its shareholders, officers, and directors, or any of them, and to the titles to the books, records, and assets of every description of any previous receiver or other legal custodian of the bank. Neither the shareholders, officers, or directors, nor any of them, shall thereafter, except as expressly provided in this section, have or exercise any rights, powers, or privileges or act in connection with any assets or property of any nature of the bank in receivership.

(2) The Commissioner may, at any time, direct the receiver (unless it is the FDIC) to return the bank to its previous or a newly constituted management and its shareholders.

(3) A receiver, other than the FDIC, may, at any time during the receivership and before final liquidation, be removed and a replacement appointed by the Commissioner.

(g) A receiver may perform any of the following acts:

(1) Demand, sue for, collect, receive, and take into possession all the goods and chattels, rights and credits, moneys and effects, lands and tenements, books, papers, choses in action, bills, instruments, notes, intangible interests, and property of every description of the bank.

(2) Foreclose mortgages, deeds of trust, and other liens granted to the bank to the extent the bank would have the right to do so.

(3) Seek injunctions and institute suits for the recovery of any property, damages, or demands existing in favor of the bank, and shall, upon the receiver's own application, be substituted as party plaintiff in the place of the bank in any suit or proceeding pending at the time of the receiver's appointment.

(4) Sell, convey, and assign any or all of the property rights and interests owned by the bank.

(5) Appoint agents and engage independent contractors.

(6) Examine papers and investigate persons.

(7) Make and carry out agreements with the FDIC for the payment or assumption of the bank's liabilities, in whole or in part, and to sell, convey, transfer, pledge, or assign assets as security or otherwise and to make guarantees in connection therewith.

(8) Perform all other acts that might be done by the employees, officers, and directors of the bank.

These powers shall be continued in effect until liquidation of the bank or until return of the bank to its prior or newly constituted management.

(h) The Commissioner may, unless the FDIC has been appointed as receiver, determine that the receivership proceedings of a bank should be discontinued and the possession of the bank returned to newly constituted management. The Commissioner shall then remove the receiver and restore all the rights, powers, and privileges of the bank's depositors, shareholders, customers, employees, officers, and directors. The return of a bank to a newly constituted management from the possession of a receiver shall, by operation of law and without any conveyance or other instrument, act, or deed, vest in the bank the title to all property held by the receiver in the capacity as receiver for the bank.

(i)   Claims against a bank in receivership shall have the following order of priority for payment:

(1)   Costs, expenses, and debts of the bank incurred on or after the date of the appointment of the receiver, including compensation for the receiver and a reasonable sum for the time of employees and agents of the OCOB.

(2)   Claims of holders of deposit accounts.

(3)   Claims of secured creditors in such order of priority as is established by applicable law or regulation.

(4)   Claims of general creditors.

(5)   Claims of holders of the bank's shares in the order of preference established by the bank's organizational documents.

(j)   All claims of each class described within subsection (i) of this section shall be paid in full so long as sufficient assets are available therefor. Members of a class for which the receiver cannot make payment in full shall be paid an amount proportionate to their total claims.

(k)   The Commissioner may direct the receiver to make payment of claims for which no provision is made in this section and may direct the payment of less than all claims within a class.

(l)   When all assets of the bank have been fully liquidated, all claims and expenses have been paid or settled, and the receiver has recommended a final distribution, the dissolution of the bank in receivership shall be accomplished in the following manner:

(1)   The receiver shall file with the Commissioner a detailed report, in a form to be prescribed by the Commissioner, of the receiver's acts and proposed final distribution of the bank's assets.

(2) Upon the Commissioner's approval of the final report of the receiver, the receiver shall make the final distribution of the bank's assets in any manner as the Commissioner may direct.

(3) When any unclaimed property, including funds due to a known but unlocated depositor, remains following the final distribution of the bank's assets, such property shall be promptly transferred to the State Treasurer to hold in accordance with the provisions of Chapter 115B of the General Statutes.

(4) Upon completion of the actions described in this subsection, the process of dissolution and liquidation of the bank shall be deemed complete, and the Commissioner shall issue a certification of completed liquidation to the Secretary of State.

(5) Upon completion of the process of dissolution and liquidation, the Commissioner shall cause an examination of the receiver's activities and records to be conducted, with which the receiver shall assist. The accounts of the receiver shall then be ruled upon by the Commissioner, and if approved, the receiver shall be given a final and complete discharge and release. (2012-56, s. 4.)

Part 4. Provisions Relating to Any Dissolution or Receivership.

§ 53C-9-401. Statute relating to receivers applicable to insolvent banks.

The provisions of G.S. 1-507.1 through 1-507.11, relating to receivers, when not inconsistent with the provisions of this Article, shall apply to the liquidation of banks under this Article. (2012-56, s. 4.)

§ 53C-9-402. Storage and destruction of records.

(a) Any record of a bank that is in or has completed the process of dissolution and liquidation may be kept in compliance with the provisions of G.S. 53C-6-14.

(b)   All records of a bank that has completed the process of dissolution and liquidation shall be held in such place as in the Commissioner's judgment will provide for their proper safekeeping and protection.

(c)   After the expiration of five years from the date of filing of the certificate of completed liquidation under G.S. 53C-9-301, the records of the liquidated bank may be destroyed by the Commissioner using commercially reasonable record destruction procedures.

(d)   Nothing in this section shall be construed to authorize the destruction by the Commissioner of any of the records of the OCOB made by it with reference to the dissolution, receivership, or liquidation of any bank. (2012-56, s. 4.)

§ 53C-9-403. Authority to serve as trustee terminated.

Whenever any bank that has been, or shall be, appointed trustee in any indenture, deed of trust, or other instrument of like character, executed to secure the payment of any bonds, notes, or other evidences of indebtedness, has been or shall be placed in receivership, a new trustee shall be appointed in the manner provided in G.S. 36C-7-704 or other applicable law, and the powers and duties of the bank as trustee in any such instrument shall immediately cease. (2012-56, s. 4; 2013-29, s. 19.)

§ 53C-9-404. Petition for new trustee; upon parties interested.

In all cases of dissolution receivership and liquidation under this Article, the clerk of superior court of any county in which an indenture, deed of trust, or other instrument of like character is recorded shall, upon the verified petition of any person interested in any such trust, either as trustee, beneficiary, or otherwise, which interest shall be set out in the petition, enter an order directing service, in the manner required by law for service of summons, on all interested parties of a notice requiring all persons having any interest in the trust to appear at the clerk's office on a day designated in the order and notice, not less than 30 days from the date of the first publication of the notice, and show cause why a new trustee shall not be appointed. The notice shall set forth the names of the parties to the indenture, deed of trust, or other such instrument, and the date the documents were executed and the place of recording. (2012-56, s. 4.)

§ 53C-9-405. Appointment of substitute trustee where no objection made.

If, upon the day fixed in the notice, no person appears and objects to the appointment of a substitute trustee, the clerk of superior court shall, upon such terms as he or she deems advisable to the best interest of all parties, appoint a competent person authorized to act as substitute trustee, who shall be vested with and shall exercise all the powers conferred upon the trustee named in the instrument. (2012-56, s. 4.)

§ 53C-9-406. Hearing where objection made; appeal from order.

If objection is made to the appointment of a new trustee under this Part, the clerk shall hear and determine the matter, and from his or her decision an appeal may be prosecuted as in cases of special proceedings generally. (2012-56, s. 4.)

§ 53C-9-407. Registration of final order.

The final order of appointment of a new trustee or trustees under this Part shall be certified by the clerk of superior court issuing the order and shall be recorded in the office of the register of deeds in the county or counties in which the instrument under which the appointment has been made is recorded. (2012-56, s. 4.)

§ 53C-9-408. Petition and order applicable to all instruments involved.

The petition and the order appointing a new trustee or trustees under this Part may apply to any number of indentures, deeds of trust, or other instruments, wherein the same trustee or trustees are named. (2012-56, s. 4.)

§ 53C-9-409. Additional remedy.

The appointment of a substitute trustee as described in this Part shall be in addition to and not substitution for any other remedy provided by law. (2012-56, s. 4.)

Article 10.

Bank Holding Companies.

Part 1. Change in Control.

§ 53C-10-101. Holdings companies.

Every holding company, as defined in G.S. 53C-1-4(39), of a bank shall register with the Commissioner and maintain that registration on an annual basis in the form prescribed by the Commissioner. (2012-56, s. 4.)

§ 53C-10-102. Holding company control transaction.

(a)   Except as otherwise expressly permitted by this section, a person shall not engage in a control transaction to which a holding company formed under the laws of this State and having a bank as a subsidiary is a party without the prior approval of the Commissioner. A person may contract to engage in a control transaction with the consummation of the control transaction being subject to receipt of the approval of the Commissioner.

(b)   The Commissioner may require a person who is obligated to file a notice or an application under this section to appoint an agent resident in this State for service of process upon the filing of the notice or application or as a condition to the acceptance of the notice or application for review. An application for approval shall be in a form required by the Commissioner and shall be accompanied by such fee as may be required by rule.

(c)   The following transactions shall not constitute a control transaction under this section requiring the prior approval of the Commissioner:

(1)   The acquisition of control over voting securities by a person who has previously engaged in a control transaction with respect to the holding company after receiving the approval of the Commissioner under this Article, which approval permits the acquisition of control over additional voting securities, or any person who is an affiliate of the person previously engaging in the approved control transaction with such permission and who is identified in the application submitted for the approval, if the acquiring person files a notice with the Commissioner, in the form required by the Commissioner, describing the transaction at least 10 days before the acquiring person or affiliate thereof first votes or directs the voting of the voting securities.

(2)   An acquisition of control over voting securities by operation of law, will, or intestate succession, if the acquiring person files a notice with the Commissioner, in the form required by the Commissioner, describing the acquisition or transfer at least 10 days before the acquiring person first votes or directs the voting of the voting securities.

(3)   Bona fide gifts.

(4)   A transaction exempted by rules, orders, or declaratory rulings of the Commissioner, issued because approval of the transaction is not necessary to achieve the objectives of this Chapter.

(5)   An acquisition of control over voting shares exempt from the prior approval requirements set forth in section 3 of the Bank Holding Company Act, as amended (12 U.S.C. § 1842), pursuant to the exceptions described in items (A), (B), or (C) of subsection (a) of that section.

(6)   An acquisition of control over voting securities in a transaction subject to approval under section 3 of the Bank Holding Company Act, as amended (12 U.S.C. § 1842).

(d)   Upon receipt of a notice described in subsection (c) of this section, the Commissioner may, before the 10th day following the receipt, notify the acquiring person of the Commissioner's objection to the exercise of control over the voting securities or may require the acquiring party to submit further information before exercising control over the voting securities. An acquiring person receiving a notice of objection shall be required to submit an application for approval of a control transaction. An acquiring person receiving a notice to submit further information may be required to provide any information that would be included in an application for approval of a control transaction. In the event such an acquiring person is comprised of a group of persons, the Commissioner may require each member of the group to submit relevant information.

(e) All voting securities over which control has been acquired by an acquiring person shall not be voted on any matter submitted to a vote of the holders of the outstanding voting securities of the holding company of a bank and shall be deemed authorized but unissued for purposes of determining the presence of a quorum of holders of voting securities until such time as follows:

(1) The Commissioner has approved an application for approval of a control transaction with respect to the voting securities.

(2) The transaction is one listed in subsection (c) of this section that does not require the filing of a notice with the Commissioner.

(3) The transaction is one listed in subsection (c) of this section that requires a notice to be filed with the Commissioner and the Commissioner has not issued an objection to the notice and any requirement of the Commissioner for the filing of further information had been determined by the Commissioner to have been satisfied. (2012-56, s. 4; 2013-29, s. 20.)

§ 53C-10-103. Application regarding a control transaction.

(a) A person seeking approval of a control transaction to which a holding company of a bank is a party under this Article shall file the following with the Commissioner:

(1) An application in the form prescribed by the Commissioner.

(2) All filing fees required by rule of the Commissioner.

(3) Any other information required by a rule of the Commissioner or deemed by the Commissioner to achieve the objectives of this Chapter.

(b) In the event a person submitting an application is a group of persons, the Commissioner may require each member of the group to submit information relevant to the application.

(c) Notwithstanding any laws to the contrary, information about the character, competence, or experience of an acquiring person or its proposed management personnel or affiliates shall be deemed a confidential record of the Commissioner subject to G.S. 53C-2-7(b). (2012-56, s. 4.)

§ 53C-10-104. Public notice.

A person filing an application for approval of a control transaction shall publish a public notice of the filing of the application not more than 30 days before nor more than 10 days after the filing of the application with the Commissioner. The public notice shall contain the following:

(1) A statement that the application has been filed with the Commissioner.

(2) The name of the applicable holding company and the address of its principal office.

(3) A statement that any interested person may make written comment on the proposed control transaction and that comments received by the Commissioner within 14 days of the publication of the public notice shall be considered. The public notice shall provide the current mailing address of the Commissioner. (2012-56, s. 4.)

§ 53C-10-105. Actions on control transaction applications.

(a) The Commissioner shall examine the proposed control transaction, including the character, competence, and experience of the acquiring person and its proposed management personnel, to determine whether the financial stability of the holding company or the interests of the customers served by one or more bank subsidiaries of the holding company would be adversely affected by the proposed control transaction. Not later than the 60th day following receipt of a completed application for approval of a control transaction unless extraordinary circumstances require a longer period of review, the Commissioner shall approve or deny the application.

(b) The Commissioner may deny an application for approval of a control for any of the following reasons:

(1) The financial condition of the person seeking approval of a control transaction could jeopardize the financial stability of the holding company, one or more bank subsidiaries of the holding company, or the financial interests of the bank's customers.

(2) An examination of the character, competence, or experience of any acquiring person or of any of the proposed management personnel of the holding company shows that it would not be in the interest of the customers of one or more of the bank subsidiaries of the holding company or in the interest of the public to permit the person to control the holding company.

(3) The plans or proposals of the person seeking approval with respect to exercising control over the holding company would not be in the best interests of the customers of one or more bank subsidiaries of the holding company.

(4) Upon the effective date of the proposed control transaction, one or more of the bank subsidiaries of the holding company would not be solvent, have inadequate capital, or not be in compliance with this Chapter or rules of the Commissioner.

(5) The application for approval is incomplete.

(6) If the acquiring person solicits votes for the approval of or consents to the control transaction from the holders of the voting securities of the holding company, adequate and complete disclosures of all material information about the proposed control transaction, together with a prominent statement that neither the control transaction nor any solicitation of such holders' votes or consents has been approved by the Commissioner and that any representation to the contrary is a criminal offense, have not been made to the holders.

(c) If an application filed under this Part is approved by the Commissioner, the control transaction may become effective. All conditions to approval set forth in the order of the Commissioner shall be enforceable against the person, and each member of a group of persons, receiving the approval. (2012-56, s. 4.)

§ 53C-10-106. Appeal.

Any order of the Commissioner denying an application for approval of a control transaction may be appealed to the Commission by the person filing the application denied, as provided in G.S. 53C-2-6. (2012-56, s. 4.)

Part 2. Combinations.

§ 53C-10-201. Combination authority.

With the approval of the Commissioner, a holding company of a bank may combine with one or more other holding companies or other companies. The application for approval shall be in the form required by the Commissioner and shall be accompanied by such fee as may be required by rule. (2012-56, s. 4.)

§ 53C-10-202. Combination application and investigation.

(a) A holding company of a bank seeking approval of a combination shall file with the Commissioner an application for approval, copies of the agreement under which the holding company proposes to effect the combination, and any additional information that the Commissioner shall require by rule or as is required by the Commissioner in connection with the application in order to achieve the objectives of this Chapter.

(b) A holding company filing an application for approval of a combination shall publish a public notice of the filing of the application not more than 30 days before nor more than 10 days after the filing of the application with the Commissioner. The public notice shall contain the following:

(1) A statement that the application has been filed with the Commissioner.

(2) The names of the parties to the proposed combination and the addresses of its principal offices.

(3) A statement that any interested person may make written comment on the proposed combination and that comments received by the Commissioner within 14 days of the publication of the public notice shall be considered. The public notice shall provide the current mailing address of the Commissioner.

(c) The Commissioner shall examine the proposed combination, including the character, competency, and experience of the proposed directors and executive officers of the surviving party of the combination, to determine whether the interests of the customers and communities served by the banks controlled by the parties to the combination would be adversely affected by the proposed combination.

(d) Notwithstanding any laws to the contrary, information about the character, competence, and experience of the directors and executive officers of the parties to a combination received by the Commissioner shall be deemed a confidential record of the Commissioner subject to G.S. 53C-2-7(b). (2012-56, s. 4.)

§ 53C-10-203. Decision on application.

Based on the application and the Commissioner's examination, the Commissioner shall enter an order approving or denying approval of the proposed combination not later than the 60th day following the date the Commissioner notifies the parties that the application is complete, unless extraordinary circumstances require a longer period of review. (2012-56, s. 4.)

§ 53C-10-204. Appeal.

Any order of the Commissioner denying an application for approval of a combination may be appealed to the Commission by a party to the combination, as provided in G.S. 53C-2-6. (2012-56, s. 4.)

Part 3. General Authority.

§ 53C-10-301. Cease and desist order.

Upon a finding that any action of a holding company subject to registration under this Article, or its nonbank affiliate, may be in violation of any banking laws, the Commissioner, after a reasonable notice to the holding company and an opportunity for it to be heard, shall have the authority to order it to cease and desist from such action. If the holding company fails to appeal the decision within 10 days of the date of the issuance of the order in accordance with G.S. 53C-2-6, and continues to engage in the action in violation of the Commissioner's order to cease and desist such action, it shall be subject to a civil money penalty of twenty thousand dollars ($20,000) for each day it remains in violation of the order. The penalty provision of this section shall be in addition to and not in lieu of any other provision of law applicable to a holding company's failure to comply with an order of the Commissioner. The clear proceeds of the civil money penalty shall be remitted to the Civil Penalty and Forfeiture Fund in accordance with G.S. 115C-457.2. (2012-56, s. 4; 2013-29, s. 21.)

§ 53C-10-302. Other control changes.

Each holding company of a bank shall report to the Commissioner any changes in its directors, president, chief executive officer, or chief financial officer by the close of the second day on which the holding company is open for business following the change. (2012-56, s. 4.)

Chapter 54.

Cooperative Organizations.

SUBCHAPTER I. BUILDING AND LOAN ASSOCIATIONS, BUILDING ASSOCIATIONS AND SAVINGS AND LOAN ASSOCIATIONS.

Article 1.

Organization.

§§ 54-1 through 54-12.1. Repealed by Session Laws 1981, c. 282, s. 1.

Article 2.

Shares and Shareholders.

§§ 54-13 through 54-18.2. Repealed by Session Laws 1981, c. 282, s. 1.

Article 2A.

Savings Accounts.

§§ 54-18.3 through 54-18.6. Repealed by Session Laws 1981, c. 282, s. 1.

Article 3.

Loans.

§§ 54-19 through 54-23. Repealed by Session Laws 1981, c. 282, s. 1.

Article 4.

Under Control of Administrator of the Savings and Loan Division.

§§ 54-24 through 54-33.3. Repealed by Session Laws 1981, c. 282, s. 1.

Article 5.

Foreign Associations.

§§ 54-34 through 54-41. Repealed by Session Laws 1981, c. 282, s. 1.

Article 5A.

Reserves.

§ 54-41.1. Repealed by Session Laws 1981, c. 282, s. 1.

Article 6.

Withdrawals.

§§ 54-42 through 54-43: Repealed by Session Laws 1981, c. 282, s. 1.

Article 7.

Statements of Financial Condition of Associations.

§ 54-44. Repealed by Session Laws 1981, c. 282, s. 1.

Article 7A.

Mutual Deposit Guaranty Associations.

§§ 54-44.1 through 54-44.14. Repealed by Session Laws 1981, c. 282, s. 1.

SUBCHAPTER II. LAND AND LOAN ASSOCIATIONS.

Article 8.

Organization and Powers.

§ 54-45. Application of term.

The term "land and loan associations" shall apply to and include all corporations, companies, societies or associations organized for the purpose of making loans to their members only, and of enabling their members to acquire real estate, make improvements thereon, and remove encumbrances therefrom by the payment of money in periodical installments or principal sums, and for the accumulation of a fund to be returned to members who do not obtain advances for such purposes, where the principles of building and loan associations and their work are adapted to the use of the farmers and the rural population.

It shall be unlawful for any corporation, company, society, or association doing business in this State not so conducted to use in its corporate name the term "land and loan association," or in any manner or device to hold itself out to the public as a land and loan association. (1915, c. 172, s. 1; C.S., s. 5204.)

§ 54-46. Incorporation and powers.

Land and loan associations shall be incorporated, supervised, and be subject to such regulations and have such privileges as are prescribed for building and loan associations under the laws of this State as they now are or may be hereafter enacted, except as prescribed in this Article. (1915, c. 172, s. 2; C.S., s. 5205.)

§ 54-47. Loans.

The board of directors of land and loan associations may contract for loans to the amount of seventy-five percent (75%) of the securities used by them as collateral, where the loans are on long time (three or more years), and for at least one percent (1%) less than is charged by such associations on their loans to shareholders; and they may make short loans to their shareholders on their shares and personal endorsement or personal property. (1915, c. 172, s. 3; C.S., s. 5206.)

§ 54-48. Reserve associations.

Associations to be known as "reserve land and loan associations" may be chartered and licensed as provided in this Article, when they are organized and the stock therein is held by local land and loan associations, and shall have such powers, rights, and privileges as are accorded to other domestic associations, and they may conform to such laws, rules, and regulations as may be prescribed by the laws of the United States, or of this State, to enable them to receive moneys, bonds, or securities to be used in loans and to secure the same. Such reserve associations shall be under the supervision of the Commissioner of Banks as are building and loan associations. (1915, c. 172, s. 4; C.S., s. 5207; 1971, c. 864, s. 17; 1989, c. 76, s. 14; 2001-193, s. 16.)

§ 54-49. Land Conservation and Development Bureau; land mortgage associations.

Recognizing that agriculture is the most fundamental wealth-producing occupation of the State and that land is the basis of agriculture, the General Assembly of North Carolina does hereby authorize and direct the State Department of Agriculture and Consumer Services to establish as a major division of its organization a Land Conservation and Land Development Bureau. The function of this Bureau shall be to promote conservation, rural home ownership, and the development of the land resources of the State through land mortgage associations under the following provisions. (1925, c. 223, s. 1; 1997-261, s. 109.)

§ 54-50. Number of incorporators; capital stock.

Any number of persons, resident freeholders of the State, not less than 15, may associate to establish an association on the terms and conditions and subject to the liabilities hereinafter prescribed. The aggregate amount of the capital stock of any such association shall not be less than twenty thousand dollars ($20,000). Such association shall mean a corporation organized under the laws of the State for the purpose of making loans upon agricultural lands, forest lands and dwelling houses within this State and known as a land mortgage association. (1925, c. 223, s. 2.)

§ 54-51. Incorporation.

The articles of incorporation shall be in writing, signed and acknowledged by the incorporators and shall contain the following:

(1)   The declaration that they are associating for the purpose of forming a land mortgage association under the provisions of this Article.

(2)   The name of such association, which shall be in no material respect similar to any other association in the same county.

(3)   The name of the village, town or city, and the county where such association is to be located.

(4)   The amount of capital stock, which shall be divided into shares of one hundred dollars ($100.00) each.

(5)   The period for which such association is organized. (1925, c. 223, s. 3.)

§ 54-52. Organization.

The incorporators at their first annual meeting shall elect by ballot from their number a board of trustees of not less than six members who shall adopt a code of bylaws and a plan of organization approved by the Commissioner of Agriculture and the Commissioner of Banks. (1925, c. 223, s. 4; 1931, c. 243, s. 5.)

§ 54-53. Corporate powers.

Said land mortgage association shall have power:

(1)   To make loans, the conditions of which shall be approved by the Commissioner of Banks if the security taken therefor is to be used as the basis for a bond issue under subdivision (3) hereof, and to accept as security for any such loan a first mortgage upon improved or partially improved agricultural lands within this State. Such loan shall not exceed, however, sixty-five percent (65%) of the value of such real estate so conveyed, according to the appraisal made as herein provided.

(2) To purchase first mortgages, heretofore or hereafter issued against North Carolina agricultural lands, either improved or partially improved, from persons or firms resident of this State or corporations organized under the laws of this State engaged in the colonization or settlement of North Carolina lands and to whom such mortgages were issued, if, after investigation, the plan of settlement or colonization followed by such person, firm or corporation is approved by the Commissioner of Agriculture as beneficial to the settler or colonist, and if the lands against which such mortgages are issued are found by the said Commissioner to be in fact agricultural lands suitable for agricultural purposes and the terms and conditions of the loans made by such person, firm or corporation are just and reasonable, or from banks or trust companies organized under the laws of this State, or of the United States, to do business in this State, to which such mortgages were issued direct by the borrowers. Each such mortgage shall be payable on the amortization plan maturing in not less than 20 years. The request for an investigation leading to such a purchase of mortgages from persons, firms or corporations engaged in the settlement or colonization of North Carolina lands shall be accompanied by a deposit, the amount of such deposit to be determined by the Commissioner of Agriculture. Upon completion of the investigation the Commissioner of Agriculture shall render a statement of expense accompanied by a remittance of any unused balance of such deposit, but no mortgage shall be purchased until the lands against which the same is issued have been appraised as hereinafter provided for the appraisal of land for a loan by the land mortgage association and such mortgage is approved by all members of the loan committee.

(3) To issue bonds secured by the pledge of the mortgage so taken or purchased.

(4) To pledge the note and mortgages so taken or purchased under the provisions of subdivisions (1) and (2) hereof as security for the bonds of the land mortgage association referred to in subdivision (3) hereof. (1925, c. 223, s. 5; 1931, c. 243, s. 5.)

§ 54-54. Restrictions.

All mortgage obligations acquired by the company shall be subject to the following restrictions:

(1) Each such mortgage shall be a first and valid lien upon improved or partially improved agricultural lands within the State of North Carolina;

(2) Each such mortgage shall be a first and valid lien upon the whole and undivided fee and upon no lesser estate;

(3) Each such mortgage shall be given to secure a principal indebtedness not exceeding in amount fifteen percent (15%) of the capital and surplus of the company;

(4) All such mortgages shall contain provisions for soil conservation;

(5) All such mortgages shall contain provisions for the time of commencing payments for annual or semiannual reduction of the indebtedness secured thereby, subject to the requirements as to repayment of loans and interest hereinafter provided;

(6) The company shall make no loan secured by mortgage of any real estate in which any officer or trustee of the company is interested either directly or indirectly, except upon the approval of two thirds of all the trustees;

(7) A sufficient amount of the proceeds of any loan made upon lands upon which are buildings in course of construction or upon which land clearing or other improvements are being made shall be retained by the association and paid out only upon construction or improvement vouchers, countersigned by a duly authorized agent of the association. (1925, c. 223, s. 6.)

§ 54-55. Mortgage forms; approval.

The mortgages to be given to the association, the bonds to be issued and the trust deed executed to secure the bonds shall be in such form and shall contain such conditions as will adequately protect all parties thereto. The trustees shall provide the forms subject to the joint approval of the Commissioner of Banks and the Attorney General. (1925, c. 223, s. 7; 1931, c. 243, s. 5.)

§ 54-56. Repayment of loan and interest.

The prospective borrower may be required to pay all expenses incidental to the examination of title and appraisal of the property. The total amount shall include (i) the rate of interest agreed upon; and (ii) a payment. (1925, c. 223, s. 8.)

§ 54-57. Terms of payment.

A borrower may repay his loan by installments of such frequency and amounts as may be agreed upon: Provided, that not less than one percent (1%) of the original amount of the mortgage shall be paid upon the principal thereof annually, and commencing not later than the sixth year succeeding the year in which the loan was made the borrower may pay a larger installment upon the principal, or the whole of it, at any interest date, such payments to be in amounts equal to additions of one or more principal amortization payments. Such payment may be made in cash, or by tendering at par bonds of the association. For failure to pay the interest or any installment required by the terms of the loan, the borrower may be fined as the bylaws may prescribe. But the borrower shall never be required to pay more than the specified installment, nor to pay the principal before it is due except as prescribed herein for partial repayment on account of depreciation and for foreclosure by the association. The borrower may on 60 days' notice repay the association his total indebtedness, or, without such notice, upon payment of 60 days' interest upon the principal unpaid. The borrower shall be entitled to a receipt for all installments as paid, and where the repayment is complete to a satisfaction of his note and mortgage. (1925, c. 223, s. 9.)

§ 54-58. Transfer of mortgaged lands.

The acquirer of any lands mortgaged to a land mortgage association shall enter at once, on the acquisition of the land, into a written agreement with the association, attested by a notary, or a justice, and assume the personal responsibility for the indebtedness to the association attaching to such lands. This document must be presented to the trustees within 14 days after demand. (1925, c. 223, s. 10.)

§ 54-59. Calling in loans before due.

Every land mortgage association shall have the power to call in loans upon 60 days' notice:

(1) When the person acquiring the lands upon which money has been loaned does not comply with the provisions of G.S. 54-58 and fulfill the obligations incumbent upon him;

(2) When the debtor does not meet the obligation imposed upon him by his contract and the bylaws of the land mortgage association;

(3) When the mortgaged premises become subject to forced sale;

(4) When the mortgaged premises are depreciating in value because of lack of care, of failure to maintain and conserve or from other cause.

The trustees of the association, whenever necessary, shall provide for an inspection of the mortgaged premises by the State Department of Agriculture and Consumer Services for an investigation of the care which is being given said premises, and may employ an expert to inspect the soil with a view of determining whether or not the same is being depleted. (1925, c. 223, s. 11; 1997-261, s. 109.)

§ 54-60. Partial recall of debt.

The association may require a suitable partial repayment of the debt if the mortgaged premises may have at any time become depreciated in value from any cause whatsoever. (1925, c. 223, s. 12.)

§ 54-61. Foreclosure.

Whenever any loan is called in and the borrower shall fail to pay the principal and interest due to the association as required by law and the notices given him, the land mortgage association may then foreclose upon the mortgaged premises as for a past-due loan. But in no case shall a borrower be liable for a sum greater than the amount of the unpaid portion of the loan with any accretions of interest thereon and expenses incidental to the collection thereof. (1925, c. 223, s. 13.)

§ 54-62. Appraisal of lands.

Upon application for a loan the land mortgage association shall cause the lands which it is proposed to mortgage to the association to be appraised by a competent appraiser furnished it by the State Department of Agriculture and Consumer Services. (1925, c. 223, s. 14; 1997-261, s. 109.)

§ 54-63. Preference prohibited; association borrowing money.

No land mortgage association, and no officer or agent thereof, shall give any preference to any creditor by pledging any of the assets of such association as collateral security, except that any such association may borrow money for temporary purposes, and may pledge assets of the association as collateral security therefor. Whenever it shall appear that any land mortgage association has borrowed habitually for the purpose of reloaning, the Commissioner of Banks may require such association to pay off such amount so borrowed. (1925, c. 223, s. 15; 1931, c. 243, s. 5.)

§ 54-64. Bond issues.

(a) The bonds to be issued by any land mortgage association may be issued for such amounts, bearing such serial number, and date or dates, and be payable at such time and times, bear such rate of interest, and be redeemable at maturity or upon notice at such times and in such manner, as the land mortgage association may, subject to the approval of the Banking Commission, deem advisable.

(b) Each land mortgage association shall keep a register for the registration and transfer of bonds issued by it in which it shall register, or cause to be registered, all bonds upon presentation thereof for such purpose; and such register shall contain the post-office address of all registered holders of bonds and shall, at all reasonable times, be open to the inspection of the Banking

Commission, or any of its deputies, and to the State Treasurer. (1925, c. 223, s. 16.)

§ 54-65. Deed of trust.

(a) To secure the payment of such bonds, the land mortgage association shall issue a collateral deed of trust to the State Treasurer, pledging as security for such bonds the notes and mortgages taken or purchased, as provided herein, in an amount equal to or exceeding the aggregate amount of bonds issued or to be issued.

(b) The total amount of bonds actually outstanding shall not at any time exceed the total amount unpaid upon the notes secured by the mortgages belonging to the association and pledged for the payment of the bonds, plus such securities and moneys as may be on deposit with the State Treasurer under the provisions hereof.

(c) The aggregate amount of the principal of all bonds issued by land mortgage associations and outstanding at any one time shall not exceed 20 times the amount of the capital and surplus of the company. (1925, c. 223, s. 17.)

§ 54-66. Collaterals deposited with State Treasurer.

All mortgages pledged to secure the payment of the bonds issued hereunder shall be deposited and left with the State Treasurer. The land mortgage association may, with the approval of the State Treasurer, remove such mortgages from the custody of the State Treasurer, substituting in place thereof other of its mortgages, or money or State of North Carolina bonds or certificates of deposit, endorsed in blank, issued by State or national banks located in North Carolina, farm mortgage bonds issued under the provisions of the Federal Farm Loan Act approved July 17, 1916, or obligations of the United States government, in an amount equal to or greater than the amount unpaid upon the notes secured by the mortgages withdrawn. (1925, c. 223, s. 18.)

§ 54-67. Redemption of bonds.

(a) Notice of redemption of bonds may on no account be given on the part of the holder thereof, but may be given by the association only for the purpose of effecting redemption in accordance with the conditions of the bonds and as provided by law and the bylaws.

(b) If the land mortgage association shall elect to redeem any bond prior to maturity, six months' notice of redemption shall be given and shall be effected by personal service upon the owner and holder of the bond, by notice mailed to his address as registered or by advertising the same three times in a newspaper selected by the State Treasurer.

(c) The numbers of the bonds of which notice of redemption is to be given shall be determined by lot, to be drawn by the president or the vice-president at a meeting of the trustees. (1925, c. 223, s. 19; 1993, c. 553, s. 15.)

§ 54-68. Validity of bonds after maturity.

In case the holder of any bond outstanding shall not have presented the same for payment within the period of two years after its maturity or within two years after the date fixed for the redemption, as the case may be, then such bonds shall cease to be a lien upon the mortgages, moneys, and securities pledged to the State Treasurer and deposited with him as security therefor, but such bond shall still constitute, until the statute of limitation running against such bonds shall have expired, a single legal money claim or demand against the land mortgage association issuing the same, and be recoverable from it in a suit at law, and in no event shall any interest be collectible upon such bond after the maturity thereof or after the date fixed for its redemption. (1925, c. 223, s. 20.)

§ 54-69. Bonds as payment.

If the association gives notice to a debtor for repayment of the mortgage loan the latter must pay to the association in cash or in its bonds at par the face of the same so far as it has not yet been covered by his assets in the amortization and payments. (1925, c. 223, s. 21.)

§ 54-70. Bonds as investments.

The bonds of a land mortgage association shall be a legal investment for savings associations, trust companies, or other financial institutions chartered under the laws of this State and shall also be a legal investment for trustees, executors, administrators, or custodians of public or private funds, or corporations, partnerships or associations. (1925, c. 223, s. 22.)

§ 54-71. Application of earnings; reserve fund.

The gross earnings of the association shall be ascertained annually, and there shall first be deducted therefrom the expenses incurred by the association for the preceding year and the balance thereof shall be set aside as a reserve fund for the payment of contingent losses, to an amount equal to two percent (2%) of the capital stock outstanding, and until such reserve fund equals twenty percent (20%) of the capital stock of such association. (1925, c. 223, s. 23.)

§ 54-72. Restriction on holding real estate.

No land mortgage association shall acquire real estate (other than for the occupation of its offices) except to protect its interest in case any of the mortgages owned by it are foreclosed and the property therein described sold to pay the indebtedness secured thereby. All real estate so acquired shall be promptly sold. (1925, c. 223, s. 24.)

§ 54-73. Banking laws applicable.

The banking laws as defined in G.S. 53C-1-4(5), insofar as applicable and not in conflict with the provisions hereof shall apply to land mortgage associations. (1925, c. 223, s. 25; 2012-56, s. 35.)

SUBCHAPTER III. CREDIT UNIONS.

Article 9.

Credit Union Division; Administrator of Credit Unions.

§§ 54-74 through 54-75.1. Repealed by Session Laws 1975, c. 538, s. 1.

Article 10.

Incorporation of Credit Unions.

§§ 54-76 through 54-81. Repealed by Session Laws 1975, c. 538, s. 1.

Article 11.

Powers of Credit Unions.

§§ 54-82 through 54-93. Repealed by Session Laws 1975, c. 538, s. 1.

Article 12.

Shares in the Corporation.

§§ 54-94 through 54-97. Repealed by Session Laws 1975, c. 538, s. 1.

Article 13.

Members and Officers.

§§ 54-98 through 54-104. Repealed by Session Laws 1975, c. 538, s. 1.

Article 14.

Supervision and Control.

§§ 54-105 through 54-109. Repealed by Session Laws 1975, c. 538, s. 1.

Article 14A.

Formation of Credit Union.

§ 54-109.1. Definition and purposes.

A credit union is a cooperative, nonprofit association, incorporated under Articles 14A to 14L of this Chapter, for the purposes of encouraging thrift among its members, creating a source of credit at a fair and reasonable rate of interest, and providing an opportunity for its members to use and control their own money in order to improve their economic and social condition. (1975, c. 538, s. 1.)

§ 54-109.2. Organization procedure.

(a) Any 12 or more residents of this State, of legal age, who have a common bond referred to in G.S. 54-109.26 may make application to organize a credit union and become charter members thereof by complying with this section.

(b) The subscribers shall execute in duplicate articles of incorporation and agree to the terms thereof, which articles shall state:

(1) The name, which shall include the words "credit union" and which shall not be the same as that of any other existing credit union in this State, and the location where the proposed credit union is to have its principal place of business;

(2) That the existence of the credit union shall be perpetual;

(3) The initial par value of the shares of the credit union.

(4) The names and addresses of the subscribers to the articles of incorporation, and the value of shares subscribed to by each, which shall be not less than five dollars ($5.00); and

(5) That the credit union may exercise such incidental powers as are necessary or requisite to enable it to carry on effectively the business for which it is incorporated, and those powers which are inherent in the credit union as a legal entity.

(c) The subscribers shall prepare and adopt bylaws for the general government of the credit union, consistent with Articles 14A to 14L of this Chapter, and execute the same in duplicate.

(d) They shall select at least five qualified persons who agree to serve on the board of directors, and at least three qualified persons who agree to serve on the supervisory committee. A signed agreement to serve in these capacities until the first annual meeting or until the election of their successors, whichever is later, shall be executed by those who so agree. This agreement shall be submitted to the administrator of credit unions.

(e) The subscribers shall forward the required charter fee and an investigation fee, as prescribed by the Credit Union Commission, and the articles of incorporation and the bylaws to the Administrator of the Credit Union Division. The Administrator may issue a certificate of approval if the articles and the bylaws are in conformity with Articles 14A to 14L of this Chapter and he is satisfied that the proposed field of operation is favorable to the success of such credit union and that the standing of the proposed organizers is such as to give assurance that its affairs will be properly administered. He shall issue to the corporation a certificate of approval, annexed to a duplicate certificate of incorporation and of the bylaws, which certificate of approval, together with the attached duplicate certificate of incorporation, shall be recorded in the office of the register of deeds of the county in which the office of such credit union is situated, and upon recordation of the incorporators shall become and be a corporation for the purposes set forth in this Article. The register of deeds of the county in which such recordation is made shall charge the same fee for such recordation as he is now allowed to charge for handling and recording a certificate of incorporation of a corporation organized under the business corporation laws of this State. The application shall be acted upon within 30 days. (1915, c. 115, ss. 2, 9; C.S., ss. 5210, 5211, 5233; 1925, c. 73, s. 3; 1935, c. 87; 1965, c. 956, ss. 1, 4, 19; 1973, c. 199, s. 8; 1975, c. 538, s. 1; 1983, c. 568, s. 1.)

§ 54-109.3. Form of articles and bylaws.

In order to simplify the organization of credit unions, the Administrator of Credit Unions shall cause to be prepared a form of articles of incorporation and a form of bylaws, consistent with Articles 14A to 14L of this Chapter, which may be used by credit union incorporators for their guidance. Such articles of incorporation and bylaws shall provide:

(1)   The name of corporation.

(2)   The purposes for which it is formed.

(3)   Qualifications for membership.

(4)   The date of the annual meeting; the manner in which members shall be notified of meetings; the manner of conducting the meetings; the number of members which constitute a quorum at the meetings, and the regulations as to voting.

(5)   The number of members of the board of directors, their powers and duties, and the compensation and duties of officers elected by the board of directors, and frequency of meetings.

(6)   The number of members of the credit committee, if any, their powers and duties.

(7)   The number of members of the supervisory committee, if any, their powers and duties.

(8)   The par value of shares of capital stock.

(9)   The conditions upon which shares may be issued, paid in, transferred, and withdrawn.

(10) The fines, if any, which shall be charged for failure to meet obligations to the corporation punctually.

(11) The conditions upon which deposits may be received and withdrawn. Whether the proposed corporation shall, in addition, have power to borrow funds.

(12) The manner in which the funds of the corporation shall be invested.

(13) The conditions upon which loans may be made and repaid.

(14) The maximum rate of interest that may be charged upon loans, not to exceed, however, the legal rate.

(15) The method of receipting for money paid on account of shares, deposits, or loans.

(16) The manner in which the reserve fund shall be accumulated.

(17) The manner in which dividends shall be determined and paid to members.

(18) The manner in which a voluntary dissolution of the corporation shall be effected.

(19) The manner in which the bylaws and articles of incorporation may be amended. (1915, c. 115, s. 2; C.S., s. 5211; 1975, c. 538, s. 1.)

§ 54-109.4. Amendments.

(a) The articles of incorporation or the bylaws may be amended as provided in the bylaws. Amendments to the articles of incorporation or bylaws shall be submitted to the Administrator of Credit Unions who shall approve or disapprove the amendments within 60 days.

(b) Amendments shall become effective upon approval in writing by the Administrator and no fee shall be charged for such approval. (1915, c. 115, s. 3; C.S., s. 5213; 1925, c. 73, s. 3; 1935, c. 87; 1965, c. 956, s. 6; 1973, c. 1331, s. 3; 1975, c. 538, s. 1.)

§ 54-109.5. Use of name exclusive.

With the exception of a credit union organized under the provisions of Articles 14A to 14L of this Chapter or of any other credit union act, or an association of credit unions or a recognized chapter thereof, any person, corporation, copartnership or association using a name or title containing the words "credit union" or any derivation thereof or representing themselves in their advertising or otherwise as conducting business as a credit union shall be guilty of a Class 1 misdemeanor, and may be permanently enjoined from using such words in its name. (1915, c. 115, s. 4; C.S., s. 5214; 1925, c. 73, s. 3; 1935, c. 87; 1941, c. 236; 1975, c. 538, s. 1; 1993, c. 539, s. 428; 1994, Ex. Sess., c. 24, s. 14(c).)

§ 54-109.6. Office facilities.

(a)   A credit union may maintain service facilities at locations other than its main office if the maintenance of such offices is reasonably necessary to furnish service to its members, subject to the approval of the Administrator of Credit Unions.

(b)   A credit union may change its place of business within this State upon written notice to the Credit Union Division. Such a change shall be recorded in the office of the register of deeds where its office was located, and a second duplicate in the office of the register of deeds of the county in which the new office is to be located, if same is changed to another county. If the change is from one location to another in the same county, then only the Administrator of Credit Unions need be notified.

(c)   A credit union may share office space with one or more credit unions and contract with any person or corporation to provide facilities or personnel. (1915, c. 115, ss. 9, 25; C.S., ss. 5215, 5233; 1925, c. 73, s. 3; 1935, c. 87; 1965, c. 956, ss. 1, 7, 19; 1967, c. 823, s. 10; 1973, c. 199, s. 8; c. 1331, s. 3; 1975, c. 538, s. 1.)

§ 54-109.7. Conducting business outside this State.

A credit union incorporated under this Subchapter may conduct business outside of this State in any state where it is permitted to conduct business as a credit union. (1991, c. 651, s. 1.)

§ 54-109.8. Reserved for future codification purposes.

§ 54-109.9. Reserved for future codification purposes.

Article 14B.

Supervision and Regulation.

§ 54-109.10. Creation and supervision of Division.

There shall be established in the North Carolina Department of Commerce a Credit Union Division which shall be under the supervision of the Administrator of Credit Unions appointed by the Secretary of Commerce. The Credit Union Division and the Administrator of Credit Unions shall be under the general direction and supervision of the Secretary of Commerce, and there shall be such assistants to the Administrator of Credit Unions as may be necessary and the salaries of the Administrator and assistants shall be fixed by the State Personnel Council. (1915, c. 115, s. 1; C.S., s. 5208; 1925, c. 73, s. 4; 1935, c. 87; 1965, c. 956, s. 1; 1971, c. 864, s. 17; 1975, c. 538, s. 1; 1989, c. 751, s. 9(c); 1991 (Reg. Sess., 1992), c. 959, s. 3.)

§ 54-109.11. Duties of Administrator.

The duties of the Administrator of Credit Unions shall be as follows:

(1) To organize and conduct in the State Department of Commerce, a bureau of information in regard to cooperative associations and rural and industrial credits.

(2) Upon request, to furnish, without cost, such printed information and blank forms as, in his discretion, may be necessary for the formation and establishment of any local credit union in the State.

(3) To maintain an educational campaign in the State looking to the promotion and organization of credit unions. Upon the written request of 12 bona fide residents of any particular locality in this State expressing a desire to form a local credit union at or in such locality, the Administrator of Credit Unions, or one of his assistants, shall proceed as promptly as may be convenient to such locality and make an investigation in order that the Administrator may determine whether or not a local credit union should be established according to the standards set forth and provided in this Article. The Administrator shall notify the applicants of his decision within 30 days after receipt of the written request. Before refusing the establishment of a credit union, the Administrator shall afford the applicants an opportunity to be heard therewith in person or by counsel and at least 60 days prior to the date set for a hearing on any such matter shall notify in writing the applicants of the date of said hearing and assign therein the grounds for the action contemplated to be taken and as to which inquiry shall be made on the date of such hearing. The determination of the Administrator shall be subject to judicial review in all respects according to the provisions and procedures set forth in Chapter 150B of the General Statutes of North Carolina, as amended.

(4) To examine at least once a year, and oftener if such examination be deemed necessary by the Administrator or his assistant, the credit unions formed under this Article. A report of such examination shall be filed with the State Department of Commerce, and a copy mailed to the credit union at its proper address.

(5) The Administrator of Credit Unions is authorized, empowered, and directed to fix the amount of a blanket surety bond which shall be required of each credit union official, committee member and employee, irrespective of whether such official, committee member and employee receives, pays or has custody of money or other personal property owned by a credit union or in the custody or control of the credit union as collateral or otherwise. The surety on the bond shall be a surety company authorized to do business in North Carolina. Any such bond or bonds shall be in a form approved by the Administrator of Credit Unions with a view to providing surety coverage to the credit union with reference to loss by reason of acts of fraud or dishonesty including forgery, theft, embezzlement, wrongful abstraction or misapplication on the part of the

person, directly or through connivance with others, and such other surety coverages as the Administrator of Credit Unions may determine to be reasonably appropriate or as elsewhere required by the Chapter. Any such bond or bonds shall be in an amount in relation to the money or other personal property involved or in relation to the assets of the credit union as the Administrator may from time to time prescribe by regulation for the purpose of requiring reasonable coverage. The Administrator may also approve the use of a form of excess coverage bond whereby a credit union may obtain an amount of coverage in excess of the basic surety coverage. No agreement, compromise or settlement of any claim or claims filed by a credit union with any surety or any surety company for less than the full amount of said claim or claims shall be entered into or made by the board of directors of any credit union unless and until the said claim or claims shall have been submitted to the Administrator of Credit Unions and his advice thereon given or transmitted to the board of directors of said credit union. The following schedule shall be deemed as the minimum fidelity and faithful performance bond requirements only:

Assets		Minimum Coverage	
$ 0,000 to 1,000	$	5,000	$
5,001 to 2,000		10,000	
10,001 to 4,000		20,000	
20,001 to 6,000		30,000	
30,001 to 8,000		40,000	
40,001 to 10,000		50,000	
50,001 to 15,000		75,000	

20,000	75,001 to	100,000
30,000	100,001 to	200,000
40,000	200,001 to	300,000
50,000	300,001 to	400,000
70,000	400,001 to	500,000
85,000	500,001 to	750,000
100,000	750,001 to	1,000,000
$100,000 plus $50,000	1,000,001 to	50,000,000

for

each million or

fraction

thereof of assets

over $1,000,000

2,500,000 plus $25,000	$50,000,001 to	$150,000,000	$

for

each million or

fraction
thereof of assets

over $50,000,000

Over $150,000,000
$5,000,000

It shall be the duty of the board of directors of each credit union to provide proper protection to meet any circumstances by obtaining adequate bond (an insurance) coverage in excess of the above minimum schedule. The treasurer and all other persons handling credit union funds or records before entering upon his or their duties shall give a proper bond with good and sufficient surety, in an amount and character to be determined by the board in compliance with regulations conditioned upon the faithful performance of his or their trust.

The Administrator may require additional coverage for any credit union when, in his opinion, the surety bonds in force are insufficient to provide adequate surety coverage, and it shall be the duty of the board of directors of any credit union to obtain such additional coverage within 60 days after the date of written notice by the Administrator to such board of directors. For good cause shown, the Administrator may extend the time to obtain additional coverage. (1915, c. 115, s. 1; C.S., s. 5209; 1925, c. 73, ss. 2, 3, 5, 6; 1935, c. 87; 1957, c. 989, s. 1; 1965, c. 956, ss. 1-3; 1971, c. 864, s. 17; 1973, c. 199, ss. 1-3; c. 1331, s. 3; 1975, c. 538, s. 1; 1977, c. 559, s. 1; 1987, c. 827, s. 1; 1989, c. 751, s. 7(2); 1991 (Reg. Sess., 1992), c. 959, ss. 4, 4.1.)

§ 54-109.12. Corporations organized hereunder subject to Administrator of Credit Unions; rules and regulations.

In addition to any and all other powers, duties and functions vested in the Administrator of Credit Unions under the provisions of this Article, the Administrator of Credit Unions shall have general control, management and supervision over all corporations organized under the provisions of Article 14A. All corporations organized under the provisions of Article 14A shall be subject to the management, control and supervision of the Administrator of Credit Unions as to their conduct, organization, management, business practices and their financial and fiscal matters. The Administrator of Credit Unions may prescribe rules and regulations for the administration of this Article, as well as rules and regulations relating to financial records, business practices and the conduct and management of credit unions, and it shall be the duty of the board of directors and of the various officers of the credit union to put into effect and to carry out such regulations. (1915, c. 115, s. 7; C.S., s. 5237; 1925, c. 73, s. 3; 1935, c. 87; 1957, c. 989, s. 6; 1965, c. 956, ss. 1, 22; 1975, c. 538, s. 1; 1979, c. 198.)

§ 54-109.13. Revocation of certificate; liquidation.

If any such corporation shall neglect to make its annual report, as provided in this Article, or any other report required by the Administrator of Credit Unions for more than 15 days, or shall fail to pay the charges required, including the fines for delay in filing reports, the Administrator of Credit Unions shall give notice to such corporation of his intention to revoke the certificate of approval of the corporation for such neglect or failure, and if such neglect or failure continues for 15 days after such notice, the said Administrator shall, at his discretion, personally or by an agent appointed by him, take possession of the property and business of the corporation and retain possession until such time as he may permit it to resume business, or until its affairs be finally liquidated as provided for in G.S. 54-109.93. (1915, c. 115, s. 7; C.S., s. 5240; 1925, c. 73, ss. 3, 8; 1935, c. 87; 1957, c. 989, s. 8; 1965, c. 956, s. 1; 1975, c. 538, s. 1.)

§ 54-109.14. Fees.

(a) Each credit union subject to supervision and examination by the Administrator of Credit Unions, including credit unions in process of voluntary liquidation, shall pay into the office of the Administrator of Credit Unions twice each year, in the months of January and July, supervision fees, except those credit unions which liquidate or convert its charter shall pay into the office of the Administrator of Credit Unions, to the date of dissolution, pro rata supervision fees. Examination fees shall be paid promptly upon receipt of the examination report and invoice.

The Administrator of Credit Unions, subject to the advice and consent of the Credit Union Commission, shall, on or before December 1 of each year, determine and fix the scale of supervisory and examination fees to be assessed during the next calendar year.

No credit union shall be required to pay any supervisory fee until the expiration of 12 months from the date of the issuance of a certificate of incorporation to such credit union.

(b)   Moneys collected under this section shall be deposited with the State Treasurer of North Carolina and expended, under the terms of the Executive Budget Act, to defray expenses incurred by the office of the Administrator of Credit Unions in carrying out its supervisory and auditing functions.

(c)   All revenue derived from fees will be placed into a special account to be administered solely for the operation of the Credit Union Division. (1915, c. 115, s. 7; C.S., s. 5238; 1925, c. 73, ss. 3, 7; 1935, c. 87; 1941, c. 235; 1955, c. 1135, ss. 3, 4; 1957, c. 989, s. 7; 1965, c. 956, ss. 1, 23, 24; 1969, c. 69, s. 6; 1971, c. 864, s. 17; 1973, c. 199, s. 12; 1975, c. 538, s. 1; 1977, c. 559, ss. 2, 3.)

§ 54-109.15. Reports.

(a)   Credit unions organized under Articles 14A to 14L of this Chapter shall, in January and in July of each year, make a report of condition to the Administrator of Credit Unions on forms supplied for that purpose. Additional reports may be required.

(b)   Any credit union that neglects to make semiannual reports as provided in subsection (a) of this section, or any of the other reports required by the Administrator of Credit Unions at the time fixed by the Administrator, shall pay a late penalty to the Administrator of Credit Unions of seventy-five dollars ($75.00) for each day the neglect continues. The Administrator of Credit Unions may revoke the certificate of incorporation and take possession of the assets and business of any credit union failing to pay a penalty imposed under this section after serving notice of at least 15 days upon the credit union of the proposed action. The clear proceeds of penalties collected pursuant to this subsection shall be remitted to the Civil Penalty and Forfeiture Fund in accordance with G.S. 115C-457.2. (1915, c. 115, s. 7; C.S., ss. 5238, 5240; 1925, c. 73, ss. 3, 7, 8; 1935, c. 87; 1941, c. 235; 1955, c. 1135, ss. 3, 4; 1957, c. 989, ss. 7, 8; 1965,

c. 956, ss. 1, 23, 24; 1969, c. 69, s. 6; 1971, c. 864, s. 17; 1973, c. 199, s. 12; 1975, c. 538, s. 1; 1991, c. 651, s. 2; 2005-276, s. 6.37(u).)

§ 54-109.16. Annual examinations required; payment of cost.

The Administrator of Credit Unions shall cause every such corporation to be examined once a year and whenever he deems it necessary. The examiners appointed by him shall be given free access to all books, papers, securities, and other sources of information in respect to the corporation; and for the purpose of such examination the Administrator shall have power and authority to subpoena and examine personally, or by one of his deputies or examiners, witnesses on oath and documents, whether such witnesses are members of the corporation or not, and whether such documents are documents of the corporation or not. The Administrator may designate an independent auditing firm to do the work under his direction and supervision, with the cost to be paid by the credit union involved. (1915, c. 115, s. 7; C.S., s. 5239; 1925, c. 73, s. 3; 1935, c. 87; 1965, c. 956, ss. 1, 25; 1969, c. 69, ss. 7, 8; 1975, c. 538, s. 1; 1977, c. 559, s. 4.)

§ 54-109.17. Records.

(a)   A credit union shall maintain all books, records, accounting systems and procedures in accordance with such rules as the Administrator from time to time prescribes. In prescribing such rules, the Administrator shall consider the relative size of a credit union and its reasonable capability of compliance.

(b)   A credit union is not liable for destroying records after the expiration of the record retention time prescribed by the Administrator.

(c)   A photostatic or photographic reproduction of any credit union records shall be admissible as evidence of transactions with the credit union. (1973, c. 98, s. 1; 1975, c. 538, s. 1.)

§ 54-109.18. Selection of attorneys to handle loan-closing proceedings.

The Administrator of Credit Unions shall establish rules and regulations relating to selection of attorneys-at-law to handle credit union loan closing proceedings. (1977, c. 559, s. 10.)

§ 54-109.19. Removal of officers.

(a) The Administrator of Credit Unions shall have the right and is hereby empowered to serve a written notice of his intention to remove from office any officer, director, committeeman or employee of any credit union doing business under Articles 14A through 15A of this Chapter who shall be found to be dishonest, incompetent, or reckless in the management of the affairs of the credit union, or who persistently violates the laws of this State or the lawful orders, instructions and regulations issued by the Administrator and/or the State Credit Union Commission.

(b) A notice of intention to remove a director, officer, committee member or employee from office shall contain a statement of the alleged facts constituting the grounds therefor and shall fix a time and place at which a hearing before the Credit Union Commission will be held thereon. Such hearing shall be fixed for a date not earlier than 30 days nor later than 60 days after the date of service of such notice unless an earlier or a later date is set by the Commission at the request of such director, officer, committee member or employee and for good cause shown. Pending this hearing, the Administrator may remove the alleged violator if he finds that it is essential to the continued well-being of the credit union or the public to do so. Unless, of course, such director, officer, committee member or employee shall appear at the hearing in person or by a duly authorized representative, he shall be deemed to have consented to the issuance of an order of such removal. In the event of such consent, or if upon the record made at any such hearing the Credit Union Commission shall find that any of the grounds specified in such notice has been determined by the greater weight of the evidence, the Commission may issue such orders of removal from office as it may deem appropriate. Any such order shall become effective at the expiration of 30 days after service upon such credit union and the director, officer, committee member or employee concerned (except in the case of an order issued upon consent, which shall become effective at the time specified therein). Such order shall remain effective and enforceable except to such extent as it is stayed, modified, terminated or set aside by action of the Credit Union Commission or a reviewing court. (1979, c. 197, s. 1.)

§ 54-109.20. Reserved for future codification purposes.

Article 14C.

Powers of Credit Union.

§ 54-109.21. General powers.

A credit union may:

(1)   Make contracts;

(2)   Sue and be sued;

(3)   Adopt and use a common seal and alter the seal;

(4)   Acquire, lease, hold and dispose of property, either in whole or in part, necessary or incidental to its operations;

(5)   At the discretion of the board of directors, require the payment of an entrance fee or annual membership fee, or both, of any person admitted to membership;

(6)   Receive savings from its members in the form of shares, deposits, or special-purpose thrift accounts;

(7)   Lend its funds to its members as provided in Articles 14A to 14L of this Chapter;

(8)   Borrow from any source in accordance with policy established by the board of directors;

(9)   Discount and sell any eligible obligations, subject to rules adopted by the Administrator;

(10) Sell all or substantially all of its assets or purchase all or substantially all of the assets of another financial institution, subject to the approval of the Administrator of Credit Unions;

(11) Invest surplus funds as provided in Articles 14A to 14L of this Chapter;

(12) Make deposits in legally chartered banks, savings institutions, trust companies and central-type credit union organizations;

(13) Assess charges to members in accordance with the bylaws for failure to meet properly their obligations to the credit union;

(14) Hold membership in other credit unions organized under Articles 14A to 14L of this Chapter or other acts, and in other associations and organizations composed of credit unions;

(15) Declare dividends; pay interest on deposits and pay interest refunds to borrowers as provided in Articles 14A to 14L of this Chapter;

(16) Sell travelers checks and money orders and charge a reasonable fee for such services, provided the travelers checks are payable at institutions other than a credit union;

(17) Perform tasks and missions requested by the federal government or this State or any agency or political subdivision thereof, when approved by the board of directors and not inconsistent with Articles 14A to 14L of this Chapter;

(18) Act as fiscal agent for and receive deposits from the federal government, this State, or any agency or political subdivision thereof;

(19) Contribute to, support, or participate in any nonprofit service facility whose services will benefit the credit union or its membership subject to rules adopted by the Administrator;

(20) Make donations or contributions to any civic, charitable or community organization as authorized by the board of directors, subject to such regulations as are prescribed by the Administrator;

(21) Act as a custodian of qualified pension funds if permitted by federal law;

(22) Purchase or make available insurance for its directors, officers, agents, employees, and members; insurance may be provided through any insurance company or through any subsidiary insurance company owned by the credit union; and

(23) Facilitate its members' purchase of goods and services in a manner which promotes the purposes of the credit union.

(24) The board of directors may expel from the corporation any member who has not carried out the engagement the member made with the corporation, has been convicted of a felony or crime involving moral turpitude, or neglects or refuses to comply with the provisions of this Article or of the bylaws. The Board may, after notice and hearing as provided in this subdivision, expel from the corporation any member who because of the member's intemperance disrupts the activities of the credit union or who because of the member's habitual neglect of financial obligations reflects discredit upon the credit union. No member shall be expelled until informed in writing of the charges made and given an opportunity, after reasonable notice, to be heard.

(25) Engage in activity permitted under this subdivision. Notwithstanding any other provision of this Chapter, the Administrator of Credit Unions, subject to the advice and consent of the Credit Union Commission, and upon a finding that action is necessary to preserve and protect the welfare of credit unions and to promote the general economy of the State, may adopt rules allowing State-chartered credit unions to engage in any activity in which they could engage if they were federally chartered credit unions.

(26) Subject to rules adopted by the Administrator, act as trustee or custodian, and receive reasonable compensation for so acting, under any written trust instrument or custodial agreement created or organized and forming a part of a deferred compensation plan for its members or groups or organizations of its members, provided the funds of the plans are invested in savings or deposits of the credit union. All funds held may be commingled for the purpose of investment, but individual records shall be kept by the credit union for each participant and shall show in proper detail all transactions engaged in under authority of this subdivision.

A member may withdraw from a credit union by filing a written notice of intent to withdraw.

The amounts paid in on shares or deposits by an expelled or withdrawing member, with any dividends credited to the shares and any interest accrued on the deposits to the date of expulsion or withdrawal shall be paid to the member, but in the order of expulsion or withdrawal, and only as funds therefor become available, after deducting any amounts due to the credit union by the member. The member shall have no other or further right in the credit union or to any of its benefits, but the expulsion or withdrawal shall not operate to relieve the member from any remaining liability to the credit union. (1915, c. 115, ss. 5, 16, 17, 23; C.S., ss. 5216-5218, 5231; 1925, c. 73, ss. 3, 10; 1935, c. 87; 1965, c. 956, s. 8; 1975, c. 538, s. 1; 1977, c. 559, s. 5; 1983, c. 568, s. 2; 1991, c. 651, s. 3; 2011-221, s. 1.)

§ 54-109.22. Incidental powers.

A credit union may exercise such incidental powers such as are necessary or requisite to enable it to promote and carry on most effectively its purposes. (1975, c. 538, s. 1.)

§§ 54-109.23 through 54-109.25. Reserved for future codification purposes.

Article 14D.

Membership.

§ 54-109.26. "Membership" defined.

(a)   The membership of a credit union shall be limited to and consist of the subscribers to the articles of incorporation and such other persons within the common bond set forth in the bylaws as have been duly admitted members, have paid any required entrance fee or membership fee, or both, have subscribed for one or more shares, and have paid the initial installment thereon, and have complied with such other requirements as the articles of incorporation or bylaws specify.

(b)   Credit union membership may include groups having a common bond of similar occupation, association or interest, or groups who reside within an identifiable neighborhood, community, or rural district, or employees of a common employer, and members of the immediate family of such persons. (1915, c. 115, s. 6; C.S., s. 5230; 1925, c. 73, s. 3; 1935, c. 87; 1965, c. 956, s. 18; 1975, c. 538, s. 1.)

§ 54-109.27. Societies and other associations.

Societies, and copartnerships composed primarily of individuals who are eligible to membership, and corporations whose stockholders are composed primarily of such individuals, may be admitted to membership in the same manner and under the same conditions as individuals, but may not borrow in excess of their shareholdings. Provided, however, secured loans in excess of shareholdings may be made to nonprofit societies, copartnerships, and corporations who are members. (1975, c. 538, s. 1; 1979, c. 809, s. 1.)

§ 54-109.28. Other credit unions.

Any credit union organized under Articles 14A to 14L of this Chapter may permit membership of any other credit union organized under Articles 14A to 14L of this Chapter or other acts. (1975, c. 538, s. 1.)

§ 54-109.29. Members who leave field.

Members who leave the field of membership may be permitted to retain their membership in the credit union as a matter of general policy of the board of directors. (1975, c. 538, s. 1.)

§ 54-109.30. Liability of shareholders.

A shareholder of any such corporation, unless the bylaws so provide, shall not be individually liable for the payment of its debts for an amount in excess of the par value of the shares which he owns or for which he has subscribed. (1975, c. 538, s. 1.)

§ 54-109.31. Meetings of members.

(a) The annual meeting and any special meetings of the members of the credit union shall be held at the time, place, and in the manner indicated by the bylaws.

(b) At all such meetings, a member shall have but one vote, irrespective of his shareholdings. No member may vote by proxy, but a member may vote by absentee ballot if the bylaws of the credit union so provide.

(c) A society, association, copartnership or corporation having membership in the credit union may be represented and have its vote cast by one of its members or shareholders, provided such person has been fully authorized by the organization's governing body.

(d) The board of directors may establish a minimum age of 16 years of age as a qualification to vote at meetings of the members.

(e) The board of directors may establish a minimum age of 18 years of age as a qualification to hold office. (1975, c. 538, s. 1.)

§§ 54-109.32 through 54-109.34. Reserved for future codification purposes.

Article 14E.

Direction of Affairs.

§ 54-109.35. Election or appointment of officials.

(a) The credit union shall be directed by a board of directors, at least five in number, to be elected at the annual members' meeting by and from the members. All members of the board shall hold office for such terms as the bylaws provide.

(b) The board of directors at its first meeting after its election shall appoint a supervisory committee from the membership (no more than one of whom may be a member of the board of directors and none a member of the credit committee) of not less than three members who shall serve for such terms as may be fixed by the bylaws; or in lieu thereof, the bylaws may authorize the board of directors to employ and use such clerical and auditing assistants as may be required to perform the duties required by G.S. 54-109.49. The board of directors may remove or suspend any member of the supervisory committee for neglect of duty, misfeasance, malfeasance, official misconduct, or for other good cause shown.

(c) The board of directors shall appoint a credit committee from the membership consisting of an odd number, not less than three, for such terms as the bylaws provide or, in lieu of a credit committee, appoint one or more loan officers from the membership and, in such instances, duties and responsibilities of the credit committee shall be carried out by such loan officer or officers. (1975, c. 538, s. 1.)

§ 54-109.36. Record of board and committee members.

Within 15 days following the board of directors' initial or annual organization meeting, a record of the names and addresses of the members of the board, committees and all other officers of the credit union shall be filed with the Credit Union Division on forms provided by that Division. (1975, c. 538, s. 1.)

§ 54-109.37. Vacancies.

The board of directors shall fill any vacancies occurring in the board until successors elected at the next annual meeting have qualified. The board shall also fill vacancies in the credit and supervisory committees. (1975, c. 538, s. 1.)

§ 54-109.38. Compensation of officials.

No member of the board of directors or of the credit committee or supervisory committee shall be compensated for his service in this position, but providing reasonable life, health, accident and similar insurance protection for a director or committee member shall not be considered compensation. Directors and committee members, while on official business of the credit union, may be reimbursed for necessary expenses incidental to the performance of the business. (1975, c. 538, s. 1.)

§ 54-109.39. Conflicts of interest.

No director, committee member, officer, agent or employee of the credit union shall in any manner, directly or indirectly, participate in the deliberation upon or the determination of any question affecting his pecuniary interest or the pecuniary interest of any corporation, partnership, or association (other than the credit union) in which he is directly or indirectly interested. (1975, c. 538, s. 1.)

§ 54-109.40. Executive officers.

(a)   At their organization meeting and within 30 days following each annual meeting of the members, the directors shall elect from their own number an executive officer, who may be designated as chairman of the board or president; a vice-chairman of the board or one or more vice-presidents; a treasurer; and a secretary. The treasurer and the secretary may be the same individual. The persons so elected shall be the executive officers of the corporation.

(b)   The terms of the officers shall be one year, or until their successors are chosen and have duly qualified.

(c)   The duties of the officers shall be prescribed in the bylaws.

(d)   The board of directors may employ an officer in charge of operations whose title shall be either president and/or general manager; or, in lieu thereof, the board of directors may designate the treasurer or an assistant treasurer to act as general manager and be in active charge of the affairs of the credit union. (1975, c. 538, s. 1.)

§ 54-109.41. Authority of directors.

The board of directors shall have the general direction of the business affairs, funds, and records of the credit union. (1975, c. 538, s. 1.)

§ 54-109.42. Executive committee.

From the persons elected to the board, the board may appoint an executive committee of not less than three directors who may be authorized to act for the board in all respects, subject to such conditions and limitations as are prescribed by the board. (1975, c. 538, s. 1.)

§ 54-109.43. Meetings of directors.

The board of directors and the executive committee shall meet as often as the bylaws prescribe. (1915, c. 115, s. 8; C.S., s. 5232; 1975, c. 538, s. 1.)

§ 54-109.44. Duties of directors.

It shall be the duty of the directors to:

(1) Act upon applications for membership or to appoint one or more membership officers to approve applications for membership under such conditions as the board prescribes. A record of a membership officer's approval or denial of membership shall be available to the board of directors for inspection. A person denied membership by a membership officer may appeal the denial to the board;

(2) Purchase a blanket fidelity bond, in accordance with any rules and regulations of the Administrator, to protect the credit union against losses caused by occurrences covered therein such as fraud, dishonesty, forgery, embezzlement, misappropriation, misapplication, or unfaithful performance of

duty by a director, officer, employee, member of an official committee, attorney-at-law or other agent;

(3) Determine from time to time the interest rate or rates consistent with Articles 14A to 14L of this Chapter, which shall be charged on loans and to authorize interest refunds, if any, to members from income earned and received in proportion to the interest paid by them on such classes of loans and under such conditions as the board prescribes;

(4) Fix from time to time the maximum amount which may be loaned to any one member;

(5) Declare dividends on shares in the manner and form as provided in the bylaws; and determine the interest rate or rates which will be paid on deposits;

(6) Set the number of shares and the amount of deposits which may be owned by a member, such limitations to apply alike to all members;

(7) Have charge of the investment of surplus funds, except that the board of directors may designate an investment committee or any qualified individual to have charge of making investments under controls established by the board of directors;

(8) Authorize the employment of such persons necessary to carry on the business of the credit union;

(9) Authorize the conveyance of property;

(10) Borrow or lend money to carry on the functions of the credit union;

(11) Designate a depository or depositories for the funds of the credit union;

(12) Suspend any or all members of the credit or supervisory committee for failure to perform their duties;

(13) Appoint any special committees deemed necessary; and

(14) Perform such other duties as the members from time to time direct, and perform or authorize any action not inconsistent with Articles 14A to 14L of this Chapter and not specifically reserved by the bylaws for the members. (1915, c.

115, s. 10; C.S., s. 5234; 1957, c. 989, s. 5; 1965, c. 956, s. 20; 1973, c. 199, s. 9; 1975, c. 538, s. 1.)

§ 54-109.45. Authority of credit committee.

The credit committee shall have the general supervision of all loans to members. (1915, c. 115, s. 11; C.S., s. 5235; 1961, c. 1187, s. 22; 1965, c. 956, s. 1; 1969, c. 69, s. 5; 1973, c. 199, s. 10; 1975, c. 538, s. 1.)

§ 54-109.46. Meetings of credit committee.

The credit committee shall meet as often as the business of the credit union requires and not less frequently than once a month to consider applications for loans. No loan shall be made unless it is approved by a majority of the committee who are present at the meeting at which the application is considered. (1915, c. 115, s. 11; C.S., s. 5235; 1961, c. 1187, s. 22; 1965, c. 956, s. 1; 1969, c. 69, s. 5; 1973, c. 199, s. 10; 1975, c. 538, s. 1.)

§ 54-109.47. Loan officers.

(a) The credit committee may appoint one or more loan officers and delegate the power to approve loans, subject to such limitations or conditions as the credit committee prescribes.

(b) Loan applications not approved by a loan officer shall be reviewed and acted upon by the credit committee. (1915, c. 115, s. 11; C.S., s. 5235; 1961, c. 1187, s. 22; 1965, c. 956, s. 1; 1969, c. 69, s. 5; 1973, c. 199, s. 10; 1975, c. 538, s. 1.)

§ 54-109.48. When credit committee dispensed with.

The credit committee may be dispensed with, and loan officer(s) empowered to approve or disapprove loans under conditions prescribed by the board of directors. In the event the credit committee is dispensed with, the procedures prescribed in G.S. 54-109.45, 54-109.46 and 54-109.47 do not apply, and no loans shall be made unless approved by the loan officer(s). (1915, c. 115, s. 11; C.S., s. 5235; 1961, c. 1187, s. 22; 1965, c. 956, s. 1; 1969, c. 69, s. 5; 1973, c. 199, s. 10; 1975, c. 538, s. 1.)

§ 54-109.49. Duties of supervisory committee.

The supervisory committee shall make or cause to be made an annual audit, in accordance with rules and regulations promulgated by the Administrator of Credit Unions, and shall submit a report of that audit to the board of directors and a summary of the report to the members at the next annual meeting of the credit union. The supervisory committee shall make or cause to be made such supplemental audits as deemed necessary by it or as may be ordered by the Administrator of Credit Unions. Any violation of this Article or of the bylaws or of any practice of the corporation which in the opinion of the supervisory committee is unsafe, unsound, or unauthorized, shall be reported to the board of directors and the Administrator of Credit Unions within seven days after its discovery. (1915, c. 115, s. 12; C.S., s. 5236; 1965, c. 956, s. 21; 1973, c. 199, s. 11; 1975, c. 538, s. 1.)

§§ 54-109.50 through 54-109.52. Reserved for future codification purposes.

Article 14F.

Savings Accounts.

§ 54-109.53. Shares.

(a)　　The capital of a credit union consists of the payments made by members on shares, undivided surplus, and reserves.

(b)　　Shares may be subscribed to, paid for and transferred in such manner as the bylaws prescribe.

(c) A certificate need not be issued to denote ownership of a share in a credit union. (1915, c. 115, s. 13; C.S., s. 5226; 1925, c. 73, s. 3; 1935, c. 87; 1965, c. 956, ss. 16, 17; 1975, c. 538, s. 1.)

§ 54-109.54. Dividends.

The board of directors of any credit union may declare dividends as its bylaws provide. (1915, c. 115, s. 22; C.S., s. 5223; 1925, c. 73, s. 3; 1935, c. 87; 1957, c. 989, s. 3; 1965, c. 956, s. 15; 1969, c. 69, ss. 3, 4; 1973, c. 199, s. 7; 1975, c. 538, s. 1; 1983, c. 568, s. 3.)

§ 54-109.55. Deposits.

A credit union may receive on deposit the savings of its members and also nonmembers in such amounts and upon such terms as the board of directors may determine and the bylaws shall provide. (1915, c. 115, s. 16; C.S., s. 5217; 1925, c. 73, s. 3; 1935, c. 87; 1975, c. 538, s. 1.)

§ 54-109.56. Thrift accounts.

Christmas clubs, vacation clubs, and other thrift accounts may be operated under conditions established by the board of directors. (1975, c. 538, s. 1.)

§ 54-109.57: Repealed by Session Laws 2011-236, s. 4, effective October 1, 2011.

§ 54-109.57A. Payable on Death (POD) accounts.

(a) Shares may be issued to and deposits received from any natural person or natural persons establishing an account who shall execute a written agreement with the credit union containing a statement that it is executed pursuant to the provisions of this section and providing for the account to be held in the name of the natural person or natural persons as owner or owners for one or more beneficiaries. Such account and any balance thereof shall be held as a Payable on Death account. The account shall have the following incidents:

(1)   Any owner during the owner's lifetime may change any designated beneficiary by a written direction to the credit union.

(2)   If there are two or more owners of a Payable on Death account, the owners shall own the account as joint tenants with right of survivorship and, except as otherwise provided in this section, the account shall have the incidents set forth in G.S. 54-109.58.

(3)   Any owner may withdraw funds by writing checks or otherwise, as set forth in the account contract, and receive payment in cash or check payable to the owner's personal order.

(4)   If the beneficiary or beneficiaries are natural persons, there may be one or more beneficiaries and the following shall apply:

a.   If only one beneficiary is living and of legal age at the death of the last surviving owner, the beneficiary shall be the owner of the account, and payment by the credit union to such owner shall be a total discharge of the credit union's obligation as to the amount paid. If two or more beneficiaries are living at the death of the last surviving owner, they shall be owners of the account as joint tenants with right of survivorship as provided in G.S. 54-109.58, and payment by the credit union to the owners or any of the owners shall be a total discharge of the credit union's obligation as to the amount paid.

b.   If only one beneficiary is living and that beneficiary is not of legal age at the death of the last surviving owner, the credit union shall transfer the funds in the account to the general guardian or guardian of the estate, if any, of the minor beneficiary. If no guardian of the minor beneficiary has been appointed, the credit union shall hold the funds in a similar interest bearing account in the name of the minor until the minor reaches the age of majority or until a duly appointed guardian withdraws the funds.

(5)   If the beneficiary is an entity other than a natural person, there shall be only one beneficiary.

(6) If one or more owners survive the last surviving beneficiary who was a natural person, or if a beneficiary who is an entity other than a natural person should cease to exist before the death of the owner, the account shall become an individual account of the owner, or a joint account with right of survivorship of the owners, and shall have the legal incidents of an individual account in a case of a single owner or a joint account with right of survivorship, as provided in G.S. 54-109.58, in the case of multiple owners.

(7) Prior to the death of the last surviving owner, no beneficiary shall have any ownership interest in a Payable on Death account. Funds in a Payable on Death account established pursuant to this subsection shall belong to the beneficiary or beneficiaries upon the death of the last surviving owner, and the funds shall be subject only to the personal representative's right of collection as set forth in G.S. 28A-15-10(a)(1). Payment by the credit union of funds in the Payable on Death account to the beneficiary or beneficiaries shall terminate the personal representative's authority under G.S. 28A-15-10(a)(1) to collect against the credit union for the funds so paid, but the personal representative's authority to collect such funds from the beneficiary or beneficiaries is not terminated.

The natural person or natural persons establishing an account under this subsection shall sign a statement containing language set forth in a conspicuous manner and substantially similar to the language set out below; the language may be on a signature card or in an explanation of the account that is set out in a separate document whose receipt is acknowledged by the person or persons establishing the account:

"CREDIT UNION (or name of institution)

PAYABLE ON DEATH ACCOUNT

G.S. 54-109.57A

I (or we) understand that by establishing a Payable on Death account under the provisions of North Carolina General Statute 54-109.57A that:

1. During my (or our) lifetime I (or we), individually or jointly, may withdraw the money in the account.

2. By written direction to the credit union (or name of institution) I (or we), individually or jointly, may change the beneficiary or beneficiaries.

3. Upon my (or our) death the money remaining in the account will belong to the beneficiary or beneficiaries, and the money will not be inherited by my (or our) heirs or be controlled by will.

_____

_____ "

(b) This section shall not be deemed exclusive. Deposit accounts not conforming to this section shall be governed by other applicable provisions of the General Statutes or the common law, as appropriate.

(c) No addition to such accounts, nor any withdrawal, payment, or change of beneficiary, shall affect the nature of such accounts as Payable on Death accounts or affect the right of any owner to terminate the account.

(d) This section does not repeal or modify any provisions of laws relating to estate taxes.

(e) Any payable on death account created under the provisions of G.S. 54-109.57, as it existed prior to October 1, 2011, shall for all purposes be governed by the provisions of this section on and after October 1, 2011, and any reference to G.S. 54-109.57 in any document concerning the account shall be deemed a reference to this section. (1915, c. 115, s. 14; C.S., s. 5227; 1975, c. 538, s. 1; 1987 (Reg. Sess., 1988), c. 1078, s. 2; 1989, c. 164, s. 6; 1989 (Reg. Sess., 1990), c. 866, s. 8; 2001-267, s. 2; 2001-487, s. 61(a); 2011-236, s. 4; 2012-168, s. 4; 2012-194, s. 63; 2013-132, s. 1.)

§ 54-109.58. Joint accounts.

(a) Shares may be issued to and deposits received from any two or more persons opening or holding an account or accounts, but no joint tenant, unless a member in his own right, shall be permitted to vote, obtain loans, or hold office or be required to pay an entrance or membership fee. The account and any balance thereof shall be held by them as joint tenants, with or without right of survivorship, as the contract shall provide; the account may also be held pursuant to G.S. 41-2.1 and have the incidents set forth in that section, provided, however, if the account is held pursuant to G.S. 41-2.1 the contract shall set forth that fact as well.

(b) Unless the persons establishing the account have agreed with the credit union that withdrawals require more than one signature, payment by the credit union to, or on the order of, any persons holding an account authorized by this section shall be a total discharge of the credit union's obligations as to the amount so paid.

(c) Funds in a joint account established with right of survivorship shall belong to the surviving joint tenant or tenants upon the death of a joint tenant, and the funds shall be subject only to the personal representative's right of collection as set forth in G.S. 28A-15-10(a)(3), or as provided in G.S. 41-2.1 if the account is established pursuant to the provisions of that section. Payment by the credit union of funds in the joint account to a surviving joint tenant or tenants shall terminate the personal representative's authority under G.S. 28A-15-10(a)(3) to collect against the credit union for the funds so paid, but the personal representative's authority to collect such funds from the surviving joint tenant or tenants is not terminated.

(d) A pledge of such account by any holder or holders shall, unless otherwise specifically agreed upon, be a valid pledge and transfer of such account, or of the amount so pledged, and shall not operate to sever or terminate the joint ownership of all or any part of the account.

(e) A credit union is not liable to joint tenants for complying in good faith with a writ of execution, garnishment, attachment, levy, or other legal process that appears to have been issued by a court or other authority of competent jurisdiction and seeks funds held in the name of any one or more of the joint tenants.

(f) Persons establishing an account under this section shall sign a statement showing their election of the right of survivorship in the account, and containing language set forth in a conspicuous manner and substantially similar to the following:

"CREDIT UNION (or name of institution)

JOINT ACCOUNT WITH RIGHT OF SURVIVORSHIP

G.S. 54-109.58

We understand that by establishing a joint account under the provisions of North Carolina General Statute 54-109.58 that:

1.   The credit union (or name of institution) may pay the money in the account to, or on the order of, any person named in the account unless we have agreed with the credit union that withdrawals require more than one signature; and

2.   Upon the death of one joint owner the money remaining in the account will belong to the surviving joint owners and will not pass by inheritance to the heirs of the deceased joint owner or be controlled by the deceased joint owner's will.

We DO elect to create the right of survivorship in this account.

_____

_____ "

The language may be on a signature card or in an explanation of the account that is set out in a separate document whose receipt is acknowledged by the person or persons establishing the account.

(g)   Any joint tenant may terminate a joint account.

(h)   Where a joint account is held by two or more individuals and a joint tenant does not wish for the account to be terminated but requests to be removed from the account, the credit union shall remove the joint tenant from the account. The joint account shall continue in the names of the remaining tenant or tenants. Any joint tenant who requested to be removed from an account remains liable for any debts incurred in connection with the joint account during the period in which the individual was a named joint tenant.

(i)   This section shall not be deemed exclusive. Deposit accounts not conforming to this section shall be governed by other applicable provisions of the General Statutes or the common law as appropriate.

(j) This section does not repeal or modify any provisions of laws relating to estate taxes. This section regulates and protects the credit union in its relationship with joint owners of accounts.

(k) No addition to such account, nor any withdrawal or payment shall affect the nature of the account as a joint account, or affect the right of any tenant to terminate the account. (1975, c. 538, s. 1; 1987 (Reg. Sess., 1988), c. 1078, s. 3; 1989, c. 164, s. 3; 1989 (Reg. Sess., 1990), c. 866, s. 7; 1998-69, s. 15; 2013-132, s. 2.)

§ 54-109.59. Liens.

The credit union shall have a lien on the shares, deposits and accumulated dividends or interest of a member in his individual, joint or trust account, for any sum past due the credit union from said member or for any loan endorsed by him. (1915, c. 115, s. 13; C.S., s. 5226; 1925, c. 73, s. 3; 1935, c. 87; 1965, c. 956, ss. 16, 17; 1975, c. 538, s. 1.)

§ 54-109.60. Repealed by Session Laws 1977, c. 559, s. 6.

§ 54-109.60A. Minors.

(a) A credit union may issue and operate a share or deposit account in the name of (i) a minor or (ii) the names of two or more individuals, one or more of which are minors. A minor who obtains a share or deposit account from a credit union under this subsection, whether individually or together with others, is bound by the terms of the account agreement to the same extent as if the minor were of full age and legal capacity.

(b) If a minor with a share account, other than a joint account with right of survivorship or a payable on death account, dies, a parent or legal guardian of the minor may access and withdraw the funds on deposit, and the credit union is discharged to the extent of any withdrawal.

(c) This section shall not affect the law governing transactions with minors in cases outside the scope of this section, including transactions that constitute an extension of credit to a minor. (2013-132, s. 3.)

§ 54-109.60B. Accounts opened by adults for minors.

(a) One or more adults may open and maintain a custodial share account for or in the name of a minor and using the minor's taxpayer identification number. Unless otherwise provided in the agreement governing the account, the following terms apply:

(1) Beneficial ownership of the account vests exclusively in the minor. All interest credited to the account shall belong to the minor and shall be reported to the appropriate taxing authorities in the name of the minor using the minor's taxpayer identification number.

(2) Except as otherwise provided, control of the account vests exclusively in the custodian whose name appears on the credit union's records for the account. If there is more than one custodian named on the credit union's account records, each may act independently. Any one or more of the custodians named on the credit union's records may turn over control of the account to the minor at any time, either before or after the minor reaches the age of majority.

(3) If the custodian has not already transferred control, then after the minor beneficiary reaches the age of majority, the beneficiary may instruct the credit union to transfer control to the beneficiary and remove the named custodian.

(4) If the custodian or, if more than one custodian is on the account, the last of the custodians to survive dies before the minor reaches the age of majority, the minor's parent or the minor's legal guardian may act as custodian or name another custodian on the account.

(b) This section shall not be deemed exclusive. Accounts not conforming to this section shall be governed by other applicable provisions of the General Statutes, including Chapter 33A, the North Carolina Uniform Transfers to Minors Act, or the common law, as appropriate. (2013-132, s. 3.)

§ 54-109.61. Reduction in shares.

(a)   Whenever the losses of any credit union, resulting from a depreciation in value of its loans or investments or otherwise, exceed its undivided earnings and reserve fund so that the estimated value of its assets is less than the total amount due the shareholders, the credit union may by a majority vote of the members present at a special meeting called for that purpose order a reduction in the shares of each of its shareholders to divide the loss proportionately among the members.

(b)   If the credit union thereafter realizes from such assets a greater amount than was fixed by the order of reduction, such excess shall be divided proportionately among the shareholders whose assets were reduced, but only to the extent of such reduction. (1975, c. 538, s. 1.)

§ 54-109.62. Payment of balance of deceased person or person under disability to personal representative or guardian.

(a)   A credit union may pay any balance on deposit to the credit of any deceased individual to the duly qualified personal representative, collector, or public administrator of the decedent who is qualified as such under the laws of any state.

(b)   A credit union may pay any balance on deposit to the credit of any individual judicially declared incompetent or otherwise under a legal disability to the duly qualified personal representative, guardian, curator, conservator, or committee of the person declared incompetent or under disability who is qualified as such under the laws of any state.

(c)   The presentation of a letter of qualification as personal representative, collector, public administrator, guardian, curator, conservator, or committee of the person issued or certified by the appointing court shall be conclusive proof of the jurisdiction of the court issuing the same and sufficient authority for the payment.

(d)   Payment by a credit union in good faith under the authority of this section discharges the liability of the bank to the extent of the payment. (2013-132, s. 3.)

§ 54-109.62A. Powers of attorney; notice of revocation; payment after notice.

(a) Any credit union may continue to recognize any act of an attorney-in-fact or other agent until the credit union receives actual notice of the principal's death or a written notice of revocation signed by the principal who granted the authority or, in the case of a company, evidence satisfactory to the credit union of the revocation. Payment by the credit union to or at the direction of an attorney-in-fact or other agent before receipt of the notice is a total discharge of the credit union's obligation as to the amount so paid.

(b) Notwithstanding that a credit union has received written notice of revocation of the authority of an attorney-in-fact or other designated agent, a credit union may, until 10 days after receipt of notice, pay any item made, drawn, accepted, or endorsed by the attorney-in-fact or agent prior to the revocation, provided that the item is otherwise properly payable. (2013-132, s. 3.)

§ 54-109.63. Personal agency accounts.

(a) A person may open a personal agency account by written contract containing a statement that it is executed pursuant to the provisions of this section. A personal agency account may be a checking account, savings account, time deposit, or any other type of withdrawable account or certificate. The written contract shall name an agent who shall have authority to act on behalf of the depositor in regard to the account as set out in this subsection. The agent shall have the authority to:

(1) Make, sign or execute checks drawn on the account or otherwise make withdrawals from the account;

(2) Endorse checks made payable to the principal for deposit only into the account; and

(3) Deposit cash or negotiable instruments, including instruments endorsed by the principal, into the account.

A person establishing an account under this section shall sign a statement containing language substantially similar to the following in a conspicuous manner:

"CREDIT UNION (or name of institution)

PERSONAL AGENCY ACCOUNT

G.S. 54-109.63

I understand that by establishing a personal agency account under the provisions of North Carolina General Statute 54-109.63 that the agent named in the account may:

1. Sign checks drawn on the account; and

2. Make deposits into the account.

I also understand that upon my death the money remaining in the account will be controlled by my will or inherited by my heirs.

_____ "

The language may be on a signature card or in an explanation of the account that is set out in a separate document whose receipt is acknowledged by the person or persons establishing the account.

(b) An account created under the provisions of this section grants no ownership right or interest in the agent. Upon the death of the principal there is no right of survivorship to the account and the authority set out in subsection (a) terminates.

(c) The written contract referred to in subsection (a) shall provide that the principal may elect to extend the authority of the agent set out in subsection (a) to act on behalf of the principal in regard to the account notwithstanding the subsequent incapacity or mental incompetence of the principal. If the principal so elects to extend such authority of the agent, then upon the subsequent incapacity or mental incompetence of the principal, the agent may continue to exercise such authority, without the requirement of bond or of accounting to any court, until such time as the agent shall receive actual knowledge that such authority has been terminated by a duly qualified guardian of the estate of the incapacitated or incompetent principal or by the duly appointed attorney-in-fact for the incapacitated or incompetent principal, acting pursuant to a durable power of attorney (as defined in G.S. 32A-8) which grants to the attorney-in-fact that authority in regard to the account which is granted to the agent by the written contract executed pursuant to the provisions of this section, at which time the agent shall account to such guardian or attorney-in-fact for all actions of the agent in regard to the account during the incapacity or incompetence of the principal. If the principal does not so elect to extend the authority of the agent, then upon the subsequent incapacity or mental incompetence of the principal, the authority or the agent set out in subsection (a) terminates.

(d)   When an account under this section has been established all or part of the account or any interest or dividend thereon may be paid by the credit union on a check made, signed or executed by the agent. In the absence of actual knowledge that the principal has died or that the agency created by the account has been terminated, such payment shall be a valid and sufficient discharge to the credit union for payment so made.

(e)   An account established under the provisions of this section does not grant to the agent the authority to vote, obtain loans, or hold office and the agent shall not be required to pay an entrance or membership fee. (1987 (Reg. Sess., 1988), c. 1078, s. 4; 1989, c. 164, s. 9; 1989 (Reg. Sess., 1990), c. 866, s. 9; 2013-132, s. 4.)

§ 54-109.64. Savings promotion raffles.

A credit union may offer a savings promotion raffle in which the sole consideration required for a chance of winning designated prizes is the deposit of a minimum specified amount of money in a savings account or other savings program offered by the credit union. A credit union shall maintain records sufficient to facilitate an audit of the savings promotion raffle, shall conduct the savings promotion raffle in a safe and sound manner, and shall fully disclose the terms and conditions of the promotion to account holders and prospective account holders of the credit union. (2011-146, s. 2.)

Article 14G.

Loans.

§ 54-109.65. Purposes, terms and interest rate.

A credit union may loan to its members for such purpose and upon such security and terms as the board of directors prescribes at rates of interest not exceeding eighteen percent (18%) annual percentage rate, unless a greater rate not to exceed the annual percentage rate permitted to be charged by federally chartered credit unions, is otherwise approved by the Credit Union Commission. Such action by the Commission will be uniform and apply to all credit unions.

The term "interest," as used in this section, shall not be deemed to include charges made by a credit union for appraisals of real or personal property; attorneys' fees for searching title to real property, preparing notes, deeds of trust, mortgages and closing loans; and recording fees. Rate of interest and terms of repayment shall appear on each note but the corporation may, for the purpose of making loans, discount and negotiate promissory notes and deduct in advance, from the proceeds of such loan, interest at a rate not to exceed the rate herein fixed, which shall be the legal rate for corporations organized under this Article, and such deductions shall be made upon the amount of the loan from the date thereof until the maturity of the final installment, notwithstanding that the principal amount of such loan is required to be repaid in such installments. (1915, c. 115, ss. 19, 20; 1917, c. 232, s. 4; C.S., ss. 5220, 5221; 1925, c. 73, s. 3; 1935, c. 87; 1955, c. 1135, s. 2; 1957, c. 989, s. 2; 1961, c. 1187, s. 1; 1965, c. 956, ss. 1, 12, 13; 1969, c. 69, s. 9; 1973, c. 199, ss. 5, 6; 1975, c. 538, s. 1; 1983, c. 568, s. 4.)

§ 54-109.66. Application.

Every application for a loan shall be made in writing upon a form, which the board of directors prescribe. The application shall state the purpose for which the loan is desired, and the security, if any, offered. Each loan shall be evidenced by a written document. (1975, c. 538, s. 1.)

§ 54-109.67. Loan limit.

No loan shall be made to any member in an aggregate amount in excess of ten percent (10%) of the credit union's unimpaired capital and surplus. In accordance with the bylaws and subject to such rules and regulations as the Administrator may prescribe, the board of directors shall determine and set the maximum unsecured loan limits subject to the limitation contained in the preceding sentence. (1915, c. 115, s. 19; 1917, c. 232, s. 4; C.S., s. 5220; 1925, c. 73, s. 3; 1935, c. 87; 1955, c. 1135, s. 2; 1961, c. 1187, s. 1; 1965, c. 956, ss. 1, 12, 13; 1969, c. 69, s. 9; 1973, c. 199, s. 5; 1975, c. 538, s. 1; 1983, c. 568, s. 5.)

§ 54-109.68. Security.

In addition to generally accepted types of security, the endorsement of a note by a surety, comaker or guarantor, or assignment of shares, in a manner consistent with the laws of this State, shall be deemed security within the meaning of Articles 14A to 14L of this Chapter. The adequacy of any security shall be determined by the board of directors subject to Articles 14A to 14L of this Chapter and the bylaws. (1975, c. 538, s. 1.)

§ 54-109.69. Installments.

A member may receive a loan in installments, or in one sum, and may pay the whole or any part of his loan on any day on which the office of the credit union is open for business. (1975, c. 538, s. 1.)

§ 54-109.70. Line of credit.

A line of credit and advances may be granted to each member within guidelines established by the board of directors. Where a line of credit has been approved, no additional loan applications are required as long as the aggregate obligation does not exceed the limit of such line of credit. (1975, c. 538, s. 1.)

§ 54-109.71. Other loan programs.

(a) A credit union may participate in loans to credit union members jointly with other credit unions, corporations, or financial organizations.

(b) A credit union may participate in guaranteed loan programs of the federal and State government.

(c) A credit union may purchase the conditional sales contracts, notes and similar instruments of its members. (1975, c. 538, s. 1.)

§§ 54-109.72 through 54-109.74. Reserved for future codification purposes.

Article 14H.

Insurance and Group Purchasing.

§ 54-109.75. Insurance for members.

(a) A credit union may purchase or make available insurance for its members in amounts related to their respective ages, shares, deposits or loan balances or to any combination of them.

(b) A credit union may enter into cooperative marketing arrangements to facilitate its members' voluntary purchase of insurance including, but not by way of limitation, life insurance, disability insurance, accident and health insurance, property insurance, liability insurance, and legal expense insurance.

(c) Insurance may be provided through any insurance company or through any subsidiary insurance company owned by the credit union. (1975, c. 538, s. 1; 2011-221, s. 2.)

§ 54-109.76. Liability insurance for officers.

A credit union may purchase and maintain liability insurance on behalf of any person who is or was a director, officer, employee, or agent of the credit union, or who is or was serving at the request of the credit union as a director, officer, employee, or agent of another corporation, partnership, joint venture, trust or other enterprise against any liability asserted against such person and incurred by such person in any such capacity or arising out of such person's status as such, whether or not the credit union would have the power to indemnify such person against such liability. (1975, c. 538, s. 1.)

§ 54-109.77. Group purchasing.

A credit union may enter into cooperative marketing arrangements to facilitate its members' voluntary purchase of such goods and services as are in the interest of improving economic and social conditions of the members. (1975, c. 538, s. 1.)

§ 54-109.78. Share and deposit insurance.

(a)   All credit unions established under this Chapter shall, no later than July 1, 1976, apply for insurance of member share and deposit accounts from any mutual deposit guaranty association which qualifies under Article 7A of Chapter 54 of the General Statutes (Mutual Deposit Guaranty Associations), or from the National Credit Union Administration under the Federal Credit Union Act. All such credit unions shall, on or before January 1, 1977, obtain and thereafter maintain the above-mentioned insurance. A credit union which is unable to obtain a commitment for insurance of the share and deposit accounts within the time limit specified above shall be dissolved by action of the Administrator of Credit Unions or permitted to merge with another credit union. Provided, the Administrator may grant additional time to obtain the insurance commitment, upon satisfactory evidence that the credit union has made or is making a substantial effort to achieve the conditions precedent to issuance of the commitment. Granting of additional time or times to obtain the insurance commitment shall not extend later than January 1, 1978.

(b)   All credit unions chartered under Articles 14A to 14L of this Chapter after ratification shall apply for and obtain insurance as a condition to granting the charter. (1975, c. 538, s. 1.)

§§ 54-109.79 through 54-109.81. Reserved for future codification purposes.

Article 14I.

Investments.

§ 54-109.82. Investment of funds.

The capital, deposits, undivided profits and reserve fund of the corporation may be invested only in any of the following ways:

(1) They may be lent to the members of the corporation in accordance with the provisions of this Chapter.

(2) In capital shares, obligations, or preferred stock issues of any agency, company, or association organized either as a stock company, mutual association, or membership corporation, provided the membership or stockholdings, as the case may be, of the agency, company, or association are confined or restricted to credit unions or organizations of credit unions, or provided the purpose for which the agency, company, or association is organized or designed is to service or otherwise assist credit union operations.

(3) In obligations of the State of North Carolina or any subdivision thereof.

(4) In obligations of the United States, including bonds and securities upon which payment of principal and interest is fully guaranteed by the United States.

(5) They may be deposited to the credit of the corporation in savings institutions, credit unions, or State banks or trust companies incorporated under the laws of the State, or in national banks located in the State.

(6) In loans to other credit unions in any amount not to exceed twenty-five percent (25%) of the shares and unimpaired surplus of the lending credit union.

(7) In an aggregate amount not to exceed twenty-five percent (25%) of the allocations to the reserve fund in any agency, company, or association of the

type described in subdivision (2) of this section provided the purposes of the agency, company, or association are designed to assist in establishing and maintaining liquidity, solvency, and security in credit union operations.

(8)   In the North Carolina Savings Guaranty Corporation.

(9)   In any form of investment allowed by law to the State Treasurer under G.S. 147-69.1. In addition, investment in corporate bonds that bear a minimum rating of A+ by at least one nationally recognized rating service is permissible. Credit unions shall monitor overall credit exposure by setting corporate bond investment limits as a percentage of assets.

(10)   Debentures issued by an agency of the United States government.

(11)   In the College Foundation in any amount not to exceed ten percent (10%) of the shares and unimpaired surplus of the investing credit union.

(12)   They may be deposited in any bank or savings institution insured by the federal government or any of its agencies. (1915, c. 115, s. 18; 1917, c. 232, ss. 2, 3; C.S., s. 5219; 1925, c. 73, ss. 12, 13, 14; 1935, c. 87; 1939, c. 400, s. 1; 1947, c. 781; 1965, c. 956, ss. 10, 11; 1969, c. 69, s. 1; 1973, c. 199, s. 4; c. 1255, s. 1; 1975, c. 538, s. 1; 1977, c. 559, s. 7; 1979, c. 467, s. 23; c. 809, s. 2; 1991, c. 651, s. 4; 1991 (Reg. Sess., 1992), c. 1030, s. 51.11; 2011-221, s. 3; 2013-132, s. 5.)

§§ 54-109.83 through 54-109.85. Reserved for future codification purposes.

Article 14J.

Reserve Allocations.

§ 54-109.86. Transfers to regular reserve.

(a)   At the end of each accounting period the gross income shall be determined. From this amount, there shall be set aside, as a regular reserve against losses on loans and against such other losses as may be specified in regulations prescribed pursuant to law, sums in accordance with the following schedule:

(1) A credit union in operation for more than four years and having assets of five hundred thousand dollars ($500,000) or more shall set aside

a. Ten per centum (10%) of gross income until the regular reserve shall equal four per centum (4%) of the total of outstanding loans and risk assets, then

b. Five per centum (5%) of gross income until the regular reserve shall equal six per centum (6%) of the total of outstanding loans and risk assets.

(2) A credit union in operation less than four years or having assets of less than five hundred thousand dollars ($500,000) shall set aside

a. Ten per centum (10%) of gross income until the regular reserve shall equal seven and one-half per centum (7 1/2%) of the total of outstanding loans and risk assets, then

b. Five per centum (5%) of gross income until the regular reserve shall equal ten per centum (10%) of the total outstanding loans and risk assets.

(3) Whenever the regular reserve falls below the stated per centum of the total of outstanding loans and risk assets, it shall be replenished by regular contributions in such amounts as may be determined by the Administrator to maintain the stated reserve goals.

(b) The Administrator, with the advice and consent of the Credit Union Commission, may increase or decrease the reserve requirement set forth in subsection (a) of this section when such an increase or decrease is deemed necessary or desirable in order to conform to the reserve requirements of federally chartered credit unions.

(c) In addition to such regular reserve, special reserves to protect the interests of members shall be established:

(1) When required by regulation; or

(2) When found by the Administrator, in any special case, to be necessary for that purpose.

(d) Nothing in this section shall be construed as limiting the amount that a credit union may set apart to its reserve fund. (1915, c. 115, s. 21; C.S., s. 5222; 1939, c. 400, s. 2; 1955, c. 1135, s. 1; 1969, c. 69, ss. 2, 10; 1975, c. 538, s. 1; 1979, c. 293; 1997-456, s. 27.)

§ 54-109.87. Use of regular reserve.

The regular reserve shall belong to the credit union and shall be used to meet losses except those resulting from an excess of expenses over income and shall not be distributed except on liquidation of the credit union, or in accordance with a plan approved by the Administrator of Credit Unions. (1975, c. 538, s. 1.)

§ 54-109.88. "Risk assets" defined.

For the purpose of establishing the reserves required by G.S. 54-109.86, all assets except the following shall be considered risk assets:

(1) Cash on hand.

(2) Deposits and shares in federal or State banks, savings and loan associations, and credit unions.

(3) Assets which are issued by, fully guaranteed as to principal and interest by, or due from the U.S. government, its agencies, Fannie Mae, or the Government National Mortgage Association.

(4) Loans to other credit unions.

(5) Loans to students insured under the provision of Title IV, Part B of the Higher Education Act of 1965 (20 U.S.C. 1071, et seq.) or similar state insurance programs.

(6)   Loans insured under Title I of the National Housing Act (12 U.S.C. 1703) by the Federal Housing Administration.

(7)   Shares or deposits in central credit unions organized under Article 14I of this Chapter of any other State act or of the Federal Credit Union Act.

(8)   Common trust investments which deal in investments authorized by Articles 14A to 14L of this Chapter.

(9)   Prepaid expenses.

(10)   Accrued interest on nonrisk investments.

(11)   Furniture and equipment.

(12)   Land and buildings.

(13)   Loans secured by shares.

(14)   Deposits in mutual savings guaranty associations which qualify under Article 7A of Chapter 54 of the General Statutes.

(15)   Investments in the College Foundation. (1975, c. 538, s. 1; 1977, c. 559, s. 8; 2001-487, s. 14(c).)

§§ 54-109.89 through 54-109.91. Reserved for future codification purposes.

Article 14K.

Change in Corporate Status.

§ 54-109.92. Suspension and conservation.

(a)   The Administrator of Credit Unions may determine in the performance of his duties under this Subchapter that a credit union is insolvent or in imminent danger of insolvency, or that an officer, director, or employee of a credit union, or the credit union itself, acting by and through an officer, director, or employee, has:

(1) Affected or is likely to affect the safety or soundness of the credit union by a violation of:

a. This Subchapter,

b. A rule adopted under this Subchapter, or

c. Any federal law or regulation applicable to credit unions;

(2) Violated, neglected, or refused to comply with a duly issued final order of the Administrator of Credit Unions or the Credit Union Commission;

(3) Refused to submit to examination under oath, or to permit examination of the credit union's books, papers, records, accounts, and affairs by the Administrator of Credit Unions or his duly authorized representative;

(4) Failed or refused to authorize and direct any other person to permit the inspection and examination of the credit union's books, papers, records, or accounts in the other person's care, possession, custody, or control by the Administrator of Credit Unions or a duly authorized representative of the Administrator, after the Administrator has requested the granting of that authority and direction to the other person; or

(5) Affected or is likely to affect the safety or soundness of the credit union by conducting the credit union's business in an unauthorized or unlawful manner.

(b) If the Administrator of Credit Unions makes any of these findings, he may issue an order temporarily suspending the credit union's operations for not more than 90 days or, if the Administrator determines that the findings are of such severity that immediate affirmative action is needed to prevent further dissipation of the assets of the credit union, the Administrator may immediately issue an order of conservation and appoint a conservator to manage the affairs of the credit union. Service of the order of suspension or the order of conservation must be by certified or registered mail, addressed to the credit union at the last known address of its principal office, or by delivery to an officer or director of the credit union. Service by mail is complete upon the deposit of the paper, enclosed in a postpaid, properly addressed wrapper, in a post office or official depository under the care and custody of the United States Postal Service. The order must clearly state the grounds for suspension or conservation.

(c) After a conservation order has been served on the credit union, the Administrator of Credit Unions shall take possession and control of the books, records, property, assets, and business of the credit union. Upon the service of the suspension order, the credit union shall cease all operations, except those authorized by the Administrator and conducted under his supervision. Not later than 15 days after the date an order of suspension or conservation is served, the board of directors shall file a written reply to the order. They may file a written request for a hearing to present to the Administrator a plan to continue operations under the control of the board of directors setting out proposed corrective actions. Under an order of suspension, the board of directors may request that a conservator be appointed for the credit union or that the credit union be closed or merged or that a liquidating agent be appointed, and may waive rights to further appeal. In that event, the Administrator may immediately appoint a conservator, or order that the credit union be liquidated and appoint a liquidating agent. Under an order of conservation, the board of directors may consent to the conservatorship and waive rights to further appeals.

(d) If the board of directors files its reply and requests a hearing as provided by subsection (c), the Administrator of Credit Unions shall set and hold the hearing not less than 10 nor more than 30 days after the date of receipt of such a request. Not later than 10 days before the hearing, the Administrator shall give notice to the credit union of the date, time, and place of the hearing. Not later than 10 days after the earlier of the date of conclusion of the hearing or the date on which the suspension expires, the Administrator shall (i) adopt the plan to continue operations under the control of the board of directors presented by the credit union, (ii) agree with the credit union on an alternative plan to continue operations under the control of the board of directors or other appropriate measures, (iii) reject the plan to continue operations under the control of the board of directors and issue an order of conservation appointing a conservator, (iv) continue a previous order of conservation, or (v) issue an order of liquidation ordering that the credit union be closed, ordering that its affairs and business be liquidated, and appointing a liquidating agent.

(e) If the Administrator of Credit Unions rejects the credit union's plan to continue operations and determines that it is in the public interest and in the best interest of the members, depositors, and creditors of the credit union to rehabilitate the credit union, he may permit the credit union to operate under his direction and control, and shall issue an order of conservation appointing a conservator to manage the affairs of the credit union. The Administrator shall serve the order of conservation in the same manner as provided for service of an order of suspension.

(f) The conservator, on behalf and under the supervision and direction of the Administrator of Credit Unions, shall take charge of the books, records, property, assets, and business of the credit union and shall conduct the business and affairs of the credit union under the direction and supervision of the Administrator. The conservator shall take steps toward the removal of the causes and conditions that have necessitated the order that the Administrator directs. During the conservatorship, the conservator shall make reports to the Administrator from time to time as the Administrator requires. The conservator shall take all necessary measures to preserve, protect, and recover the assets or property of the credit union, including claims or causes of action belonging to or that may be asserted by the credit union. In addition, the conservator may deal with that property in his own name as conservator and may file, prosecute, or defend against a suit by or against the credit union if the conservator considers this action necessary to protect the interested parties or property affected by the suit.

(g) The Administrator of Credit Unions shall determine the cost incident to the conservatorship. The cost is a charge against the assets and funds of the credit union, and shall be paid as the Administrator directs.

(h) A suit filed against a credit union or its conservator while a conservatorship order is in effect must be brought in a court of proper jurisdiction in Wake County. The conservator may file suit in a court of proper jurisdiction in Wake County against any person for the purpose of preserving, protecting, or recovering assets or property of the credit union, including a claim or cause of action belonging to or that may be asserted by the credit union.

(i) The conservator shall serve for the period necessary to accomplish the purposes of conservatorship consistent with the intent of this section. If the credit union is rehabilitated, it shall be returned to the management of the board of directors under the terms that are reasonable and necessary to prevent recurrence of the conditions that occasioned the conservatorship.

(j) If the Administrator of Credit Unions determines that the credit union in conservatorship is not in a condition to continue business and cannot be rehabilitated as provided by this section, he shall issue, as he deems appropriate, either an order of merger or an order of liquidation, appointing a liquidating agent.

(k)   If, after a hearing under this section, the board of directors of the credit union is dissatisfied with the decision of the Administrator of Credit Unions, the board may appeal to the Credit Union Commission by filing with the Administrator a written appeal, including a duly certified resolution of the board, not later than 10 days after the day that the Administrator's order is served. If the appeal is duly filed, the Administrator shall set a date for a hearing on the appeal not more than 30 days after the date on which the appeal is filed. The Administrator shall promptly give notice of the date, time, and place of the hearing to the credit union and any other interested party. The filing of an appeal does not suspend the effect of the order of the conservation and this order remains in force pending final disposition of the appeal by the Commission. At the conclusion of the hearing, the Commission may reverse the order of the Administrator and adopt and approve the credit union's plan to continue operations, affirm the Administrator's order of conservation, or order that other appropriate action be taken.

(l)   If the board of directors of the credit union does not file a reply to the order of suspension or an order of conservation as required by this section or fails to request and appear at the hearing provided for by this section, the Administrator of Credit Unions may dispose of the matter as he considers appropriate. The credit union is presumed to have consented to the action and may not contest it.

(m)   The period of suspension and the date and time of the hearings provided for by this section may be extended by agreement of the parties and the Administrator of Credit Unions.

(n)   The Administrator of Credit Unions shall notify the members of the Credit Union Commission of any suspension. (1975, c. 538, s. 1; 1977, c. 559, s. 9; 1989, c. 72.)

§ 54-109.93. Liquidation.

(a)   A credit union may elect to dissolve voluntarily and liquidate its affairs in the manner prescribed in this section.

(b) The board of directors shall adopt a resolution recommending the credit union be dissolved voluntarily, and directing that the question of liquidation be submitted to the members.

(c) Within 10 days after the board of directors decides to submit the question of liquidation to the members, the president shall notify the Administrator of Credit Unions thereof in writing, setting forth the reasons for the proposed action. Within 10 days after the members act on the question of liquidation, the president shall notify the Administrator in writing as to whether or not the members approved the proposed liquidation.

(d) As soon as the board of directors decides to submit the question of liquidation to the members, payment on shares, withdrawal of shares, making any transfer of shares to loans and interest, making investments of any kind, and granting loans shall be suspended pending action by members on the proposal to liquidate. On approval by the members of such proposal, all such business transactions shall be permanently discontinued. Necessary expenses of operation shall, however, continue to be paid on authorization of the board of directors or liquidating agent during the period of liquidation.

(e) For a credit union to enter voluntary liquidation, approval by a majority of the members in writing or by a two-thirds majority of the members present at a regular or special meeting of the members is required. Where authorization for liquidation is to be obtained at a meeting of the members, notice in writing shall be given to each member, by first-class mail, at least 10 days prior to such meeting.

(f) A liquidating credit union shall continue in existence for the purpose of discharging its debts, collecting and distributing its assets, and doing all acts required in order to wind up its business and may sue and be sued for the purpose of enforcing such debts and obligations until its affairs are fully adjusted.

(g) The board of directors or the liquidating agent shall use the assets of the credit union to pay: first, expenses incidental to liquidating including any surety bond that may be required; second, any liability due nonmembers; third, deposits and special purpose thrift accounts as provided in Articles 14A to 14L of this Chapter. Assets then remaining shall be distributed to the members proportionately to the shares held by each member as of the date dissolution was voted.

(h) As soon as the board of directors or the liquidating agent determines that all assets from which there is a reasonable expectancy of realization have been liquidated and distributed as set forth in this section, the Administrator of Credit Unions shall issue to such corporation, in duplicate, a certificate of dissolution which shall be filed by the corporation in the office of the register of deeds of the county in which the corporation has its place of business. The corporation shall then be dissolved and its certificate of incorporation revoked. All pertinent books and records of the liquidating credit union shall be retained by the liquidating agent and/or filed with the Credit Union Division and kept for a minimum period not to exceed five years. The liquidating agent's fee, if any, shall be set by the Administrator of Credit Unions. (1915, c. 115, s. 24; C.S., s. 5224; 1925, c. 73, ss. 3, 15; 1935, c. 87; 1957, c. 989, s. 4; 1965, c. 956, s. 1; 1967, c. 823, s. 11; 1975, c. 538, s. 1.)

§ 54-109.94. Merger.

Any credit union may, with the approval of the Administrator of Credit Unions, merge with another credit union subject to the rules and regulations set forth by the Administrator of Credit Unions. (1975, c. 538, s. 1.)

§ 54-109.95. Conversion of charter.

(a) A credit union chartered under the laws of this State may be converted to a credit union chartered under the laws of any other state or under the laws of the United States, subject to regulations issued by the Administrator of the Credit Union Division.

(b) A credit union chartered under the laws of the United States or of any other state may convert to a credit union chartered under the laws of this State. To effect such a conversion, a credit union must comply with all the requirements of the jurisdiction under which it was originally chartered and the requirements of the Administrator of Credit Unions and file proof of such compliance with said Administrator. (1965, c. 956, s. 9; 1975, c. 538, s. 1.)

§§ 54-109.96 through 54-109.98. Reserved for future codification purposes.

Article 14L.

Taxation.

§ 54-109.99. Restriction of taxation.

The corporation shall be deemed an institution for savings, and together with all accumulations therein shall not be taxable under any law which shall exempt building and loan associations or institutions for savings from taxation; nor shall any law passed taxing corporations in any form, or the shares thereof, or the accumulations therein, be deemed to include corporations doing business in pursuance of the provisions of this Article, unless they are specifically named in such law. The shares of credit unions, being hereby regarded as a system for saving, shall not be subject to any stock-transfer tax either when issued by the corporation or transferred from one member to another. (1915, c. 115, s. 26; C.S., s. 5225; 1925, c. 73, ss. 3, 16; 1935, c. 87; 1975, c. 538, s. 1.)

§§ 54-109.100 through 54-109.104. Reserved for future codification purposes.

Article 14M.

Confidential Information.

§ 54-109.105. What information deemed confidential; disclosure; certain information deemed public; exchange of information.

(a) The following records of information of the credit union division, the Administrator or the agent(s) of either shall be confidential and shall not be disclosed:

(1) Information obtained or compiled in preparation of, during, or as a result of an examination, audit or investigation of any credit union;

(2) Information reflecting the specific collateral given by a named borrower, or specific withdrawable accounts held by a named member;

(3) Information obtained, prepared or compiled during or as a result of an examination, audit or investigation of any credit union by an agency of the United States, if the records would be confidential under federal law or regulation;

(4) Information and reports submitted by credit unions to federal regulatory agencies, if the records or information would be confidential under federal law or regulation;

(5) Information and records regarding complaints from the members received by the division which concern credit unions when the complaint would or could result in an investigation, except to the management of those credit unions;

(6) Any other letters, reports, memoranda, recordings, charts or other documents or records which would disclose any information of which disclosure is prohibited in this subsection.

(b) A court of competent jurisdiction may order the disclosure of specific information.

(c) The information contained in an application for a new credit union shall be deemed to be public information.

(d) Nothing in this Article shall prevent the exchange of information relating to credit unions and the business thereof with the representatives of the agencies of this State, other states, or of the United States, or with reserve or insuring agencies for credit unions. Nothing in this Article shall prevent the Administrator, in his discretion, from disclosing pertinent information relating to a credit union and the business thereof with directors, officers, or members of the credit union. The private business and affairs of an individual or company shall not be disclosed by any person employed by the credit union division, or by any person with whom information is exchanged under the authority of this subsection.

(e) Any official or employee violating this section shall be liable to any person injured by disclosure of such confidential information for all damages sustained thereby. Penalties provided shall not be exclusive of other penalties.

(f) The willful or knowing violation of the provisions of this Article by any employee of the credit union division shall be a Class 1 misdemeanor. (1981, c. 512; 1993, c. 539, s. 429; 1994, Ex. Sess., c. 24, s. 14(c).)

Article 14N.

Foreign Credit Unions.

§ 54-109.106. Foreign Credit Unions.

(a) A credit union organized under the laws of another state or territory of the United States may conduct business as a credit union in this State with the approval of the Administrator, provided credit unions incorporated under Articles 14A through 14M of this Chapter are allowed to do business in the other state under conditions similar to these provisions. Before granting the approval, the Administrator must find that the foreign credit union:

(1) Is a credit union organized under laws similar to Articles 14A through 14M of this Chapter;

(2) Is financially solvent;

(3) Has account insurance through the federal government or any agency thereof;

(4) Is examined and supervised by a regulatory agency of the state in which it is organized;

(5) Will serve a field of membership not being served in this State or to adequately serve its members in this State;

(6) Operation by the credit union will not have adverse impact on the financial, economic or other interests of residents of this State.

(b) No foreign credit union may conduct business in this State unless it:

(1) Makes loans at such terms allowed under the provisions of Article 14G of this Chapter;

(2)   Complies with the rules and regulations applicable to credit unions incorporated under Articles 14A through 14M of this Chapter;

(3)   Agrees to furnish the Administrator a copy of the report of examination of its regulatory agency and such other documents or reports as may be requested or to submit to an examination as the Administrator deems necessary;

(4)   Designates and maintains an agent for the service of process in this State.

(c)   The Administrator may deny or revoke approval of a credit union to conduct business in this State if the Administrator finds that:

(1)   The credit union fails to meet the requirements of subsection (a);

(2)   The credit union fails to comply with the laws of this State or lawful rules or orders issued by the Administrator;

(3)   The credit union has engaged in a pattern of unsafe or unsound credit union practices. (1991, c. 271.)

Article 15.

Central Associations.

§ 54-110: Recodified as §§ 54-110.1 through 54-110.10.

Article 15A.

Corporate Credit Union.

§ 54-110.1. Definition and purposes.

(a)   A corporate credit union may be incorporated under this Article and shall be subject to all parts of this Chapter not inconsistent with this Article.

(b) A corporate credit union is a cooperative nonprofit association whose members consist primarily of other credit unions and whose purposes are:

(1) To accumulate and prudently manage the liquidity of its member credit unions through interlending and investment services;

(2) To act as an intermediary for credit union funds between members and other corporate credit unions;

(3) To obtain liquid funds from other credit union organizations, financial intermediaries, and other sources;

(4) To foster and promote in cooperation with other state, regional, and national corporate credit unions and credit union organizations or associations the economic security, growth and development of member credit unions; and

(5) To perform such other financial services of benefit to its members which are authorized by the Administrator of Credit Unions. (1983, c. 470.)

§ 54-110.2. Membership.

(a) Membership in the corporate credit union shall be institutional and be limited to the subscribers to the articles of incorporation, credit unions organized under Chapter 54 of the General Statutes, the Federal Credit Union Act or any other credit union act, organizations or associations of credit unions, and such other persons or organizations provided for in the articles of incorporation unless the bylaws otherwise prescribe.

(b) The board of directors of each credit union, organization or association becoming a member of the corporate credit union shall designate one person to be a voting representative in the corporate credit union. Such voting representatives shall be eligible to hold office in the corporate credit union as if such person were himself a member of the corporate credit union. (1983, c. 470.)

§ 54-110.3. Charter and name exclusive.

Only one corporate credit union shall be incorporated under this Article; and no other credit union may use the term "corporate credit union" as a part of its name. (1983, c. 470.)

§ 54-110.4. Organization.

(a) Application to form a corporate credit union shall be made in writing to the Administrator of Credit Unions. The application shall contain the names of at least 15 credit unions which have agreed to subscribe to shares in the corporate credit union at the time the application is made.

(b) The application shall be accompanied by articles of incorporation, bylaws, and articles of association or other appropriate documents.

(c) The bylaws shall provide for the selection of a board of directors of a least five members and shall require credit unions applying for membership to subscribe to shares in a minimum amount as specified in the bylaws. (1983, c. 470.)

§ 54-110.5. Powers and privileges.

(a) A corporate credit union shall enjoy the powers and privileges of any other credit union incorporated under Chapter 54 of the General Statutes in addition to those powers enumerated in this Article, notwithstanding any limitations or restrictions found elsewhere in this Article.

(b) A corporate credit union may:

(1) Accept shares or deposits in any form from its members, other state, regional or national corporate credit unions, and credit union organizations or associations;

(2) Make loans to its members and other credit unions and other State, regional or national corporate credit unions, organizations and associations of credit unions;

(3) Establish lines of credit for members and participate with other credit unions in making loans to its members under the terms and conditions determined by the board of directors;

(4) Invest in the shares of or make deposits in credit unions;

(5) Buy and sell any form of marketable debt obligations of domestic or foreign corporations or of federal, state or local government units;

(6) Borrow from any source without limitation, accept demand deposits from any source and issue notes or debentures;

(7) Acquire or sell the assets and assume the liabilities of a member; and

(8) Enter into agreements with credit unions to discount or purchase loans made pursuant to government-guaranteed loan programs, real estate loans made by members or any obligations of the United States or any agency thereof held by members.

(c) A corporate credit union shall not be taxable under any law which shall exempt any other credit union.

(d) The board of directors shall meet at least quarterly and shall have the general direction and control of the affairs of the corporation.

(e) The corporate credit union may exercise such incidental powers or privileges conferred upon a federal corporate credit union. (1983, c. 470.)

§ 54-110.6. Participation in central system.

The corporate credit union may enter into agreements for the purpose of participation in any state or federal central liquidity facility or central financial system for credit unions, and for the purpose of aiding credit unions in establishing concentrated lines of credit with other financial institutions and act as a depositor and transmitter of funds to carry out such agreements. (1983, c. 470.)

§ 54-110.7. Right of set-off; security interest.

(a) The corporate credit union shall have a right of immediate set-off against the balances of the share and deposit accounts of each member for any amounts due from the member to the corporate credit union.

(b) The corporate credit union shall have a lien on all share and deposit accounts of each member in the amount of the total indebtedness of the member to the corporate credit union. The lien created herein shall attach to such accounts and be effective whenever the member is indebted to the corporate credit union. The lien shall have priority over any interests of all members and unsecured creditors of the member credit unions of the corporate credit union.

(c) The board of directors or credit committee may require and accept additional security for loans to a member in the form of a pledge, assignment, hypothecation or mortgage of any assets of the member or a guarantor. (1983, c. 470.)

§ 54-110.8. Fees.

The operating fees established by the Administrator of Credit Unions shall make allowances for the special purposes and operations of a corporate credit union. (1983, c. 470.)

§ 54-110.9. Reserves.

A corporate credit union shall be exempt from the regular reserve requirements of Article 14J, but shall be required to establish and maintain an equity reserve to meet losses, in accordance with regulations prescribed by the Administrator of Credit Unions. (1983, c. 470.)

§ 54-110.10. Applicability of Article.

Nothing in this Article shall be construed as affecting the status of a central association formed prior to the enactment of this Article pursuant to former G.S. 54-110. For the purposes of this Article, the corporate credit union authorized by G.S. 54-110.3 shall be the central association in existence on June 8, 1983. (1983, c. 470.)

SUBCHAPTER IV. COOPERATIVE ASSOCIATIONS.

Article 16.

Organization of Associations.

§ 54-111. Nature of the association.

Any number of persons, not less than five, may associate themselves as a mutual association, society, company, or exchange, for the purpose of conducting any agricultural, housing (including apartment housing), horticultural, forestry, dairy, mercantile, mining, manufacturing, telephone, electric light, power, storage, refrigeration, flume, irrigation, water, sewerage, or mechanical business, or purchase, maintain and use fire-fighting equipment, or for any other lawful purpose, on the mutual plan. For the purposes of this Subchapter, the words association, company, corporation, exchange, society, or union shall be construed to mean the same; provided that the membership of agricultural organizations incorporated under this Subchapter shall consist of producers of agricultural products, handled by such organizations or by organizations owned and controlled by such producers. (1915, c. 144, s. 1; C.S., s. 5242; 1925, c. 179, ss. 1, 2; 1931, c. 447; 1949, c. 1042, ss. 1, 2(a); 1955, c. 746, s. 1; 1959, c. 991; 1985, c. 542, s. 1.)

§ 54-111.1. Repealed by Session Laws 1959, c. 991.

§ 54-112. Use of term restricted.

No corporation or association hereafter organized or doing business for profit in this State shall be entitled to use the term "mutual" as part of its corporate or other business name or title, unless it has complied with the provisions of this Subchapter; and any corporation or association violating the provisions of this section may be enjoined from doing business under such name at the instance of any shareholder of any association legally organized under this Subchapter. (1915, c. 144, s. 18; C.S., s. 5243; 1925, c. 179, s. 1; 1945, c. 635.)

§ 54-113. Articles of agreement.

The persons desiring to organize such association shall sign and acknowledge written articles which shall contain the name of the association and the names and residences of the persons forming the same. Such articles shall also contain a statement of the purposes of the association and shall designate the city, town, or village where its principal place of business shall be located. The articles shall also state the amount of authorized capital stock, the number of shares authorized, and the par value of each. No shareholder in any corporation organized under this Subchapter shall be personally liable for any debt of the corporation. (1915, c. 144, s. 2; C.S., s. 5244; 1985, c. 542, s. 2.)

§ 54-114. Certificate of incorporation.

The original articles of incorporation of corporations organized under this Subchapter, or a true copy thereof, verified as such by the affidavits of two of the signers thereof, shall be filed with the Secretary of State. A like verified copy of such articles and certificate of the Secretary of State, showing the date when such articles were filed with and accepted by the Secretary of State, within 30 days of such filing and acceptance, shall be filed with and recorded by the register of deeds of the county in which the principal place of business of the corporation is to be located, and no corporation shall, until such articles be left for record, have legal existence. The register of deeds shall forthwith transmit to the Secretary of State a certificate stating the time when such copy was recorded. Upon a receipt of such certificate, the Secretary of State shall issue a certificate of incorporation. (1915, c. 144, s. 3; C.S., s. 5245; 1967, c. 823, s. 12.)

§ 54-115. Fees for incorporation.

(10) The manner in which the reserve fund shall be accumulated.

(11) The manner in which the dividends shall be determined and paid to members.

(12) Associations, societies, companies or exchanges, organized hereunder to engage in the telephone or electric light business upon a mutual basis, shall adopt a bylaw limiting the patrons and subscribers to members of the association.

(13) In the case of apartment housing, regulations governing the rental of apartments. (1915, c. 144, s. 5; C.S., s. 5247; 1925, c. 179, s. 4; 1959, c. 991.)

§ 54-117. General corporation law or general nonprofit corporation law applied; dealing in products of, or renting to, nonmembers.

All mutual associations shall be maintained in accordance with the general corporation law or general nonprofit corporation law, except as otherwise provided for in this Subchapter. And no corporation or association hereafter organized under this Subchapter for doing business in this State shall be permitted to deal in the products of nonmembers to an amount greater in value than such as are handled by it for members: Provided, no housing corporation or association hereafter organized under this Subchapter shall be permitted to rent to nonmembers for a period longer than 90 days. (1915, c. 144, s. 17; C.S., s. 5248; 1925, c. 179, s. 1; 1931, c. 447, s. 2; 1949, c. 1042, s. 2(b); 1985, c. 542, s. 3.)

§ 54-118. Other corporations admitted.

All mutual corporations, companies, or associations heretofore organized and doing business under other incorporation statutes, or which have attempted to so organize and do business, shall have the benefit of all of the provisions of this Subchapter, and be bound thereby on filing with the Secretary of State a written declaration, signed and sworn to by the president and secretary, to the effect that the mutual company or association has by a majority vote of its shareholders decided to accept the benefits of and to be bound by the provisions of this Subchapter. No association organized under this Subchapter shall be required to do or perform anything not specifically required herein, in order to become a corporation. (1915, c. 144, s. 16; C.S., s. 5249; 1925, c. 179, s. 1; 1985, c. 542, s. 4.)

§ 54-118.1. License taxes.

On and after June 1, 1955, the provisions of Article 2, Subchapter I of Chapter 105 of the General Statutes of North Carolina shall apply to an association or corporation organized under the provisions of this Subchapter. (1955, c. 1313, s. 1.)

§ 54-118.2. Franchise taxes.

On and after July 1, 1955, the provisions of Article 3, Subchapter I of Chapter 105 of the General Statutes of North Carolina shall apply to an association or corporation organized under the provisions of this Subchapter. (1955, c. 1313, s. 1.)

Article 17.

Stockholders and Officers.

§ 54-119. Certificate for stock fully paid.

Certificates of stock shall not be issued to any subscriber until fully paid, but the bylaws of the association may allow subscribers to vote as shareholders: Provided, part of the stock subscribed for has been paid in cash. (1915, c. 144, s. 11; C.S., s. 5250.)

§ 54-120. Ownership of shares limited.

No shareholder in any such association shall own shares of a greater aggregate par value than twenty percent (20%) of the paid-in capital stock, except as hereinafter provided, or be entitled to more than one vote. A mutual association shall reserve the right of purchasing the stock of any member whose stock is for sale, and may restrict the transfer of stock to such persons as are made eligible to membership in the bylaws. (1915, c. 144, s. 9; C.S., s. 5251; 1925, c. 179, s. 1.)

§ 54-121. Shares issued on purchase of business.

Whenever an association, created under this Subchapter, shall purchase the business of another association or person, it may pay for the same in whole or in part by issuing to the selling association or persons shares of its capital stock to an amount which at par value would equal the fair market value of the business so purchased, and in such case the transfer to the association of such business at such valuation shall be equivalent to payment in cash for the shares of stock so issued. (1915, c. 144, s. 10; C.S., s. 5252.)

§ 54-122. Absent members voting.

At any regularly called general or special meeting of the shareholders a written vote received by mail from any absent shareholder, and signed by him, may be read in such meeting, and shall be equivalent to a vote of such of the shareholders so signing: Provided, he has been previously notified in writing of the exact motion or resolution upon which such vote is taken, and a copy of same is forwarded with and attached to the vote so mailed by him. In case of sickness or other unavoidable absence of a member, he shall be allowed to vote by proxy in writing; but no member shall vote more than one such proxy. (1915, c. 144, s. 12; C.S., s. 5253.)

§ 54-123. Directors and other officers.

Every such association shall be managed by a board of not less than five directors. The directors shall be elected by and from the stockholders of the association at such time and for such term of office as the bylaws may prescribe, and shall hold office for the time for which elected and until their successors are elected and shall enter upon the discharge of such duties as are prescribed in the bylaws; but a majority of the stockholders shall have the power at any regular or special stockholders' meeting, legally called, to remove any director or officer for cause, and fill the vacancy, and thereupon the director or officer so removed shall cease to be a director or officer of the association. The officers of every such association shall be a president, one or more vice-presidents, a secretary and treasurer, who shall be elected annually by the directors, and each of the officers must be a director of the association. The office of secretary and treasurer may be combined, and when so combined the person filling the office shall be secretary-treasurer. (1915, c. 144, s. 6; C.S., s. 5254.)

Article 18.

Powers and Duties.

§ 54-124. Nature of business authorized.

An association created under this Subchapter shall have power to conduct any agricultural, housing, horticultural, forestry, dairy, mercantile, mining, manufacturing, telephone, electric light, power, storage, refrigeration, flume, irrigation, water, sewerage, or mechanical business, or purchase, maintain and use fire-fighting equipment, or conduct any other lawful business, on the mutual plan. (1915, c. 144, s. 8; C.S., s. 5255; 1925, c. 179, ss. 1, 3; 1949, c. 1042, s. 2; 1955, c. 746, s. 2; 1985, c. 542, s. 5.)

§ 54-125. Amendment of articles.

The association may amend its articles of incorporation by a majority vote of its shareholders at any regular shareholders' meeting, or any special shareholders' meeting called for that purpose, on 10 days' notice to the shareholders. The power to amend shall include the power to increase or diminish the amount of capital stock and the number of shares: Provided, the amount of the capital stock shall not be diminished below the amount of the paid-up capital at the time the amendment is adopted. Within 30 days after the adoption of an amendment to its articles of incorporation, an association shall cause a copy of such amendment adopted to be recorded in the office of the Secretary of State and of the register of deeds of the county where the principal place of business is located. (1915, c. 144, s. 7; C.S., s. 5256; 1967, c. 823, s. 14.)

§ 54-126. Apportionment of earnings.

The net earnings or losses shall be apportioned among the members in accordance with the ratio which each member's patronage during the period involved bears to total patronage by all members during the period. "Patronage" means amount of purchases, sales, business, labor, wages or other similar criteria. (1915, c. 144, s. 13; C.S., s. 5257; 1925, c. 179, s. 5; 1985, c. 542, s. 6.)

§ 54-127. Time of allocation.

The profits or net earnings of such association shall be allocated to those entitled thereto, at such times as the bylaws shall prescribe, which shall be as often as once in 12 months. (1915, c. 144, s. 14; C.S., s. 5258; 1985, c. 542, s. 7.)

§ 54-128. Annual reports.

Every association organized under the provisions of this Subchapter shall annually, on or before the first day of March of each year, make a report to the Secretary of State; such report shall contain the name of the company, its principal place of business in this State, and generally a statement as to its business, showing total amount of business transacted, amount of capital stock subscribed for and paid in, number of shareholders, total expenses of operation, amount of indebtedness or liabilities, and its profits and losses. A copy of such report shall also be filed with the division of markets in the Department of Agriculture and Consumer Services. (1915, c. 144, s. 15; C.S., s. 5259; 1997-261, s. 109.)

subchapter v. marketing associations.

Article 19.

Purpose and Organization.

§ 54-129. Declaration of policy.

In order to promote, foster, and encourage the intelligent and orderly producing and marketing of agricultural products through cooperation, and to eliminate speculation and waste, and to make the distribution of agricultural products as direct as can be efficiently done between producer and consumer, and to stabilize the marketing problems of agricultural products, this Subchapter is enacted. (1921, c. 87, s. 1; C.S., s. 5259(a); 1935, c. 230, s. 1.)

§ 54-130. Definitions and nature.

As used in this Subchapter-

(1) Agricultural Products. - The term "agricultural products" shall include horticultural, viticultural, forestry, dairy, livestock, poultry, bee, and any farm products.

(2) Association. - The term "association" means

a. Any corporation organized under this Subchapter; or

b. Any foreign corporation which

1. Is organized under any general or special act of another state or the District of Columbia as a cooperative association for the mutual benefit of its members and other patrons,

2. Confines its operations in this State to the purposes specified in, and restricts the return on the stock or membership capital and the amount of its business with nonmembers to the limits placed thereon by, this Subchapter for corporations organized hereunder, and

3. Is authorized to transact business in this State pursuant to G.S. 54-139.

(3) Charter. - The term "charter" includes the original articles of incorporation, together with all amendments thereto and articles of merger or consolidation.

(4) Member. - The term "member" shall include actual members of associations without capital stock and holders of stock in associations organized with capital stock.

(5) Person. - The term "person" shall include individuals, firms, partnerships, corporations, and associations.

Associations organized or domesticated hereunder shall be deemed nonprofit, inasmuch as they are not organized to make profits for themselves, as such, or for their members, as such, but only for their members as producers.

This Subchapter shall be referred to as the "Cooperative Marketing Act." (1921, c. 87, s. 2; C.S., s. 5259(b); 1935, c. 436, s. 1; 1963, c. 1168, ss. 1-3.)

§ 54-131. Who may organize.

Three or more persons engaged in the production of agricultural products may form a nonprofit, cooperative association, with or without capital stock, under the provisions of this Subchapter. (1921, c. 87, s. 3; C.S., s. 5259(c); 1979, c. 908, s. 1.)

§ 54-132. Purposes.

An association may be organized to engage in any activity in connection with the producing, marketing or selling of the agricultural products of its members and other farmers, or with the harvesting, preserving, drying, processing, canning, packing, storing, handling, shipping, or utilization thereof, of the manufacturing or marketing of the by-products thereof; or in connection with the manufacturing, selling, or supplying to its members of machinery, equipment, or supplies; or in the financing of the above-enumerated activities; or in any one or more of the activities specified herein. (1921, c. 87, s. 4; C.S., s. 5259(d); 1933, c. 350, s. 2; 1935, c. 230, s. 2.)

§ 54-133. Preliminary investigation.

Every group of persons contemplating the organization of an association under this Subchapter is urged to communicate with the Chief of the Division of Markets, who will inform it whatever a survey of the marketing conditions affecting the commodities to be handled by the proposed association indicates regarding probable success. (1921, c. 87, s. 5; C.S., s. 5259(e).)

§ 54-134. Articles of incorporation.

Each association formed under this Subchapter must prepare and file articles of incorporation, setting forth:

(1)   The name of the association.

(2)   The purposes for which it is formed.

(3)   The place where its principal business will be transacted.

(4)   The period of duration, which may be perpetual. When the articles of incorporation fail to state the period of duration, it shall be considered perpetual. Any association heretofore or hereafter organized for a period less than perpetual, may by amendment to its articles of incorporation, extend the period of its duration for a specified period or perpetually.

(5)   The names and addresses of those who are to serve as directors for the first term or until the election of their successors.

(6)   If organized without capital stock, whether the property rights and interest of each member shall be equal or unequal; and if unequal, the article shall set forth the general rule or rules applicable to all members by which the property rights and interests, respectively, of each member may and shall be determined and fixed; and this association shall have the power to admit new members who shall be entitled to share in the property of the association with the old members in accordance with such general rule or rules. This provision of the articles of incorporation shall not be altered, amended, or repealed except by the written consent or the vote of three-fourths of the members.

(7)   If organized with capital stock, the amount of such stock and the number of such shares into which it is divided and the par value thereof. The capital stock may be divided into preferred and common stock. If so divided, the articles of incorporation must contain a statement of the number of shares of stock to which preference is granted and the number of shares of stock to which no preference is granted and the nature and extent of the preference and the privileges granted to each.

In addition to the foregoing, the petition for articles of incorporation may contain any provision consistent with law with respect to management, regulation, government, financing, indebtedness, membership, the establishment of voting districts and the election of delegates for representative purposes, the issuance, retirement and transfer of its stock, if formed with capital stock, or any provisions relative to the way or manner in which it shall operate with respect to its members, officers, or directors, and any other provisions relating to its affairs; provided that nothing set forth in this paragraph shall be construed as limiting any of the rights or powers otherwise given to such associations.

The articles must be subscribed by the incorporators and acknowledged by one of them before an officer authorized by the law of this State to take and certify acknowledgments of deeds and conveyances; and shall be filed as provided in G.S. 55A-4; and when so filed the said articles of incorporation, or certified copies thereof, shall be received in all the courts of this State, and other places, as prima facie evidence of the facts contained therein, and of the due incorporation of such association. A certified copy of the articles of incorporation shall also be filed with the Chief of the Division of Markets. (1921, c. 87, s. 8; C.S., s. 5259(f); 1935, c. 230, ss. 3, 4; 1963, c. 1168, ss. 4, 5; 1979, c. 908, s. 2.)

§ 54-135. Amendments to articles of incorporation.

(a)   An association may amend its charter from time to time in any and as many respects as may be desired, so long as its charter as amended contains only such provisions as are lawful under this Subchapter.

(b)   Amendments to the charter shall be made as follows: The board of directors shall by a vote of not less than two-thirds of all of the members of the board, adopt a resolution approving the proposed amendment or amendments and directing that the proposed amendment or amendments be submitted to a vote at a meeting of members, which may be either an annual or a special meeting. Written or printed notice setting forth the proposed amendment or amendments, or a summary of the changes to be effected thereby shall be given to each member entitled to vote at such meeting, within the time and in the manner provided in this Subchapter for the giving of notice of meetings of members. The proposed amendment shall be adopted upon receiving at least a majority of the votes entitled to be cast by members present or represented by proxy at such meeting.

(c) The articles of amendment shall set forth:

(1) The name of the association;

(2) The amendment or amendments so adopted;

(3) A statement setting forth the date of the meeting of the board of directors at which the amendment or amendments were approved by the board, that a quorum was present at such meeting, and that such approval received a vote of not less than two-thirds of all the members of the board;

(4) A statement setting forth the date of the meeting of members at which the amendment was adopted, that a quorum was present at such meeting, and that such amendment received at least a majority of the votes entitled to be cast by members present or represented by proxy at such meeting;

(5) The articles of amendment shall be executed by the association and shall be filed all as provided in G.S. 55A-4;

(6) A certified copy of the articles of amendment shall be filed with the Chief of the Division of Markets. (1921, c. 87, s. 9; C.S., s. 5259(g); 1935, c. 230, s. 5; 1963, c. 1168, s. 6.)

§ 54-136. Bylaws.

Each association incorporated under this Subchapter must, within 30 days after its incorporation, adopt for its government and management a code of bylaws, not inconsistent with the powers granted by this Subchapter. A majority vote of a quorum of the members or stockholders attending a meeting, of which notice of the proposed bylaw or bylaws shall have been given, is sufficient to adopt or amend the bylaws. Each association under its bylaws may also provide for any or all of the following matters:

(1)   The time, place, and manner of calling and conducting its meetings.

(2)   The number of stockholders or members constituting a quorum.

(3)   The right of members or stockholders to vote by proxy or by mail, or by both, and the conditions, manner, form, and effects of such votes.

(4)   The number of directors constituting a quorum.

(5)   The qualifications, compensations, and duties and terms of office of directors and officers; time of their election, and the mode and manner of giving notice thereof.

(6)   Penalties for violations of the bylaws.

(7)   The amount of entrance, organization, and membership fees, if any; the manner and method of collection of the same, and the purposes for which they may be used.

(8)   The amount which each member or stockholder shall be required to pay annually or from time to time, if at all, to carry on the business of the association, the charge, if any, to be paid by each member or stockholder for services rendered by the association to him, and the time of payment and the manner of collection; and the marketing contract between the association and its members or stockholders which every member or stockholder may be required to sign.

(9)   The number and qualification of members or stockholders of the association and the conditions precedent to membership or ownership of common stock; the method, time, and manner of permitting members to withdraw or the holders of common stock to transfer their stock; the manner of assignment and transfer of the interest of members, and of the shares of common stock; the conditions upon which, and the time when membership of any member shall cease; the automatic suspension of the rights of a member when he ceases to be eligible to membership in the association, and mode, manner, and effect of the expulsion of a member; manner of determining the value of a member's interest and provision for its purchase by the association

upon the death or withdrawal of a member or stockholder, or upon the expulsion of a member or forfeiture of his membership, or at the option of the association, by conclusive appraisal by the board of directors.

Upon the death, withdrawal or expulsion of a member, the board of directors of the association shall, within one year, cause to be paid to such member or his estate one hundred percent (100%) of all amounts due him for any and all raw products which have been delivered by him to the association. All other amounts which might be due for capital stock, certificates of interest, reserves or on account of any other equity credits shall be payable in accordance with the charter or bylaws of the association.

Notwithstanding the foregoing provisions of this section, any association may amend its articles of incorporation to provide that thereafter any bylaw or bylaws of the association may be amended or repealed, or any new bylaw may be adopted, either by the members or by the board of directors, but if the members amend any bylaw or bylaws or adopt any new bylaw or bylaws, such bylaw or bylaws shall not thereafter be amended or repealed by the board of directors, and if the members repeal any bylaw or bylaws, such bylaw or bylaws shall not be readopted by the board of directors; provided, however, that no bylaw shall be adopted by the board of directors which shall require a higher number or percentage of members to be present or represented at a members' meeting for the purpose of constituting a quorum, or a higher number or percentage of such quorum to take action, than was the case before the power to alter, amend, or repeal the bylaws was conferred upon the board of directors. (1921, c. 87, s. 10; C.S., s. 5259(h); 1935, c. 230, s. 6; 1963, c. 1168, s. 7; 1979, c. 543.)

§ 54-137. General and special meetings; how called.

In its bylaws each association shall provide for one or more regular meetings annually. The board of directors shall have the right to call a special meeting at any time, and ten percent (10%) of the members or stockholders may file a petition stating the specific business to be brought before the association, and demand a special meeting at any time. Such meeting must thereupon be called by the directors. Notice of all meetings, together with a statement of the purposes thereof, shall be mailed to each member at least 10 days prior to the meeting: Provided, however, that the bylaws may require instead that such notice may be given by publication in a newspaper of general circulation, published at the principal place of business of the association. (1921, c. 87, s. 11; C.S., s. 5259(i).)

§ 54-138. Conflicting laws not to apply.

Any provisions of law which are in conflict with this Subchapter shall not be construed as applying to the associations herein provided for. (1921, c. 87, s. 20; C.S., s. 5259(j).)

§ 54-139. Foreign cooperative corporations; limitation on use of word "cooperative."

(a) A foreign corporation (with or without capital stock) that can qualify as an association, as defined in G.S. 54-130(2)b1 and 2, may be authorized to transact business in this State under the provisions of Chapter 55A of the General Statutes.

(b) No person other than an association organized under this Subchapter, or a foreign corporation authorized to transact business in this State pursuant to subsection (a) of this section, or an electric or telephone membership corporation domesticated pursuant to G.S. 117-28, or an organization created under or governed by Subchapter IV of Chapter 54 of the General Statutes, shall be entitled to organize, domesticate, or transact business in this State if the corporate or other business name or title of such person contains the word "cooperative." (1921, c. 87, s. 21; C.S., s. 5259(k); 1963, c. 1168, s. 8; 1985, c. 542, s. 8; 1993, c. 552, s. 20.)

§ 54-140. Association heretofore organized may adopt the provisions of this Subchapter.

Any corporation or association organized under previously existing statutes may, by a majority vote of its stockholders or members, be brought under the provisions of this Subchapter by limiting its membership and adopting the other restrictions as provided herein. It shall make out in duplicate a statement signed and sworn to by its directors, upon forms supplied by the Secretary of State, to the effect that the corporation or association has by a majority vote of its stockholders or members decided to accept the benefits and be bound by the provisions of this Subchapter. Articles of incorporation shall be filed as required in G.S. 54-134, except that they shall be signed by the members of the board of directors. The filing fee shall be the same as for filing an amendment to articles of incorporation. (1921, c. 87, s. 24; C.S., s. 5259(l).)

§ 54-141. Associations not in restraint of trade.

No association organized hereunder shall be deemed to be a combination in restraint of trade or an illegal monopoly; or an attempt to lessen competition or fix prices arbitrarily, nor shall the marketing contracts or agreements between the association and its members, or any agreements authorized in this Subchapter be considered illegal or in restraint of trade. (1921, c. 87, s. 26; C.S., s. 5259(m).)

§ 54-142. Application of North Carolina Business Corporation Act to cooperative associations with capital stock.

The provisions of the North Carolina Business Corporation Act (Chapter 55 of the General Statutes) shall apply, so far as appropriate, to every cooperative association with capital stock heretofore or hereafter organized or domesticated under this Subchapter, except where the provisions of that act are in conflict with or inconsistent with the express provisions of this Subchapter. (1921, c. 87, s. 28; C.S., s. 5259(o); 1963, c. 1168, s. 9; 1989 (Reg. Sess., 1990), c. 1024, s. 3.)

§ 54-142.1. Application of Nonprofit Corporation Act to cooperative associations without capital stock.

The provisions of the Nonprofit Corporation Act (Chapter 55A of the General Statutes) shall apply, so far as appropriate, to every cooperative association without capital stock heretofore or hereafter organized or domesticated under this Subchapter, except where the provisions of that act are in conflict with or inconsistent with the express provisions of this Subchapter. (1963, c. 1168, s. 9.)

§ 54-143. License taxes.

On and after June 1, 1955, the provisions of Article 2, Subchapter I of Chapter 105 of the General Statutes of North Carolina shall apply to an association or corporation organized under the provisions of this Subchapter. (1921, c. 87, s. 29; C.S., s. 5259(p); 1955, c. 1313, s. 1.)

§ 54-143.1. Franchise taxes.

On and after July 1, 1955, the provisions of Article 3, Subchapter I of Chapter 105 of the General Statutes of North Carolina shall apply to an association or corporation organized under the provisions of this Subchapter. (1955, c. 1313, s. 1.)

§ 54-144. Filing fees.

For filing articles of incorporation, an association organized hereunder shall pay ten dollars ($10.00); and for filing an amendment to the articles, two and one-half dollars ($2.50). (1921, c. 87, s. 30; C.S., s. 5259(q).)

Article 20.

Members and Officers.

§ 54-145. Members.

(a) Under the terms and conditions prescribed in its bylaws, an association may admit as members, or issue common stock, only to persons engaged in the production of agricultural products, including the lessees and tenants of land used for the production of such products and any lessors and landlords who receive as rent part of the crop raised on the leased premises.

(b)   If a member of a nonstock association be other than a natural person, such member may be represented by any individual, associate, officer, or member thereof, duly authorized in writing.

(c)   One association organized hereunder may become a member or stockholder of any other association or associations, organized hereunder. (1921, c. 87, s. 7; C.S., s. 5259(r); 1963, c. 1168, s. 10.)

§ 54-146. Directors; election.

(a)   The affairs of the association shall be managed by a board of not less than three directors, elected by the members or stockholders from their own number. The bylaws may provide that the territory in which the association has members shall be divided into districts, and that the directors shall be elected according to such districts. In such case the bylaws shall specify the number of directors to be elected by each district, the manner and method of reapportioning the directors and of redistricting the territory covered by the association. The bylaws may provide that primary elections should be held in each district to elect the directors apportioned to such districts, and the result of all such primary elections must be ratified by the next regular meeting of the association.

(b)   The bylaws may provide that one or more directors may be appointed either by the Director of the Agricultural Extension Service or by such public official or public board or commission as may be designated by the bylaws. The directors so appointed need not be members or stockholders of the association, but shall have the same powers and rights as other directors.

(c)   An association may provide a fair remuneration for the time actually spent by its officers and directors in its service. No director, during the term of his office, shall be a party to a contract for profit with the association differing in any way from the business relations accorded regular members or holders of common stock of the association, or to any other kind of contract differing from terms generally current in that district.

(d) When a vacancy on the board of directors occurs, other than by expiration of term, the remaining members of the board, by a majority vote, shall fill the vacancy, unless the bylaws provide for an election of directors by districts. In such case the board of directors shall immediately call a special meeting of the members or stockholders in that district to fill the vacancy: Provided, that this subsection shall not apply to the director or directors appointed under the provisions of subsection (b) of this section: Provided further, that any vacancy occurring in the office of a director appointed under subsection (b) of this section shall be filled in the same manner as the original appointment was made. (1921, c. 87, s. 12; C.S., s. 5259(s); 1963, c. 1168, s. 11; 1979, c. 908, s. 3.)

§ 54-147. Election of officers.

The directors shall elect a president, one or more vice-presidents, a secretary and treasurer who need not be directors, and they may combine the offices of secretary and treasurer designating the combined office as secretary-treasurer. They shall elect from their number a chairman and vice-chairman unless the president and vice-presidents are members of the board. The board may elect or appoint such additional officers as are necessary and appropriate. The treasurer may be a bank or any depository, and as such shall not be considered an officer, but as a function of the board of directors. In such a case the secretary shall perform the usual accounting duties of the treasurer, excepting that the funds shall be deposited only as authorized by the board of directors. (1921, c. 87, s. 13; C.S., s. 5259(t); 1971, c. 925.)

§ 54-148. Stock; membership certificates; when issued; voting; liability; limitation on transfer of ownership.

(a) When a member of an association established without capital stock has paid his membership fee in full, he shall receive a certificate of membership.

(b) No association shall issue stock to a member until it has been fully paid for. The promissory notes of the members may be accepted by the association as full or partial payment. The association shall hold the stock as security for the payment of the note, but such retention as security shall not affect the members' right to vote.

(c) Except for debts lawfully contracted between him and the association, no member shall be liable for the debts of the association to an amount exceeding the sum remaining unpaid on his membership fee or his subscription to the capital stock, including any unpaid balance on any promissory notes given in payment thereof.

(d) A cooperative association, incorporated under this Subchapter, may fix or limit in its bylaws the amount of stock which one member might own in said association.

(e) No member or stockholder shall be entitled to more than one vote; provided, however, that any association organized hereunder, all of whose members are other associations organized hereunder shall have power to determine by its bylaws the number of votes to which each member association shall be entitled and to provide for the appointment or election of delegates to cast such votes and to represent the member associations at all members' meetings.

(f) Any association organized with stock under this Subchapter may issue preferred stock, with or without the right to vote. Such stock may be redeemable or retirable by the association on such terms and conditions as may be provided for by the articles of incorporation and printed on the face of the certificate.

(g) The bylaws shall prohibit the transfer of the common stock of the association to persons not engaged in the production of agricultural products, and such restrictions must be printed upon every certificate of stock subject thereto.

(h) The association may at any time, except when the debts of the association exceed fifty percent (50%) of the assets thereof, buy in or purchase its common stock at book value thereof as conclusively determined by the board of directors, and pay for it in cash within one year thereafter. (1921, c. 87, s. 14; C.S., s. 5259(u); 1935, c. 436, s. 2; 1955, c. 596; 1963, c. 1168, s. 12.)

§ 54-149. Removal of officer or director.

Any member may bring charges against an officer or director by filing them in writing with the secretary of the association, together with a petition signed by ten percent (10%) of the members, requesting the removal of the officer or director in question. The removal shall be voted upon at the next regular or special meeting of the association, and by a vote of a majority of the members, the association may remove the officer or director and fill the vacancy. The director or officer against whom such charges have been brought shall be informed in writing of the charges previous to the meeting, and shall have an opportunity at the meeting to be heard in person or by counsel, and to present witnesses; and the person or persons bringing the charges against him shall have the same opportunity.

In case the bylaws provide for election of directors by districts, with primary elections in each district, then the petition for removal of a director must be signed by twenty percent (20%) of the members residing in the district from which he was elected. The board of directors must call a special meeting of the members residing in that district to consider the removal of the director. By a vote of the majority of that district, the director in question shall be removed from office: Provided, that this section shall not apply to directors appointed under subsection (b) of G.S. 54-146. (1921, c. 87, s. 15; C.S., s. 5259(v).)

§ 54-150. Referendum.

Upon demand of one third of the entire board of directors, any matter that has been approved or passed by the board must be referred to the entire membership of the stockholders for decision at the next special or regular meeting: Provided, however, that a special meeting may be called for the purpose. (1921, c. 87, s. 16; C.S., s. 5259(w).)

Article 21.

Powers, Duties, and Liabilities.

§ 54-151. Powers.

Each association incorporated under this Subchapter shall have the following powers:

(1) To engage in any activity in connection with the producing, marketing, selling, harvesting, preserving, drying, processing, canning, packing, storing, handling, or utilization of any agricultural products produced or delivered to it by its members and other farmers; or the manufacturing or marketing of the by-products thereof; or in connection with the purchase, hiring, or use by its members of supplies, machinery, or equipment; or in the financing of any such activities; or in any one or more of the activities specified in this section. No such association, during any fiscal year thereof, shall deal in or handle products, machinery, equipment, supplies, and/or perform services for and on behalf of nonmembers to an amount greater in value than such as are dealt in, handled, and/or performed by it for and on behalf of members during the same period.

(2) To borrow money and to make advances to members and other farmers who deliver agricultural products to the association.

(3) To act as the agent or representative of any member or members in any of the above-mentioned activities.

(4) To purchase or otherwise acquire, and to hold, own, and exercise all rights or ownership in, and to sell, transfer, or pledge shares of the capital stock or bonds of any corporation or association engaged in any related activity or in the handling or marketing of any of the products handled by the association, or engaged in the financing of the association.

(5) To establish reserves and to invest the funds thereof in bonds or such other property as may be provided in the bylaws.

(6) To buy, hold, and exercise all privileges of ownership, over such real or personal property as may be necessary or convenient for the conducting and operation of any of the business of the association, or incidental thereto.

(7) To do each and everything necessary, suitable, or proper for the accomplishment of any one of the purposes or the attainment of any one or more of the objects herein enumerated; or conducive to or expedient for the interest or benefit of the association; and to contract accordingly; and in addition, to exercise and possess all powers, rights, and privileges necessary or incidental to the purposes for which the association is organized or to the activities in which it is engaged; and in addition, any other rights and powers, and privileges granted by the laws of this State to ordinary corporations, except such as are inconsistent with the express provisions of this Subchapter; and to

do any such thing anywhere. (1921, c. 87, s. 6; C.S., s. 5259(x); 1933, c. 350, ss. 3, 4; 1935, c. 230, ss. 7-9.)

§ 54-152. Marketing contract.

(a) The association and its members may make and execute marketing contracts, requiring the members to sell, for any period of time, not over 10 years, all or any specified part of their agricultural products or specified commodities exclusively to or through the association or any facilities to be created by the association. The contract may provide that the association may sell or resell the products of its members, with or without taking title thereto, and pay over to its members the resale price, after deducting all necessary selling, overhead, and other costs and expenses, including dividends on preferred stock, not exceeding ten percent (10%) per annum, and reserve for retiring the stock, if any; and other proper reserves; and dividends not exceeding ten percent (10%) per annum upon common stock.

(b) The bylaws and the marketing contract may fix, as liquidated damages, specific sums to be paid by the member or stockholder to the association upon the breach by him of any provision of the marketing contract regarding the sale or delivery or withholding of products; and may further provide that the member will pay all costs, premiums for bonds, expenses and fees in case any action is brought upon the contract by the association; and any such provisions shall be valid and enforceable in the courts of this State.

(c) In the event of any such breach or threatened breach of such marketing contract by a member, the association shall be entitled to an injunction to prevent the further breach of the contract, and to a decree of specific performance thereof. Pending the adjudication of such an action, and upon filing a verified complaint showing the breach or threatened breach, and upon filing a sufficient bond, the association shall be entitled to a temporary restraining order and preliminary injunction against the member.

(d) In the event that a member of an association incorporated under this chapter shall have died; and that, at a time more than six months after his death, such cooperative corporation has in its hands moneys not in excess of one hundred dollars ($100.00) which would have been distributable and payable to such member except for his death; and that there has been appointed no administrator of his estate or that the administration of his estate has been

For filing the articles of incorporation of corporations organized under this Subchapter, there shall be paid the Secretary of State ten dollars ($10.00) and his fees allowed by law, and for the filing of an amendment to such articles, five dollars ($5.00) and his fees allowed by law: Provided, that when the authorized capital stock of such corporations shall be less than one thousand dollars ($1,000), such fee for filing either the articles of incorporation or amendments thereto shall be two dollars ($2.00). (1915, c. 144, s. 4; C.S., s. 5246; 1967, c. 823, s. 13.)

§ 54-116. Bylaws adopted.

At the time of making the articles of incorporation the incorporators shall make bylaws which shall provide:

(1)   The name of the corporation.

(2)   The purposes for which it is formed.

(3)   Qualifications for membership.

(4)   The date of the annual meeting; the manner in which members shall be notified of meetings; the manner of conducting the meetings; the number of members which shall constitute a quorum at the meetings, and regulations as to voting.

(5)   The number of members of the board of directors; powers and duties; the compensation and duties of officers elected by the board of directors.

(6)   In the case of selling agencies or productive societies, regulations for grading.

(7)   In the case of selling agencies or productive societies, regulations governing the sale of products by the members through the organization.

(8)   The par value of the shares of capital stock.

(9)   The conditions upon which shares may be issued, paid in, transferred, and withdrawn.

closed at such time; then such corporation, without making any publication of notice, may disburse such moneys (not in excess of one hundred dollars ($100.00)) in the following order:

(1) To the widow of the deceased if there is a widow,

(2) To pay any unsatisfied claims for funeral expenses or reimburse any person for the payment thereof, and

(3) To any adult person of the class of those nearest of kin to the deceased, for the benefit of all members of such class.

In making such disbursements the said corporation shall be responsible and liable only for the exercise of good faith and reasonable care and shall have no further responsibility or liability with respect to such moneys or their application or disbursement. (1921, c. 87, s. 17; C.S., s. 5259(y); 1959, c. 1174; 1979, 2nd Sess., c. 1302, ss. 1, 2.)

§ 54-153. Purchasing business of other associations, persons, firms, or corporations; payment; stock issued.

Whenever an association organized hereunder with preferred capital stock shall purchase the stock or any property, or any interest in any property of any person, firm, or corporation or association, it may by agreement with the other party or parties to the transaction discharge the obligations so incurred, wholly or in part, by exchanging for the acquired interest shares of its preferred capital stock to an amount which at par value would equal a fair market value of the stock or interest so purchased, as determined by the board of directors. In that case the transfer to the association of the stock or interest purchased shall be equivalent to payment in cash for shares of stock issued. (1921, c. 87, s. 18; C.S., s. 5259(z).)

§ 54-154. Annual reports.

Each association formed under this Subchapter shall prepare and make out an annual report on forms furnished by the Division of Markets, containing the name of the association, its principal place of business, and a general statement of its business operations during the fiscal year, showing the amount of capital stock paid up, and the number of stockholders of a stock association or the number of members and the amount of membership fees received, if a nonstock association; the total expenses of the operations; the amount of its indebtedness, or liability, and its balance sheets. (1921, c. 87, s. 19; C.S., s. 5259(aa).)

§ 54-155. Interest in other corporations or associations.

An association may organize, form, operate, own, control, have interest in, own stock of, or be a member of any other corporation or corporations, with or without capital stock, and engaged in preserving, drying, processing, canning, packing, storing, handling, shipping, utilizing, manufacturing, marketing, or selling of the agricultural products handled by the association, or the by-products thereof. If such corporations are warehousing corporations, they may issue legal warehouse receipts to the association, or to any other person, and such legal warehouse receipts shall be considered as adequate collateral to the extent of the current value of the commodity represented thereby. In case such warehouse is licensed or licensed and bonded under the laws of this State or the United States, its warehouse receipt shall not be challenged or discriminated against because of ownership or control, wholly or in part, by the association. (1921, c. 87, s. 22; C.S., s. 5259(bb).)

§ 54-156. Contracts and agreements with other associations.

Any association may, upon resolution adopted by its board of directors, enter into all necessary and proper contracts and agreements, and make all necessary and proper stipulations, agreements and contracts and arrangements with any other cooperative corporation, association, or associations, formed in this or in any other state, for the cooperative and more economical carrying on of its business, or any part or parts thereof. Any two or more associations may, by agreement between them, unite in employing and using or may separately employ and use the same methods, means, and agencies for carrying on and conducting their respective businesses. (1921, c. 87, s. 23; C.S., s. 5259(cc).)

§ 54-157. Breach of marketing contract of cooperative association; spreading false reports about the finances or management thereof; misdemeanor.

Any person or persons, or any corporation whose officers or employees knowingly induces or attempts to induce any member or stockholder of an association organized hereunder to breach his marketing contract with the association, or who maliciously and knowingly spreads false reports about the finances or management thereof shall be guilty of a Class 2 misdemeanor and subject only to a fine of not less than one hundred dollars ($100.00), and not more than one thousand dollars ($1,000), for such offense and shall be liable to the association aggrieved in a civil suit in the penal sum of five hundred dollars ($500.00) for each such offense: Provided, that this section shall not apply to a bona fide creditor of any member or stockholder of such association, or the agents or attorney of any such bona fide creditor, endeavoring to make collection of the indebtedness, or to any communication, written or oral, between a business company or concern and persons with whom it has an existing contractual relationship which communication relates to the performance of that contractual relationship and duties and responsibilities arising therefrom. (1921, c. 87, s. 25; C.S., s. 5259(dd); 1963, c. 1168, s. 14; 1993, c. 539, s. 430; 1994, Ex. Sess., c. 24, s. 14(c).)

§ 54-158. Cooperative associations may form subsidiaries.

Nothing in this Subchapter shall prevent an association organizing, forming, operating, owning, controlling, having an interest in, owning stock of, or being a member of any other corporation (hereinafter referred to as a subsidiary corporation) from including or having included in the charter or bylaws of such subsidiary corporation provisions for the control or management of said subsidiary corporation by such association to such extent as shall by votes of the board of directors of such association, and the majority of the stockholders of such subsidiary corporation, be declared to be for the best interests of said association and said subsidiary corporation respectively. Such provisions may be so included in any such charter or bylaws and may by way of illustration, but not of limitation, include the following:

(1) Representation of said association on the board of directors or other governing body of said subsidiary corporation, upon such terms as may be deemed advisable.

(2) Ownership by an association of an interest or interests in a subsidiary corporation represented by stock of any class thereof, or otherwise, to such extent and upon such terms, and with such voting power, as may be deemed advisable.

(3) Participation by said association in the profits of such subsidiary corporation to such extent and upon such terms as shall be deemed advisable. (1933, c. 350, s. 1.)

Article 22.

Merger, Consolidation and Other Fundamental Changes.

§ 54-159. Procedure for merger.

(a) Any two or more domestic associations organized under this Subchapter, either with or without capital stock, may merge into any one of such associations pursuant to a plan of merger approved in the manner provided in this Article.

(b) The board of directors of each association shall, by resolution adopted by each such board, approve a plan of merger setting forth:

(1) The names of the association proposing to merge, and the name of the association into which they propose to merge, which is hereinafter designated as the surviving association.

(2) The name which the surviving association is to have, which name may be that of any of the associations involved in the merger or any other available name, subject, however, to the limitations of G.S. 54-139 and 55A-10.

(3) The terms and conditions of the proposed merger.

(4) A statement of any changes in the charter of the surviving association to be effected by such merger.

(5) Such other provisions not inconsistent with law as are deemed necessary or desirable. (1963, c. 1168, s. 13.)

§ 54-160. Procedure for consolidation.

(a) Any two or more domestic associations organized under this Subchapter, either with or without capital stock, may consolidate into a new association pursuant to a plan of consolidation approved in the manner provided in this Article.

(b) The board of directors of each association shall, by resolution adopted by each such board, approve a plan of consolidation setting forth:

(1) The names of the associations proposing to consolidate, and the name of the new association into which they proposed to consolidate, which is hereinafter designated as the new association. The name of the new association may be that of any of the associations involved in the consolidation or any other available name, subject, however, to the limitations of G.S. 54-139 and 55A-10.

(2) The terms and conditions of the proposed consolidation.

(3) With respect to the new association, all of the appropriate statements required to be set forth in articles of incorporation for associations organized under this Subchapter.

(4) Such other provisions not inconsistent with law as are deemed necessary or desirable. (1963, c. 1168, s. 13.)

§ 54-161. Approval of merger or consolidation; abandonment.

(a) A plan of merger or consolidation shall be adopted in the following manner: The board of directors of each merging or consolidating association shall adopt a resolution approving the proposed plan, and directing that it be submitted to a vote at a meeting of members having voting rights, which may be either an annual or a special meeting. Written or printed notice of the meeting shall be given to each member entitled to vote at such meeting. The notice shall state that the proposed plan of merger or consolidation will be considered and acted upon at the meeting, and a copy or a summary of the plan of merger or plan of consolidation, as the case may be, shall be included in or enclosed with such notice. Such notice shall contain a statement, displayed with reasonable prominence, to the effect that objecting members are entitled, upon compliance with G.S. 54-166, including the 20-day demand requirement, to be paid the fair market value of their stock or other property rights or interest in the association, but failure of the notice to contain such a statement shall not invalidate the merger or consolidation. Each such notice shall be mailed by first-class mail at such a time that not less than 10 full days shall elapse between the date of mailing the notice and the date of the meeting, and shall be mailed to the member at his last address as it appears on the records of the association. The proposed plan shall be adopted upon receiving at least two-thirds of the votes entitled to be cast by members present at each such meeting where a quorum is present.

(b)   After such approval, and at any time prior to the filing of the articles of merger or consolidation, the merger or consolidation may be abandoned pursuant to provisions therefor, if any, set forth in the plan of merger or consolidation. (1963, c. 1168, s. 13.)

§ 54-162. Articles of merger or consolidation.

(a)   Upon such approval, articles of merger or articles of consolidation shall be executed by each association and filed as provided in G.S. 55A-4, except that a copy thereof certified by the Secretary of State shall also be recorded in the office of the register of deeds of each county wherein the constituent associations have their principal places of business or their registered offices.

(b)   The articles of merger or consolidation shall set forth:

(1)   The plan of merger or the plan of consolidation; and

(2)   A statement setting forth the date of the meeting of the members of each association at which the plan was adopted, that a quorum was present at such meeting, and that such plan received at least two-thirds of the votes entitled to be cast by members present at each such meeting where a quorum was present.

(c)   The time when the merger or consolidation is effected is determined by the provisions of G.S. 55A-4. (1963, c. 1168, s. 13; 1967, c. 823, s. 15.)

§ 54-163. Effect of merger or consolidation.

When such merger or consolidation has been effected:

(1) The several associations, parties to the plan of merger or consolidation, shall be a single association which, in the case of a merger, shall be that association designated in the plan of merger as the surviving association, and, in the case of a consolidation, shall be the new association provided for in the plan of consolidation.

(2) The separate existence of all associations which are parties to the plan of merger or consolidation, except the surviving or new association, shall cease.

(3) Such surviving or new association shall have all the rights, privileges, immunities, and powers and shall be subject to all the duties and liabilities of an association organized under this Subchapter.

(4) Such surviving or new association shall thereupon and thereafter, to the extent consistent with its charter as established or changed by the merger or consolidation, possess all the rights, privileges, immunities, and franchises, as well of a public as of a private nature, of each of the merging or consolidating associations; and all property, real and personal, and all debts due on any account, and all other choses in action, and all and every other interest, of or belonging to or due to each of the associations so merged or consolidated, shall be taken and deemed to be transferred to and vested in such single association without further act or deed; and the title to any real estate, or any interest therein, vested in any of such associations shall not revert or be in any way impaired by reason of such merger or consolidation.

(5) Such surviving or new association shall thenceforth be responsible and liable for all the liabilities, contracts or other obligations, and penalties of each of the associations so merged or consolidated; and any claim existing or action or proceeding, civil or criminal, pending by or against any of such associations may be prosecuted as if such merger or consolidation had not taken place, or such surviving or new association may be substituted in its place; and any judgments rendered against any of the merged or consolidated associations may be enforced against the surviving or new association. Neither the rights of creditors nor any liens upon the property of any merged or consolidated association shall be impaired by such merger or consolidation.

(6) In the case of a merger, the charter of the surviving association shall be deemed to be amended to the extent, if any, that changes in its charter are stated in the plan of merger. In the case of a consolidation, the articles of consolidation shall be deemed to be the articles of incorporation of the new association. (1963, c. 1168, s. 13.)

§ 54-164. Merger or consolidation of domestic and foreign associations.

(a) One or more domestic associations organized under this Subchapter and one or more foreign corporations engaging in any activity such as is described in G.S. 54-132, and which is a nonprofit cooperative in the sense that the term "nonprofit" is used in G.S. 54-130, may be merged or consolidated into an association of this State or an association or corporation of another state if such merger or consolidation is permitted by the laws of the state under which each such foreign association or corporation is organized.

(b) Each domestic association shall comply with the provisions of this Article with respect to the merger or consolidation, as the case may be, of domestic associations, and each foreign association or corporation shall comply with the applicable provisions of the laws of the state under which it is organized.

(c) If the surviving or new association or corporation, as the case may be, is an association or corporation of any state other than this State, it shall comply with the provisions of this Subchapter with respect to foreign corporations if it is to transact business in this State; and if after the merger or consolidation it transacts no business in this State, the courts of this State shall have jurisdiction in actions to enforce any obligation of any constituent association of this State and process therein may be served as provided in G.S. 55-145.

(d) The effect of such merger or consolidation shall be the same as in the case of the merger or consolidation of domestic associations, if the surviving or new corporation is to be an association of this State. If the surviving or new association or corporation is to be an association or corporation of any state other than this State, the effect of such merger or consolidation shall be the same as in the case of the merger or consolidation of domestic associations except insofar as the laws of such other state provide otherwise.

(e) If the new or surviving association or corporation is not an association of this State, then notwithstanding anything in the foregoing provisions of this section:

(1) The rights of any member of any constituent association that is an association of this State to receive notice of objectors' rights, to file his objection, upon such objection to demand and receive payment of the fair market value of his stock or other property rights or interests in the association, or to avail himself of any equitable relief to which he would be entitled if the surviving or new association or corporation were an association of this State, shall not be impaired; and

(2) The courts of this State shall have jurisdiction in actions to enforce the aforesaid rights against the surviving or new association or corporation regardless of whether or not said association or corporation is otherwise subject to the jurisdiction of the courts of this State and in any such action service of process may be made in the manner provided in G.S. 55-145 that would be applicable if said association or corporation were transacting business in this State. (1963, c. 1168, s. 13.)

§ 54-165. Sale, lease or exchange of assets; mortgage or pledge of assets.

(a) A sale, lease, or exchange of all, or substantially all, the property and assets of an association organized under the provisions of this Subchapter may be made upon such terms and conditions and for such consideration, which may consist in whole or in part of money or property, real or personal, including shares of any corporation for profit, domestic or foreign, as may be authorized in the following manner: The board of directors shall adopt a resolution recommending such sale, lease, or exchange and directing that it be submitted to a vote at a meeting of members, which may be either an annual or a special meeting. Written or printed notice of the meeting shall be given to each member entitled to vote at such meeting. The notice shall state that the proposed sale, lease, or exchange will be considered and acted upon at such meeting, and a statement of the terms of the proposed sale, lease, or exchange, as the case may be, shall be included in or enclosed with such notice. Each such notice shall be mailed by first-class mail at such a time that not less than 10 full days shall elapse between the date of mailing the notice and the date of the meeting, and shall be mailed to the member at his last address as it appears on the records of the association. The proposed sale, lease, or exchange, as the case may be, shall be adopted upon receiving at least two-thirds of the votes entitled to be cast by members present at the meeting, if a quorum is present.

(b)   A mortgage or pledge of, or any other security interest in, all or any part or parts of the property of the association may be made by authority of the board of directors of the association without authorization of the members, unless otherwise provided in the charter or bylaws adopted by the members. (1963, c. 1168, s. 13.)

§ 54-166. Rights of objecting members.

(a)   Any member of an association effecting a merger or consolidation may give to the association prior to or at the meeting of the members to which the proposal of merger or consolidation is submitted to a vote, written notice that he objects to such proposal. Within 20 days after the date on which the vote was taken, such member may, unless he votes in favor of the proposal, make written demand on the association for payment of the fair market value of his stock or other property rights or interest in the association. Such demand shall state the number and class of shares of stock owned by him or the nature and amount of other property rights or interest owned by him in the association. In addition to any other right he may have in law or equity, a member giving such notice shall be entitled, if and when the merger or consolidation is effected, to be paid by the surviving or new association, the fair market value of such stock, or other property rights or interests, as of the day prior to the date on which the vote was taken, subject only to the surrender by him of the certificate or certificates or other evidence of ownership of such stock or other property rights or interests.

(b)   If within 30 days after the date upon which the objecting member becomes entitled to payment for such stock or other property rights or interest, the fair market value of such stock or other property rights or interests is agreed upon between the member and the surviving or new association, as the case may be, payment therefor shall be made within 60 days after the agreement, upon surrender of the certificate or other evidence of such property rights or interests, whereupon the member shall cease to have any interest in such stock or other property rights or interests in the association.

(c)   If within the 30-day period mentioned in subsection (b) of this section the member and the association do not agree as to the fair market value of the stock or other property rights or interests, the member may, within 60 days after the expiration of the 30-day period, file a petition in the superior court of the county in which the association has its registered office or principal place of business asking for the appointment by the clerk of the superior court of that county of three qualified and disinterested appraisers to appraise the fair market value of the stock or other property rights or interests. A summons as in other cases of special proceedings, together with a copy of the petition, shall be served on the association at least 10 days prior to the hearing of the petition by the court. The award of the appraisers, or a majority of them, if no exceptions are filed thereto within 10 days after the award is filed in court, shall be confirmed by the court, and when confirmed shall be final and conclusive. The member, upon depositing with the court the proper stock certificates or other evidence of property rights or interests, shall be entitled to judgment against the association for the appraised value thereof as of the day prior to the date on which the vote was taken, together with interest thereon to the date of the confirmation. If either party files exceptions to the award within 10 days after the award is filed in court, the case shall be transferred to the civil issue docket of the superior court for trial during term and shall be there tried in the same manner, as near as may be practicable, as is provided in Chapter 40A of the General Statutes for the trial of cases under the eminent domain law of this State, and with the same right of appeal to the appellate division as is permitted in that Chapter. The court shall assess the cost of the proceedings as it shall deem equitable. Upon payment of the judgment, the owner of the stock or other property rights or interests shall cease to have any interest in the association and the association shall be entitled to have the stock certificates or other evidence of the property rights or interests surrendered to the association by the clerk of court. Unless the member files a petition within the time herein prescribed, the member and all persons claiming under the member shall have no right of payment hereunder, but in that event nothing herein shall impair the member's status as a member.

(d)   If in the notices sent to members in connection with the meeting to vote upon a proposed merger or consolidation no reference is made as required by this Article to the provisions of this section, any member entitled to but who did not avail himself of the provisions of this section, unless he voted for the proposal, is entitled, if he so demands in writing within one year after the effective date of the merger or consolidation, to recover from the surviving or new association, as the case may be, any damage which he suffered from failure of the association of which he was a member to make the aforesaid reference.

(e) The liability to pay for shares or to pay damages imposed by this section on an association extends to the successor association which acquires the assets of the predecessor, whether by merger or consolidation.

(f) Shares of stock acquired by an association pursuant to payment of the agreed fair market value thereof or to payment of the judgment entered therefor as in this section provided, may be held and disposed of by the association as in the case of other treasury shares.

(g) The provisions of this section shall not apply to a merger if on the date of the filing of the articles of merger the surviving association is the owner of all the outstanding shares of the other association, domestic or foreign, participating in the merger and if such merger makes no changes in the relative rights of the members of the surviving association.

(h) Notwithstanding any of the foregoing provisions of this section, no member of an association effecting a merger or consolidation, who objects thereto and makes written demand for payment of the fair market value of his stock or other property rights or interests in the association, as hereinbefore provided in this section, shall be entitled to such payment at any time prior to the time that he would otherwise be entitled to payment pursuant to valid provisions of such stock, or valid provisions of the charter or the bylaws of the association, in effect on the date of the vote for such merger or consolidation. However, in any case where the owner of such stock or other property rights or interests in the association is not entitled, because of valid provisions of his stock, or because of valid provisions of the charter or bylaws of the association, to payment at the time hereinbefore provided in this section, the fair market value of such stock or other property rights or interests in the association, as of the day prior to the date on which the vote was taken, may be determined in any manner hereinbefore provided in this section, and the amount so determined, without interest, shall be an obligation of the surviving or new association, as the case may be, and shall be due and payable at the time that the owner thereof would be entitled to payment pursuant to valid provisions of such stock, or valid provisions of the charter or the bylaws of the association. (1963, c. 1168, s. 13; 1973, c. 108, s. 19; 2001-487, s. 38(c).)

Chapter 54A.

Capital Stock Savings and Loan Associations.

§§ 54A-1 through 54A-27. Repealed by Session Laws 1981, c. 282, s. 2.

Vision Books Order Form

Fax Orders:	1-980-299-5965
Phone Orders:	1-704-898-0770
E-mail Orders:	www.visionbooks.org
Mail Orders:	Vision Books, LLC P.O. Box 42406 Charlotte, NC 28215

Shipp To:
Name_____
Address_____
City_____State_____Zip_____
Phone_____Fax_____
Email_____@_____

Bill To: We can bill a third party on your behalf.
Name_____
Address_____
City_____State_____Zip_____
Phone____(_____)_____Fax_____
Email_____@_____

Pamphlet Number ($15.00 Each)	Qty	Total Cost
_____	_____	_____
_____	_____	_____
_____	_____	_____
_____	_____	_____
_____	_____	_____
_____	_____	_____
_____	_____	_____
_____	_____	_____
<u>Full Volume Set 1-92</u>	<u>92 Pamphlets</u>	<u>1,380.00</u>

Free Shipping Shipping & Handling on Full Volume Orders
Add $1.00 Shipping & Handling per pamphlet $_____

Total Cost $_____

Thank you for your support. Management!

DID YOU ENJOY THIS BOOK?

Vision Books, LLC would like to hear from you! If you or someone you know has been fasely imprisoned, we would like to hear your story. If the 'North Carolina Criminal Law and Procedure' has had an effect in your life or if you have suggestions, we would like to hear from you. Send your letters to:

Vision Books, LLC
Attn: Staff Writers
P.O. Box 42406
Charlotte, NC 28215
Email: staff@visionbooks.org

Order Additional Copies:

Fax Orders: 1-704-921-9271

Phone Orders: 1-704-921-9271

E-mail Orders: www.visionbooks.org

Mail Orders: Vision Books
                       P.O. Box 42406
                       Charlotte, NC 28215

www.ingramcontent.com/pod-product-compliance
Lightning Source LLC
Chambersburg PA
CBHW051638170526
45167CB00001B/240